Sonata

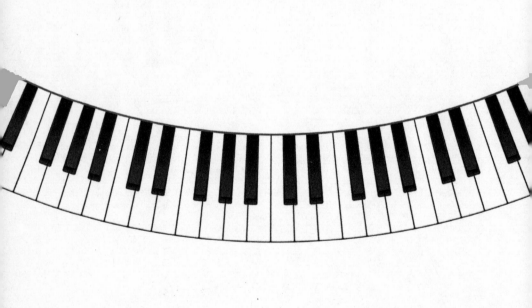

Sonata

A Memoir of Pain and the Piano

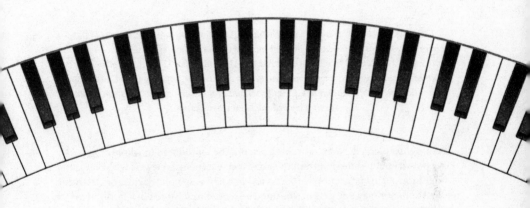

ANDREA AVERY

PEGASUS BOOKS
NEW YORK LONDON

SONATA

Pegasus Books Ltd.
148 W 37th Street, 13th Floor
New York, NY 10018

First Pegasus Books cloth edition May 2017

Interior design by Maria Fernandez

Library of Congress Cataloging-in-Publication Data is available.

ISBN: 978-1-68177-409-1

10 9 8 7 6 5 4 3 2 1

Printed in the United States of America
Distributed by W. W. Norton & Company

For Mom and Dad

Contents

PRELUDE/BEFORE

> *Imagine that you were in pain and simultaneously hearing*
> *a piano being tuned in the next room. You say, "It'll stop*
> *soon." It surely makes quite a difference whether you mean*
> *the pain or the piano-tuning.*
>
> —*Ludwig Wittgenstein,*
> Philosophical Investigations

There was a painfully short before, and then the rest came after.

The first twelve years of my life, I lived in another body. Those twelve years before 1989 get smaller and smaller in the rearview mirror: They were once all I'd known, then the better half, now just a blip. Like matter itself, they will never entirely disappear.

In this "before," I was going to be a pianist. I was not crazy to think so. By some magic of genetics and environment, the keys rose to meet my fingers and music came. And then, too soon, by some inverted miracle of genetics and environment, rheumatoid arthritis appeared. The keys still rose to meet my fingers, but my curling fingers recoiled. For too long, I tried to be arthritic and a pianist. For too long, I refused to believe that I could not be both. For decades, with swelling and crumbling hands, I groped at the piano, kneading, fearing that if I lost it, I would lose the only thing I liked about myself. Well into foolish adulthood, music swelled up inside me, infectious, a boil in need of lancing, and I kept one bruised and brutalized hand on the keyboard. With the other hand, I tried to fend off the disease—as precocious as my musical talent itself—that threatened to become the most notable thing about me.

These scenes are the notes that spell the chord of me; these are the pitches to which I'm tuned. Three notes: one, three, five. Place your hands on the white-topped keys of the piano—wrists up, loose, that's good—and play them one by one: first thumb, then middle finger, then pinkie. One, three, five: Wellness, injury, illness. One, three, five. *Do, mi, sol.*

In musical terms:

ONE (I): This is the tonic, the tonal center, home.

THREE (III): This is the mediant, halfway between the tonic and the dominant.

FIVE (V): This is the dominant, second in importance to the tonic.

One, three, five. Play each note alone, roll the notes like the strings of a harp, or smash your searing hand on them all at once, a virulent virtuoso:

SONATA

(I)

This is home, the note to which it must all resolve. To be satisfactory, to feel finished, I must get back here.

It's a swampy Maryland summer, 1985. It's hot in my room. I can't sleep. I have the window open. My dad is stingy with the air-conditioning, and my room is full of things that generate their own heat: green pile carpeting and hand-me-down stuffed animals and clothes spilling from closet doors and draped over chair backs. The scalloped edging on the pink-and-white gingham canopy of my bed flutters in the occasional breeze through the window, and the white bedposts gilded with chintzy gold bands sweat when a passing car spotlights them. I can hear the neighbor boy and his buddies in the driveway next door. They laugh and chuck something—beer cans?—skittering into the bed of a truck. I turn my pillow over. I kick the flimsy plaid bedspread to the floor. I flail and flop and the tips of my hair get stuck in the sweaty creases of my armpits. "When you have a house of your own," my dad likes to say, "you can run the air-conditioning as much as you damn well please." I am eight. A house of my own is a long way off. I'm going to be fever-hot forever. I extend my long, suntanned legs. Reflexively, I deploy the muscles I don't yet know are called *quads* so that my knees effortlessly hyperextend, so the slick crease behind them presses into my bedsheet. Many years later, in a future I can't imagine on this hot night, I will laboriously perform this same stretch twenty times in a row at the orders of a physical therapist. But tonight, I stretch my legs gloriously straight just once, a flash, and then I curl my feet up to my bottom like a potato bug. The tops of my feet, itchy with mosquito bites and spackled with calamine lotion, prick with sweat.

It is late. The black-and-white TV in my parents' bedroom at the end of the hall, perched on my dad's dresser next to his change and ChapStick, is still on, but it's well past the eleven o'clock news now. Some late-night show is on. I can't hear the jokes, but I can hear television antiphony: the call-and-response of setup, silence, punch line, laughter. My dad is snoring a low rumble. My mom is snoring in alto counterpoint on her side of the bed.

I get out of bed. There is no sound from the room Chris and Matthew share, or Erica's room—how can they sleep in this heat?—so I go down the hall, to the bathroom. I drink cup after cup of tepid tap water from a waxy Dixie cup. I pull up my Strawberry Shortcake nightgown and sit on the closed toilet lid, letting the porcelain chill my thighs. I put my cheek on the marbled countertop. I think it would be nice to sleep in the bathtub. I consider it; it would be nothing to lower myself into the cool, blue porcelain and I know I would be able to haul myself up and out of the slick, hard tub like I do most nights, like I did just hours before. What stops me tonight is the knowledge that I would probably get in trouble. I don't know why, exactly, but I know: we are a not family who sleeps in the bathtub.

Heat rises. Matthew has told me that. That's why hot-air balloons work. So I descend. I walk sideways down the carpeted stairs, stepping as close to the wall as possible to avoid creaking. Chris taught me that. I support myself with one arm against the grass wallpaper. Not so very much later, I will find I have to walk up and down all stairways sideways to minimize the pain in the balls of my feet and because my knees will freeze, incapable of the fluid perpetual motion of leaving one step even as I reach for the next. But tonight, my body is not calling the shots. Tonight, my body is incidental.

The foyer is about one hundred square feet of brown linoleum, but already the heat has spread from the bottoms of my feet to the floor. I will have to move on to somewhere cooler. The family room is down another set of stairs, these carpeted in dull brown. The family room is full of hot textiles in late-seventies colors: wheaty macramé plant holders and itchy gold afghans and the brown tweed couch. I cannot stand the thought of any of it in this heat.

Outside, it is hot and humid; the moonlight is steamy. I roam. I turn left and go into the living room. I choose it because it is a cave; it doesn't have windows. I sit on the piano bench. I put my feet over the brass pedals of the Wurlitzer upright. The pedals are cold, and they fit into the space between my foot and my toe. I open the fallboard. My piano books are stacked on top of the piano. I open a book to find the solo I played at my first competition, at Peabody Conservatory in Baltimore, in the spring: "Flamenco." I won a first-place ribbon. On the page, above the title of the piece, are the twin "Excellent!" stickers Mrs. Feltman gave me: one when I learned the piece, and another when I memorized it for competition.

The piano smells of ammonia because our two cats, Shadow and Tinkerbelle, have taken to spraying the base of the piano, above the pedals, but I do not mind the smell. It is like other warm smells that are the by-product of work and creation: the sawdust in my dad's basement workshop or the chemical stink of grass cuttings.

I put my fingers on the plastic keys. They are not cold. They are the same temperature as my body. I depress a key slowly so it will not make a sound. I will get in trouble if I wake anyone up. But now that I am here, I must play. I cannot stand it.

I push a key again, this time a little harder. I keep my left foot on the una corda, or soft pedal. This is my bargain. I will go back to sleep in my own hot room if I can play for a few minutes. I cannot go back to sleep if I do not hear the piano first.

I make a sound, and then I must hear another. I keep one foot on the soft pedal and another on the damper pedal, because I love the way it sounds when the notes are all mushed together like coins in a piggy bank.

I play chords as softly as I can, and then my eyes fall on a book of the greatest hits of the 1970s that I left out earlier in the afternoon. I will go back to bed, I promise myself and my dad—who is probably going to wake up at any second and come bounding down the stairs two at a time in his underpants, his red-brown chest hair a cherry tree across his thin chest, stage-whispering, "Judas Priest, what the hell is going on down here?"—if I can play "I Write the Songs" once. Just once. I promise.

I get through the song without turning on the piano lamp, using only the white-hot moonlight that is streaming into the living room through the foyer from the row of square windows above the front door. Then I use my thumb to riffle the thick book's pages, and this creates a gust of dusty-cool wind on my face, so I do it again and again and then, mid-riffle, I spot "Bridge Over Troubled Water," and I know I must play that one too before I go back to sleep. The song has a part at the end where my left hand is supposed to *tromp, tromp, tromp* big octaves all up and down the bottom half of the keyboard, and I haven't been able to do it right yet—my hands are lean and strong and healthy but still too small—but now that I have spotted the song in the book in the half dark—doesn't that mean I should try? Sotto voce, pianissimo, I promise. I reach up and turn on the piano light, which instantly makes me hotter and stickier.

But the heat makes the muscles in my fingers limber, and the sweat on the pads of my fingers makes them fleet. They move quickly over the tops of the keys, nearly slipping off. I try to stay quiet, but I am playing. Playing is not the same as practicing. I am very good at playing, less so at the slower, more deliberate act of practicing. Playing is a series of games and magical thinking; it is he-loves-me, he-loves-me-not; it is eeny-meeny-miney-mo: Can I play the first four measures perfectly with no mistakes? If so, I am allowed to go on to the next four. If I finish the song perfectly, I am allowed to go on to the next song. No, not allowed: I am required. I am compelled.

I wish it were the middle of the day, and I wish I were home alone, because if I were, I could pound the notes out as loud as I wanted, as many times as I wanted. I could add glissandos and trills wherever I wanted. I could press my foot down on the damper pedal and let all the notes run together into a beautiful watercolor mess.

Tomorrow, maybe, when my mom and dad are at work, maybe Erica will go to her job as a locker room attendant at the public pool, and maybe Chris will go with her, and Matthew will go on a long bike ride with his camera around his neck, and somehow I will resist the desperate little-sister need to tag along with one of them—even if it is just an hour—and maybe then I can play.

But tonight, sated, I return to my bedroom upstairs and I lie on my back on the floor because heat rises. I push the palms of my hands together and stretch my arms out in front of my face, and I wait to fall asleep and I urge time to accelerate and make me a grown-up with my own house and my own air conditioner and I command my hands to grow.

This is home. This is the tonic. Tonic: taken in doses, it restores you to health.

(III)

This is the third note of the scale, the second note sounded in the triad I am playing for you. If we are in B-flat major—and it feels like we are—the third note of the scale is D. We can modulate to this third note, D, and let it become its own home note of the related key of D minor. Where the key of B-flat is plump, round, and warm, the key of D minor is reedy, jaundiced, and empty. This is not a key to stay in; it is a stop on the way to somewhere else. It is a tense detour, leading somewhere—home, if you're lucky.

It's 1983. My brother Chris and I are playing in the backyard, climbing a hill that has been built to separate our yard from a new roadway. When they cut down the woods brimming with wild blackberries and rogue rhubarb and put in West Gude Drive, they left a thin strip of woods at the edge of the backyards on our street. Then they built a sound-barring hill—"a *berm*," my dad said, and from then on it was the Berm—and cut little wedges out of it to accommodate the row of orphaned trees they'd left behind.

The wedges were made of crisscrossed chicken wire that held back large stones. This created a little space behind each tree, perfect for forts if you attached a tarp or a sheet to the tree above your head and then tied the other end to the heavy-gauge wire. The Berm was planted with baby trees and long grasses. In the winter, we made valiant attempts to sled the sad little hill. In the summer, we settled for scrambling up it in our bathing suits and shorts.

This late-summer afternoon, Chris and I are horsing around on the Berm with a boy from across the street. I fall and start to slide quickly down the hill on my belly. A piece of wire catches on my leg and cuts it open as I slide, inscribing a bloody gash about nine inches long on the outside of my left leg. I scream; we run across the yard and through the screen porch into the house.

My dad quickly sends the neighbor boy home and then starts grilling Chris: "What did you do to her?" Through hiccupping sobs, I can't explain that Chris hasn't done anything; it just happened—if anyone did it, I did it to myself—and anyway I am too distracted by the fact that my mom has swept me into her arms and plunked me on the kitchen counter next to the sink. I am sitting on the counter! We are not a counter-sitting kind of a family. She cleans it up ("It's not as bad as it looks," she says) and bandages it.

When I cut my leg on the Berm, I don't even go to the hospital— we aren't much of an emergency-room family, either—but when the pediatrician looks at it days later, he christens my bumpy scar *keloids* and says we can talk about plastic surgery when I am older, which sounds ridiculous even to me, even then.

But that's it for good, old-fashioned scars I earned for myself, outdoors, through feats of athleticism or stupidity or derring-do.

Injury and illness are not the same, and—before—I was as sick as frequently and as routinely as any kid. No more, no less. There were no signs, no foreshadowing, no hints of the modulation to come. Or were there? Were the ordinary childhood illnesses—those errant, rumbling fevers—foreshadowing a lifetime of sickness?

On Tuesday, January 28, 1986, I was home alone, sick, from school. I was almost nine. I don't remember feeling sick. It must have been no more than a routine January cold. The only sensations I recall of that January day are the nubby tweed of the couch; my bare feet in the cool crevasse between the cushions; the dusty, wooly warmth of a pile of afghans; a purring old black cat on my belly. I think I'd been in school the previous day, and I know for sure I went back to school the next day.

Because that Tuesday was the day the *Challenger* exploded upon takeoff and I watched it fall apart. It wasn't live: we didn't have CNN or any other cable channel. But the broadcast stations ran taped coverage of the disaster over and over again all day. I watched as much as I could; I wondered if I should call one of my parents at work, and then I decided to get off the couch and go to the piano, where, for the most part, I played chromatic scales to organize my mind: orderly inching up the keyboard, every note in turn—white, black, white, black, white, white, black, white, black, white, black, white, white—easy on the way up but trickier on the way down.

I went back to school on Wednesday. Ms. Kalo talked to us about the shuttle disaster, and someone from the school's front office told us they were available to listen if we wanted to talk more, and we ordered special packets from NASA that had stickers, which came a few weeks later.

But I always felt separate from my classmates, because they'd seen it together—live—and I'd seen it alone, a beat later.

And when it came up in conversation, in dorms and bars ten, twenty, twenty-five years later, I felt separate from my peers, who reminisced about television carts being wheeled into the classroom, still a novelty in 1986.

When I think about how, just three years after that cold Tuesday—perhaps it was beginning even then?—my body began its self-defeating process of inflammation and degeneration, I think of the *Challenger*.

A few precious seconds after takeoff, a few measly years after birth—it's never too soon for things to fall apart.

A vessel can betray its contents.

(V)

This is the fifth of the chord I am building, its relation to the home note known as the *dominant*. Dominant:

I am fourteen; it has been two years since my diagnosis of rheumatoid arthritis. The cut on the outside of my leg from where I fell on the Berm has nearly faded, retreated into my skin. It has not turned out to be the disfigurement the pediatrician was worried about. It is not the wrongest thing about my body.

I'm home sick, again, from school, but I will not spend the day at the Wurlitzer. I know I am truly, differently sick, because even though I am older, I am not home alone. My dad is downstairs, having taken time off work. He is probably in the kitchen, standing at the sink, eating a piece of toast over his upturned hand. I'm in the upstairs bathroom, trying to get into my bathing suit. I can't do it. The elastic is too restrictive, and every contortion, every manipulation I have to make to wriggle the tight-but-not-extraordinarily-tight one-piece over my hips causes a riot of pain in my arms and elbows and back and neck and hands. Even trying to grip the blue Lycra hurts. My hands are too weak to hold on and pull.

I want to get into my bathing suit so I can go soak in the hot tub. I want to soak in the hot tub because I want to be surrounded by something hotter than my own skin, because I want to boil off the stiffness and pain that greeted me when I awoke this morning. Water is the kindest atmosphere; in water, less is asked of me. Water buoys my joints. In water I can almost forget the horrible, heavy fact of lugging a body around. I get the bathing suit up to my belly button. My arms are through the armholes, but the armholes are down by my waist, so my arms are strapped to my side and I'm in a straitjacket. I'm stuck. I can't get the bathing suit up or down. I will be like this forever.

The girl in the mirror has ragamuffin hair stuck to her face because her face is wet with tears and sweat and fever, and I see her bare shoulders and brand-new, inadequate breasts and her hunched form and I am disgusted. I think, No one will ever want you.

I don't know how I got out of the bathing suit, whether it went up or down, or if I ever got into the hot tub that day. In the more than twenty-five years since I received a diagnosis of rheumatoid arthritis at twelve, this point—in my disease's infancy—is among my lowest. I am ashamed of it. Not because of my helplessness—after all, a kid can get stuck in a bathing suit and it can be a funny story—or because of what it reveals about my body or how sick I really was. I am ashamed of what I thought. What I said, even silently, to a helpless, hurting kid, even if that kid was me.

I am ashamed that this moment, this raw note, is not truly discordant, that it suggests a key to which I could easily modulate, a key I was, and am always, in danger of living in.

Sonata

Movement I

ALLEGRO GIOCOSO /
QUICK, LIVELY; JOYFUL

I wouldn't say of the movement of my arm . . . that it comes when it comes, and so on. . . . I don't need to wait for my arm to rise—I can raise it.

—Ludwig Wittgenstein,
Philosophical Investigations

Chapter 1

The day that I began modulating from the key of wellness to the key of illness was May 25, 1989. This is the day I received my official diagnosis of rheumatoid arthritis, though the first diagnosis would be broad, unspecific, and ultimately inadequate. Rheumatoid arthritis is notoriously difficult to diagnose, and my case was no different. "This is a diagnosis of exclusion," the rheumatologist wrote in the follow-up she sent to my pediatrician that day.

I know details like these, and I can trace my disease's debut in my life, thanks to an astoundingly comprehensive set of notes taken by my mother, a notetaker by nature and a nurse by training. The late-winter and early-spring months of my sixth-grade year were marked by a crescendo of pain and swelling in various joints, each with a plausible explanation. Right thumb hurts: *jammed it playing basketball at recess?* Left shoulder hurts: *delayed-onset muscular soreness after basketball practice?* A visit to the family pediatrician on April 25, 1989, yielded this in my mom's notebook: *probably myalgia that will resolve (growing pains?).*

Throughout the winter and spring, as I turned from eleven to twelve and waited impatiently to turn into a teenager, my body screamed and hushed. Symptoms flared and then quieted. My thumb swelled and then it unswelled. My shoulder hurt and then it stopped hurting. I was not worried, until the morning of May 22, 1989, a Monday. On that morning, I see now, my body had already modulated from before to after: the days of ignorable, passing symptoms were gone, and I had awoken to my new life—though for months or years, I would display eroding rubber resilience, an uncanny ability to forgive and forget when it came to my body and its stunts, including this one.

On that Monday morning, I jumped down from the top bunk and found that I could not put weight on my feet. I fell. My dad was downstairs and my mom was at work, but I pulled myself up to my knees by the posts of the bunk beds so I could reach the white phone attached to the wall—the phone Erica had received as a sixteenth birthday present and then left behind when she'd gone off to Rutgers to major in philosophy—to call my mom. "I can't stand up," I told her.

It is difficult to remember exactly how I felt in this moment. If I was panicked, I am sure my panic subsided when I heard my mother on the phone. I was afraid—why were my legs suddenly traitors?—but faithful: there was an explanation, and my mother would know what it was.

"Stay home," she told me. "Put Dad on."

Is it significant that I didn't have to persuade her of the seriousness of my predicament? That she didn't suspect that I was conniving to stay home alone so I could eat chocolate chip cookies and watch *I Love Lucy* reruns and play the piano all day? That she didn't tell me to stop dawdling, get dressed, get a move on, get to school, stop with the hysterics? Had the come-and-go episodes made her more worried than she'd let on?

I pulled myself back into bed in my absent sister's always-empty, always-made lower bunk, and I stayed there until my mom got home from her night shift. By then my dad had gone to work, his government-issued CIA ID tucked in the breast pocket of his blue short-sleeve dress shirt. I don't know if he waited until my mom got there or if he left me there, alone. It doesn't matter. If the house was empty, all my own, I did not take advantage of it. I did not take cereal down to the family room (forbidden) or binge on Chopin intermezzos at the piano. I went back to hot, sticky-faced, teary sleep and waited for my mom.

My mom's notebooks, the first pages of which record that very morning, depict the intersection of mother and nurse. Over the course of hundreds of pages, the nurse in her allows this professional shorthand to come naturally: *Hx = history. Rx = prescription. Dx = diagnosis. Tx = treatment. C/O = complain(s) of. R/O = rules out.* But only a mother could write *Still walking down stairs sideways* or *8/21 danced the Charleston.* Only a mother would bother to switch to red ink to record *Andrea announced a pain-free day!*

On that Monday, my mom wrote this:

> ↑ *pain in multiple sites: R. shoulder (upper arm), L. wrist, neck, hip?, foot, toes.*
> *Temp 99.2 at 7:30 (crying, however), 99 at 1* P.M.
> *Tylenol × 3 to relieve pain. (Called Mom in tears in* A.M.*)*
> **swelling noted in L. wrist (heat, Ø redness).*
> *Pain began to* ↓ A.M. *of ⁵⁄23, remaining only in wrist and fingers. (esp. 4th finger of L. hand).*
> ↑ *pain after extensive playing in piano recital (out of school most of week).*

I can picture her at the table that day in May, home early and still in her work clothes with her own government-issued NIH ID around her neck, a cup of black coffee or a bowl of cantaloupe in front of her, a cat buttering her calves under the table, her yellow pad cocked at an angle to accommodate the writing posture of a natural leftie forced as a child to learn to write right-handed. At the table, she decided: she'd had enough. She called a local rheumatologist's office and found out that the earliest appointment was two months off. Because she was my mother, she knew my pain was real. And because she was a nurse—a nurse who had, fortuitously, encountered a kid with rheumatoid arthritis in the course of her nursing training, just once—she knew kids could get arthritis. For both reasons, she knew two months would be excruciating for us both. So she made an appointment for later that week at the pediatric rheumatology clinic at Children's National Medical Center in Washington, DC.

But over the three days between that Monday morning and our appointment at Children's, I'd recovered—my body had gotten its act somewhat together, and I had forgiven it its trespasses. I was, as I would tell this and many doctors, "fine." *Fine.*

On the day we went to our appointment at the rheumatology clinic at Children's—it was Thursday of that same week—I was not scared or nervous. I wasn't even curious. Up to that point, doctors' appointments had been a kind of holiday, notable more for what they excused me from than what happened at them. A doctor's appointment in the middle of the school day could mean a deferred math quiz or a rare trip to a drive-through. I liked doctors, I liked meeting new people, and I really liked talking about myself, and I'm sure that's what I expected to get out of our visit to the *specialist* in the big hospital in the city. I didn't even pay attention to the very significant fact that my mother had requested that my dad take the day off work and come with us, and he had.

My mother knew what diagnosis we were there to collect. "I didn't want to be right," she tells me now, sadly. "I really, really hoped that they would tell me I was wrong." My mom is rarely—and never when it comes to medicine or her children—wrong.

We parked in the garage beneath the hospital and rode long escalators up from the dark, exhaust-scented garage into the bright lobby. There were colorful murals on the walls and play equipment at the center of an antiseptic-smelling atrium, and I knew that very sick and dying kids—like the angelic bald kind I'd seen on a PBS special about St. Jude—were treated here. I hoped to spot one and dreaded meeting one. Terror and thrill: it was a safari.

The doctor I met that day, the impossibly named Patience White, was a kind, no-frills woman with a round, young face and thick salt-and-pepper hair always swept up into a tortoise clip. She gave me the kind of attention I loved, commenting on my shoes or the ballpoint doodles on my jeans, calling me by the epithets I loved so much when they came from my dad: I was "a character." I was "something else."

I must have been at least a little convincing, but not alarming, on that first visit, because Dr. White sent me on my way with a prescription for a nonsteroidal anti-inflammatory drug; ordered X-rays of my wrists and fingers to check for erosions or deformities in my bones and joints; and ordered blood tests intended to rule out infections, Lyme disease, and lupus. She told my mom to get me an over-the-counter wrist brace; she instructed me to sit out from running and soccer and basketball if I was sore. As for an official diagnosis, that would have to wait until the results of the blood tests and X-rays came back.

You can't always identify a day of consequence when you're living it, and it didn't feel at all like the big deal it's turned out to be.

No one told me not to play the piano.

The next week, on May 30, Dr. White and her associate dictated a measured, jargony letter to my pediatrician, blandly reciting their findings upon my appearance in their clinic.

If you have ever read your own medical records or any other document written about you that you aren't supposed to see, like parent-teacher conference notes, you know how disconcerting it is to find that you are not *you-the-person* but a set of pronouns. Especially disconcerting to me now are the standard medical syntax and punctuation: *She denies any abdominal pain, diarrhea, or dysphasia.* "Denies," as if I might be lying. Why not *She reports no diarrhea?* Because to doctors, there is always the possibility that I might be covering for my body. I can't be trusted to report on my body. What do I know? After all, I just live here.

In medical-speak, the patient is an ignorant denizen, an unso-
phisticated owner-operator whose words must be stripped away so
doctors and nurses can get down to the business of treating the real
thing: the body. Medical professionals are always aware that what a
patient reports—even with detail, passion, authority, or intelligence,
even if (particularly if) you borrow their words to tell them about it—
might be baloney. *On May 22,* the letter says, *I developed "unbearable"
pain in the right shoulder.* I know that the quotes are there to indicate
that I used exactly this phrase, but they introduce an offensive tone
of skepticism, as if pain exists separate from how I perceive it, as if
doctors could get rid of this complicating, complicated, mouthy,
full-of-feelings *me,* exculpate the pain with their shiny tools, lay it
on one of those napkins like on the dentist's tray and coo, "There.
See? It wasn't 'unbearable.' We classify this as a low-to-moderate,
and definitely bearable, pain." I was allowed to describe *some pain in
the hips* without the doubt-casting quotes—by their logic, shouldn't
"pain" always be in quotes, even if unqualified? The pain is unbearable if I say it is. I am its bearer, and I say "un."

And words aren't really adequate for expressing pain, anyway.
"How are you feeling?" doctors ask. "What does arthritis feel like?"
people ask. My only choices are to liken my pain to something the
questioner has experienced: a stubbed toe, a broken heart. To talk
about my pain, I have to make it *like* something you know, so the
language of pain is inherently figurative. Richard Selzer, a physician, writes that the only full expression of pain is in nonverbal
cries, moans, gasps, and sobs. "Giuseppe Verdi knew that," writes
Selzer, "and made his librettist write lines full of easily singable
vowels and diphthongs. It is the sung vowel that carries to the last
row of La Scala."

Dr. Selzer turned to writing at fifty-eight, after he began to lose
the dexterity required of a surgeon to, as he once put it, "open a
person's body and rummage around with your hands." Though
he was by profession a surgeon and not a musician himself, it was
his second career as a writer that strikes me as nearly the perfect
product of his parents, a physician and a singer.

Pain makes a special kind of sense to a musician: When you are in the hospital, doctors will ask you to locate your pain on a scale.

And when you are in emotional pain, people will tell you to "Let it out." They will invite you to open wide your jaws, as Selzer writes, and let the "noise be carried away from the body on a cloud of warm, humid air that had been within the lungs." Of course, your jaw is a joint and therefore arthritis can make even the widely opened jaws impossible, so your cries of pain—if you make them—are muted, trapped inside the resonating chamber of your mouth or chest, reverberating against the sick tissue itself.

When the lab results from my initial visit came back on June 2, my blood count was normal (no increase in white blood cells, which would indicate infection), and the Lyme disease assay was negative. My antinuclear antibody (ANA) test was slightly elevated but, my mother was reassured, would be much higher if I had lupus. The X-rays that had been taken on that first visit to the hospital in May suggested some bone mineral loss, but not bone erosions that would be more in keeping with rheumatoid arthritis.

And so the diagnosis of exclusion they settled on, "seronegative" arthritis, they chose because they weren't worried enough to order the blood test for the "rheumatoid factor." Decisive-sounding name aside, even that test isn't perfect; there is no lab test that conclusively proves rheumatoid arthritis.

Seronegative arthritis, or arthritis with a blood test showing a negative "rheumatoid factor," can still mean arthritis. Pain is pain, even if unchristened. A rose by any other name, you know. But seronegative rheumatoid arthritis means permission to hope that the pain will be moderate, the disease less crippling.

6/5 white bumps on finger joints
6/6 swollen glands, coated tongue
6/8 dry patches on skin on chest
6/11 right elbow swollen
6/12 both hips

All summer, my mother scratched out accidental poetry, tracking the development of my blooming symptoms in her notebooks. By the time we went to a follow-up appointment at the hospital's satellite clinic in July, the picture had worsened: nearly every day a new joint was implicated. My mom noticed, and wrote down, that I was walking down stairs sideways. We added Tylenol to my diet of nonsteroidal anti-inflammatories.

On that visit, blood was taken to test my rheumatoid factor. I know from my mom's notes that it cost my parents $52.05 to find out that I was positive. Dr. White underlined the rheumatoid factor results twice and wrote, *Due to her + rheumatoid factor she needs to be watched closely and may need earlier, more aggressive treatment.*

The date on that letter is mistyped as *July 12, 1898.* But in truth, it does feel like more than a hundred years ago.

Nevertheless, on July 18, 1989, my mom wrote *but still could go away.*

And so I began to see a lot more doctors, and the novelty of doctor's-visit-as-field-trip began to wear off. But I always loved seeing Dr. White. She'd ask me how I was, and I'd chirp, "Fine, thanks. You?" And she'd turn to my mom, jerking her thumb at me, eyes big, and say, "How about this one, huh? Always with the 'Fine, thanks.' She is *something else.*"

And then she'd turn back to me, friendly but serious, and place her warm, soft hands on my poisoned, bony knees, and say, "OK. Tell me what's going on."

My mom, tentatively at first, testing the waters, not wanting to take even this from me when so much was being taken from me already—she of course knew what I could not, which is that so much more would be taken from me—would answer for me: her ankles have been hurting; her wrist is swollen; she says she has a stomachache. My answer was always "I'm fine," and it was rarely the right answer. Dr. White wanted to know what new joints were hurting, was I taking my medicine, was I having side effects, had I lost any significant range of motion, what did the last blood workup say, was I anemic? But these were not the things I wanted to talk about. Those were boring things; those things had nothing in the world to do with me, fabulous me.

The episodes that had gotten us to Children's National Medical Center—the episodes of acute pain in my fingers, feet, and knees, pain that would attack suddenly and then decay—had seemed tentative, as if arthritis was testing me out to see if I'd let it set up camp in my body. When we'd gone and named it—favoring that diagnosis of exclusion, "a diagnosis of seronegative arthritis"—we gave it a foothold; we told it to stay.

If doctors really want to know what's going on with your disease, they shouldn't ask, "How are you?" First of all, the only socially acceptable answer to "How are you?" is "Fine, thanks. You?" No one who asks you how you are—except, maybe, your doctor—wants to hear "I'm in pain all the time." And, unfortunately for those doctors, we're all well trained very early on. It's a kindergarten skill, and one that's particularly well taught by good Midwestern Lutherans to their progeny: memorize your address and your phone number, mind your p's and q's, learn your "Howdy do" and "Fine, thank you." Don't bother other people with your pain. They've got their own. Bodies and their failings are not topics for polite conversation.

"*I'm* fine," I said to Dr. White, every time. I was grasping for a distinction between my self and my disease, a distinction I couldn't have articulated then. How am I? *I* am happy, busy, scooping up ribbons and trophies and certificates at every piano competition I enter, worried about algebra, crushing on Jordan Katon, afraid of the Catholic girls from Holy Cross who pick on me at the public pool, starting a Gulf War protest at school. How's my *arthritis*? Oh, well, that's different. That sucks. My ankles are throbbing and swollen and Naprosyn makes my stomach hurt.

Of course there is some overlap: How am *I*? Well, I'm pissed that my BFF told everyone that my arthritis was contagious because now Jordan will never French-kiss me ever.

These visits gave me my first, rudimentary understanding of what was going on—and what continues to go on—in my arthritic body, the cheery pamphlet-script I read from even now when people ask me why I have arthritis (and, hey, was it from all the piano playing I did? Did I crack my knuckles? As if that could possibly explain the scars on my hands, shoulder, hip, and knees).

The truth is that my body is a liar. It has received bad intel. For some mysterious reason, something in my body has told my immune system to fight. It senses (erroneously) a foreign and threatening presence in my body, and it attacks. The attacks are played out most obviously in my joints, but more subtly in my muscles, tendons, and bones. The joints themselves become craggy and the bones decalcified. Casualties in this messy war. The slick, lubricating substance between the bones, the synovium of the joint space, leaks all over the damn place, weakening tendons, ligaments, and other soft tissues. Compounding casualties. The spaces between my opposing bones (the joint spaces), what should be roomy gray-white gaps on an X-ray, eclipse. They close up and eventually disappear as the misshapen, knobby, feathered white edges of the bones come together. Bone on bone. And that hurts—sometimes like a stubbed toe, sometimes like heartbreak.

Here is the pamphlet that doesn't exist, the one I'd be happy to write: Rheumatoid arthritis is a disease that cries wolf. Given an inch, it takes a mile. This is how you lose several degrees of extension in a joint: One day, your (choose one) elbow / knee / hip / fourth finger hurts. Your body says, *That hurts. Protect me.* So you let that joint off the hook for the day; you find a different way to carry your backpack or you don't practice piano that night or you say, "No, no, I *wanted* to spend the whole birthday party at the bowling alley playing Ms. Pac-Man" because playing Ms. Pac-Man allowed you to sit on a stool for hours. Maybe you try an ice pack, if you've gotten wise to the fact that inflammation is the real problem, not the pain that comes with it.

If you're lucky, after a day or two the swelling goes down and you can play piano again, you can reach your feet to pull on a sock again. If you're not lucky, the next day is worse and you wear slip-on sandals and turn your eyeglass case into a maraca rattling with ibuprofen. You don't move the joint because you can't move the joint. Eventually, you stop trying, because it hurts. Your "great attitude" helps you find a way around it, a way to type with nine fingers. Or six. Or two thumbs and three fingers, as I am doing now. And after a while, I don't know how long it takes, you can't move it. There's the rub. You didn't move the joint because you couldn't move the joint, but now you *can't* move the joint because you *didn't* move the joint.

And yet, the problem isn't really in the joints at all. Rheumatoid arthritis is an autoimmune disease and therefore has more in common, both progression and treatment-wise, with multiple sclerosis than with your grandma's achy gardening hands. The glucosamine supplements peddled for osteoarthritis probably won't help rheumatoid arthritis very much. Bee-venom therapy—which originated centuries ago and is still used in Eastern and "alternative" therapies for forms of arthritis—might.

Thorough Internet research will uncover a loud body of unscientific devotees and a quiet body of peer-reviewed scientists who argue that bee-venom might work, and that it might work by inhibiting the production of an inflammation-producing chemical called tumor-necrosis factor, or TNF. This makes some sense: the most current "biologic" medications for rheumatoid arthritis, such as Remicade, Enbrel, Humira, and Simponi, also work by inhibiting the production of TNF. Nevertheless, bee-venom therapy for RA is, in the West, not a widely accepted treatment. I have been on almost every TNF inhibitor, though. They work incredibly well, until they don't. The last one of these I have taken is Simponi, which abruptly stopped working. I have one last dose of it still in my refrigerator, which I refuse to throw out because it's my "unfinished Simponi."

The loveliness of being aided by something that most people avoid—bee stings—has its appeal. Though my experience of Western medicine suggests bee-venom treatment has never truly been accepted (in almost thirty years of visits to rheumatologists, not one has mentioned it), there have been accepted treatments for RA that are similarly fascinating. For many years, and at the time I was diagnosed in 1989, a leading treatment for RA was gold.

Gold therapy was, and is, available in both injected and oral forms. At least one doctor suggested it for me in those early days of the disease.

However, having heard (probably from a pamphlet or in a waiting room) that the shots were extraordinarily painful, I dug in my heels and refused gold treatment. I was unwilling to admit that I was afraid of painful shots, so I rolled my eyes and insisted that the treatment seemed "primitive" to me. And my refusal was accepted. During the heyday of gold treatment for RA—essentially the 1960s through the 1990s, when TNF inhibitors took the stage—the treatment was thought to both alleviate symptoms and slow disease progression, if started early enough in the disease process. If I ever regretted my decision not to take gold way back then, I no longer did when a leading rheumatologist told me that the treatment had more side effects than benefits.

Treating RA means modifying, subduing, or overriding malfunctioning parts of the immune system. Treating its *symptoms* means ice packs and ibuprofen. These are two different, but simultaneous, wars. They are Iraq and Afghanistan. But people get those confused, too.

At the time that I received my diagnosis ("This was before the Internet, kids!"), my principal sources for information about rheumatoid arthritis were my doctors and the endless pamphlets they provided. Immediately after receiving my diagnosis, I checked in both our *Encyclopedia Britannica* and *World Book Encyclopedia* volumes, but I found nothing new or helpful. My mother had an impressive selection of medical books within my reach. One, a red volume called *Symptoms*, had provided hours of fear-based entertainment and schadenfreude for Chris and me as we lay on our bellies on the brown carpet, flipping the pages and diagnosing ourselves and each other. But whereas the pamphlets, with their cartoonish covers and conversational Q and A formats, were reassuringly upbeat, the medical books were frightening, favoring black-and-white photographs of gnarled, bumpy hands.

Eventually, of course, the Internet was born, and in a fraction of a second, Google can provide thousands of perfectly terrifying image results for "arthritic hands" or 8,790 chipper Web results for "how to beat arthritis" (though most refer to osteoarthritis, not rheumatoid arthritis, and suggestions include "eat your fruits and veggies").

I've had my fill of the Internet's arthritis specialties, horror-show pictures, and ignorant "just eat a banana every day and then rub the peel on your knees" advice. But the Internet has been able to provide fascinating perspectives on the much-debated history and treatment of this disease. Tantalizing mysteries abound: Why does RA affect about three times as many women as men? And why does it seem to go into remission in about 75 percent of pregnant women and then, in most cases, flare with a vengeance after delivery? The disease affects men, but it (as do most autoimmune diseases) appears to have a special relationship with women.

One author of a book about women and autoimmune disease that I read argues that this is the case because women's immune systems are simply more complex than men's—after all, a woman's immune system is designed so that she can carry around a thing that is 50 percent foreign genetic material and not reject it. Scientifically, the childbearing design of a woman's body probably does play a big role in autoimmunity, but that author's rhapsodic awe of the complexity of a woman's body, in the context of discussing devastating autoimmune diseases, feels a bit like the boy who once told me, "You need to have arthritis, or else you'd be, like, *too much*." We women need to be taken down a peg.

There is much discussion, but there is little consensus. Even the basics—what rheumatoid arthritis is, what causes it, how long it's been around, who gets it and why—are the topics of much debate.

For example, when I was diagnosed with arthritis in 1989—and until very recently, actually—I assumed that rheumatoid arthritis had always been around. In world studies class in seventh grade, I wondered if eugenicists would, or did, sterilize women with the mangled joints of RA. In Sunday school, even as my congenital faith waned, I wondered if Jesus cured anybody of RA among all those lepers.

Although there's evidence (some four-thousand-year-old rheumatoid-looking bones in Tennessee, for example) that Native Americans get it bad and always have—incidence and severity of RA in the Native American population is still strikingly elevated—the age of the disease is just one of the many mysteries that cloud the boggy history of rheumatoid arthritis.

Doctors and historians have combed European history looking for conclusive ancient, or even really old, evidence of rheumatoid arthritis and have found no definitive portrayals. None in the Bible; none in Shakespeare. There are a few suspicious hands in a few Flemish paintings, and an emperor—Constantine IX—who probably had something like it. And there is a female mummy named "Braids Lady," dead since the sixteenth century but excavated from beneath an Italian church in the 1990s, who seems to have the signs—both skeletal and genetic—of rheumatoid arthritis, lending credence to the theory that RA is an Old World ailment.

In high school, a sneakily kind art teacher mentioned to me that there was a theory that the sixteen-year-old girl who stood for Botticelli's *Birth of Venus*, Simonetta Vespucci, displayed the classic symptoms of the disease, like the twisted pinkie on her right hand, her swollen wrist, and a "sausage finger" on her left hand. This teacher was probably inspired by a *Washington Post* article from 1990 that featured the observations of Jan Dequeker, a Catholic University rheumatologist, writer, and art buff who had taken up a magnifying glass to pin down evidence of pre-nineteenth-century rheumatoid arthritis.

Almost ten years after Dequeker's article was published in the *Post*, art historian James Elkins sniffed in *Pictures of the Body: Pain and Metamorphosis* that Dequeker's diagnosis of Vespucci was "cold" and that it reduced her to a specimen, "an illustration of a kind of arthritis." I am not sure why Elkins seems to think Vespucci is reduced by the suggestion of her arthritis, or why to him the mere suggestion that the real woman who posed for the painting may have been in excruciating pain to do so threatens to overshadow "the original context and intentions of this painting." Then again, I have plenty of experience myself of being reduced to a specimen by virtue of my arthritis.

I would like both Dequeker and Elkins to know what it meant to me, an arthritic girl, to think that one of the world's most adored figures shared my plight. How comforted I was, upon learning of Dequeker's theory, to scrutinize the painting, convincing myself I could see my fingers in hers, how desperately grateful. Venus is still my patron saint of rheumatism, even though I'm not Catholic, and even though the theory has never been thoroughly confirmed or even widely accepted.

Part of the problem is that arthritis—even today—is a word that covers a range of symptoms and experiences. Arthritis is the word for the retired-at-thirty-six quarterback's bum knee, your grandpa's hitch in his giddyup, and my debilitating, multisystem chronic illness. A fairly recognizable depiction of rheumatoid arthritis by current diagnostic standards turned up in Paris in 1800, but until some terminology was settled on (the term *rheumatoid arthritis* was coined in the late nineteenth century), people wrote about pain and stiffness and swelling and deformity in whatever language came naturally to them—and of course there are only so many ways to describe the limp of a caddish emperor, even if he limped because of a nonrheumatoid, reactive arthritis probably caused by an STD, not a misfiring immune system.

As for the age of the disease, there are those ancient American bones, and some people insist that there are convincing descriptions of the disease in ancient Greece or India, as though to concede that it's a new disease, or a post-Columbian New World disease, is to engage in a kind of victim-blaming: "You're saying I brought this upon myself, with my tobacco or my Amerindian diet or my Industrial Revolution? No, no, we arthritics have always been here in your midst!" And here we are: It's estimated that 1.5 million adults in the United States alone have rheumatoid arthritis; approximately 294,000 children have juvenile arthritis or another rheumatic condition.

Rheumatoid arthritis is a wily disease, and it generates wily statistics. Despite being christened in the nineteenth century, RA was not established as its own "disease entity" until the middle of the twentieth century. Then, for decades, diagnosis depended on a patient's displaying markers of fairly advanced disease, meaning people who were a little bit arthritic were not counted. The American College of Rheumatology and the European League Against Rheumatism created revised RA classification criteria in 2010 to increase the ability of physicians to diagnose people with RA before they are in really bad shape with RA. But a true picture of the disease's prevalence now and over time remains elusive.

Some researchers suggest that prevalence of RA has been on the decline for some four decades—perhaps because of the availability of oral contraceptives, which appear to have a protective effect. Then again, some of the studies included in this research use the old classification criteria, some the new. Some studies don't include people who have been diagnosed but are experiencing treatment-induced remission. And prevalence and incidence rates are, literally, all over the map: lower in Northern Europe than in North America, lower still in Southern Europe. Markedly low in rural Africa.

Several studies point out that there is much less RA in "developing countries." In these places where infectious diseases are more common, immunological diseases appear to be less common. One theory to explain this correlation, as well as RA's presence in the modern world, is the hygiene hypothesis. The hygiene hypothesis states that a lack of early childhood exposure to infectious agents, microorganisms, and parasites leaves a person with a wimpy, untested immune system that is then defenseless against disease. As sanitation improves in these developing countries, rates of autoimmune disease increase. In short, cleanliness is next to sickliness.

Genetics also plays some part in producing RA, but no one's sure how big a part. One doctor explained to me that the prevailing theory is one they call the "bad luck" theory: genetics predispose a person to autoimmunity, but then some event in the person's life determines what autoimmune response is kicked off, and when, and how severely. To use the most overused (but appropriately violent, I assure you) metaphor of causality, genetics loaded the gun and then something—what? a childhood illness, a playground scrape, the mumps I had on my first Christmas or the cold I had the day the *Challenger* exploded or my bloody tumble down the Berm?—pulled the trigger and aggravated my bad-luck immune system toward arthritis. But why arthritis and not multiple sclerosis or lupus or fibromyalgia or Crohn's disease or psoriasis? I don't know. No one knows, exactly.

Music-theory pop quiz: What do you call a note that shows up where it doesn't belong? G-flat, say, totally out of place in the key of B-flat major? *Accidental.*

As lonely as it makes me to think that there weren't people of my kind populating the streets of Jesus's Jerusalem or fair Verona, I sort of like the idea that rheumatoid arthritis is relatively new. I'm an early adopter. I like to get in on the ground floor. Also, to think that this disease is relatively young gives me hope for the progress that's already been made in treating it. We may be less than two centuries in to this thing, but we've already had some pretty dark ages.

Though I love shirtdresses, pillbox hats, beaded cocktail sweaters, and little white gloves, I'm desperately grateful not to have had rheumatoid arthritis in any prior decade—in the 1940s, when, judging by a 1947 article in *The American Journal of Nursing*, I would have been hospitalized, advised not to exercise or work, and given some sedatives and some therapy to determine what combination of unsatisfactory hygiene (ironic), low income, and childhood emotional trauma (probably deprivation of emotional security paired with excessively strict parents) caused me to express my unhappiness this way; or in the 1950s, when one theory held that the severity of rheumatoid arthritis corresponded to the patient's inability to express aggressive fantasies.

Oh, I can express my aggressive fantasies.

Certainly these weren't the only theories being advanced, and good, hard work during these years yielded credible treatments—the use of steroids, for example. By the middle of the twentieth century, amazingly anti-inflammatory corticosteroids were the standard treatment of rheumatoid arthritis, but these drugs masked infection and depleted bone density and fell out of favor (as a primary treatment, anyway) for RA not long before I turned up at Children's National Medical Center that day.

The Internet may have persuaded me that Simonetta "Venus" Vespucci probably didn't have rheumatoid arthritis, but it also told me that Kathleen Turner does, and Jamie Farr, of *M*A*S*H*, does. Someday, I think, I'll get an enormous back tattoo of Farr's *M*A*S*H* character, Klinger, rising demurely from a clam shell, covering his nipples with swollen fingers, a portrait of RA that makes private sense to me—an inside joke between me and my disease.

Or maybe I'll commission a painting, a knockoff of the *Sgt. Pepper* album cover, with all the people the Internet has told me have or had rheumatoid arthritis: Jamie Farr and Kathleen Turner, Lucille Ball, James Coburn, Glenn Frey, Sandy Koufax, Edith Piaf, Renoir, a Lindbergh grandson, Baby Jessica from the well.

When I was first diagnosed, teachers and doctors and guidance counselors were always hovering, always telling me it was OK to ask, "Why me?" But that's a grown-up question, not a kid question. Kids don't have—at least I didn't have—any expectation that life would be fair. It's adults who believe they've struck some deal with God, who believe that what they've been getting is what they'll continue to get. It's the nature of childhood to expect that things will change without warning—to hope, even to *pray*, that things will change without warning: a snow day, a surprise party, a secret-admirer note. It's adults who say things like "This is not in my contract!" I get that now, now that secondary and tertiary syndromes, fatigue and dry eyes and muscle loss and anemia, pack girth onto the snowball of my original disease and add insult, insult, insult to injury, injury, injury. But kids—kids are used to being powerless. Kids take what's thrown at them and they hold on. I didn't question the justice in my getting arthritis any more than I questioned the justice in my getting two older brothers and an older sister—Chris, Matthew, Erica—even if I didn't always like it. I was a child who fully expected only extraordinary things.

Long before a diagnosis of RA confirmed it, I just knew I was a statistical oddity, an unprecedented phenomenon; I knew the rest of the world—and the "Kids Did It!" section of *National Geographic World* magazine—would figure it out soon enough.

But now that I know how it's turned out—how it's turning out—I can't help but feel for the kid in those pages of my mom's notebooks, and I allow myself to feel (What? Pity?) only because she is not me. *Don't do handstands*, one of my mom's notes reads. Another: *Much jumping today.* Oh, to even feel like doing handstands now. Why her?

I still don't think "Why me?" in anything more than a biological sense (Does it have something to do with those mumps? Being delivered by C-section? Or my not having been breastfed? All of the above?). Maybe it's not pity after all. Maybe I envy this girl in the notebooks, or I don't want to lose whatever part of her is still in me, or maybe I want to protect her. Didn't she see how hopeless it was to keep playing soccer, to try out for cheerleading, to practice piano for hours a day? Why *her*?

On the very day of my initial visit to Children's, just days after that terrifying Monday morning, only my right wrist was hurting and, because I was a kid and kids can be resilient almost to the point of being amnesiacs, I thought of it as a visit about my wrist, not about my life. I'd forgotten about calling my mom in tears after collapsing when I jumped out of bed, or any of the other symptoms she'd recorded. We went to the doctor: I brought the body with the simmering disease and a bored expression, and my mom brought her ubiquitous yellow legal pad and a concerned expression, and we collected our (tentative, inaccurate) diagnosis, and then I was deposited back at school with a letter on Children's letterhead and I showed it around to teachers so they would let me chew gum to loosen my jaw or get up to walk around the classroom if I was getting stiff or sit out of PE or be a few minutes late to class. And I showed it to the kids at school and one of them scanned it skeptically till he got to the word *chronic* and then said, nodding,

"Chronic. That means serious." Matt Bryant, wherever you are, you were right.

At that time we were all, apparently, putting our money on a just-passing-through arthritis. No one said, in so many words: This is chronic. This is progressive. Lost ground can't be re-won. This will get worse.

No one said: You will always be hammering out new terms, your body and you.

Autoimmune disease is civil war. In rheumatoid arthritis the battles are fought in the theater of the joints. Oh, but if only it stopped at the joints.

Do I wish that Dr. White had grabbed me by the shoulders (ouch), fixed her gaze, and told me that mine would be a story of invasion and encroachment, betrayal and reconciliation, negotiation and détente? I'm not sure I would have handled all that very well back then.

And how much did they know, anyway? Could Dr. White and my mother even know, coming at my illness as they did, with their muscled hands and lab coats and notepads and pens and diagnostic shorthand, about the plaguing doubt, the awful question that really matters to a person with a disabling chronic illness: Is this—this inelegant and ugly, unbidden and ultimately uninteresting, crafty and not-at-all charming medical accident—is *this* what will be most remarkable about me?

And what if someone had said, then, "You will not be a pianist. Stop now"? It would have been no use. I was too far gone by then, too in love with the piano—congenitally, incurably musical.

It's sort of lovely, really, I can see that: music is intrinsic, genetic, coded into my very DNA, and encouraged by every aspect of my childhood environment, but the expression of that music, the ability to play it, has been endangered by that same DNA and, perhaps, my environment. There is so little difference—two tiny vowels—between *melody* and *malady*.

It's algebra: If girl X sets out on her trip in 1984 carrying a cargo of not insignificant talent, genetic predisposition, and obsessive enthusiasm, and girl Y sets out in 1989 carrying a prodigious varia-tion of rheumatoid arthritis, which girl will you remember and why? Note that X = Y.

The questions I really had, no one could answer. I wanted to know if I was going to end up disabled (though the vernacular of the time was *handicapped*). That has turned out to be a more complicated question than I even knew to worry about, with more ever-changing answers than I thought possible. I went into my ill-ness with the only definition of *disabled* available to me at the time, the medical model of disability. The medical model of disability declares a person disabled if her body refuses to do something "normal" bodies do: she can't hear, or create insulin, or walk right. But that is not the only way—in fact, it is the bleakest, most hope-less way—to define disability.

And immediately after my diagnosis, I began to worry about sex. The truth is, even by age ten I had been worried about sex, but my arthritis added another shameful complication to my sneaking suspicion that I was not destined for sex (or, therefore, love). I may have been only twelve when I was diagnosed but I was not, as some girls are, an especially young twelve. I was five-four and still growing. I had OK breasts. A cute college friend of my sister's had asked me what my "major" was. Though I hadn't ditched my beloved teddy bear, Huggy (nor have I still), by the date of my diagnosis, the woven canvas cover of my three-ring binder was a many-times redacted declaration of love: "I ♥ Shane Tom Kris Brad Jeff Geoff Phil Richard Shane again." These were not unrequited romances; sixth grade, my last (mostly) arthritis-free school year, had turned out to be a newly sophisticated world lined with shining lockers where I suddenly, surprisingly, had cur-rency and nine sequential, chaste, and moon-eyed "boyfriends" to my name. This wasn't *Go Ask Alice* by a long shot, but I was doing OK: a seventh grader named Kris had French-kissed me at the Halloween dance, felt me up during Christmas break, and dumped me before New Year's. I had my eye on Jordan Katon. I was right on schedule.

I had been relieved that the terms of dating for now seemed to be the external rites for which I thought I'd been prepared by the radio: loving, touching, squeezing. I hadn't heard any radio songs about probing, tearing, bleeding. But I knew the clock had started. As are many girls, I was simultaneously terrified both of the inevitability of sex and of the possibility that I would die a virgin. Like many girls, I scrutinized my naked body in the mirror. I cocked my head and adjudicated my breasts. By thirteen, though, it wasn't my soft dots—mouth, breasts, butt—that were all wrong but the long stretches of line meant to connect them: my arms, my legs. Just one year into my life with arthritis, my limbs had thinned unappealingly; my knees jutted out in hot, red orbs; my fingers sprung bumps; and I walked in a halting limp. I could cover a flat butt with an oversize Hypercolor T-shirt. But I couldn't cover my unsexy old-lady hands.

Which may explain my fascination with little white gloves.

The coincidence of rheumatoid arthritis and puberty in my case is not unusual; in fact, the hormonal changes at puberty may be part of what turns on the disease process in some people. But my rheumatologist recently told me that I was lucky that I had already begun puberty when arthritis descended on me: I'd grown to an acceptable, fully adult height (though I would still gain four more inches), and the bones in my cheeks and chin had finished growing, saving me from the chipmunk look some kids with RA get. He seems to know that I am glad that arthritis has not assaulted my face, that I like my face just fine, though I have never told him that.

On the doorstep of the 1990s, a *Sassy* reader, newly pubescent, and even more newly arthritic, I knew that sex stood between me and love, and I knew my problematic body sat between me and sex. So when Dr. White asked me how everything was going, I said "Fine" because I didn't know how to ask, or whom to ask, or if it was OK to ask, if this arthritis business was going to mean that no one would ever love me or want to have sex with me. And it would take me nearly fifteen years to even figure out what answer I wanted: Did I want to be told I was conscripted to sex-partner status and eligible for consideration as a wife? Or did I want to hear that I was doomed to virginity, that I could use my brain and time for other things, that I was nobly, happily exempt from more carnal pursuits?

Multiplying my worries further: Even if I *could* swing the sex part, could I conceive, bear, care for a baby? What, exactly, was off the table?

Here is a truth I learned alone in my bed, worrying myself to tears: When you are a chronically ill child preparing for a life of disease, you get old before you grow up. Impossibility comes before possibility, no before yes: I got arthritis before I got my period.

It should be clear by now that I had the kind of mother I could have talked to about these things. And I'm sure there was an "Arthritis and Sexuality" pamphlet in a drawer at the children's hospital if I'd only asked for it. *Well, kiddo,* I tell my body and my former self, *some things you have to figure out on your own.* I sometimes talk to my body like I'm its brassy, no-nonsense, single working mother, doing her best and I'm-the-mommy-that's-why. Yes, a body is a family.

After all, I am my body's champion, its cheerleader, its aider and abettor, its enabler, its biggest fan, its defender. I am all it has. I am ashamed to say that sometimes at night I wonder if I hate it. Frequently and silently I disown it, for all the good that does. I wonder what connects it to me; I wonder if we are the same; I wonder if I did this and how. I wonder if it is my job to rescue it. I am sometimes guilty and frequently beguiled.

But I am ultimately, if not always, on my body's side. I have a soft spot for its hard spots. In public, I gamely defend its good qualities. I send it to school in designer duds. I am in my body's corner. I am its only chance of not being a total loss, a lifetime fuckup.

Just the way so many women, in their first days or weeks or months of motherhood, enlist the help of their own mothers to help them get their footing, my mother has been teaching me how to mother this body of mine the same way she has mothered me: with patience and tenderness and sturdiness and smarts. She has been tough-loving my illness the way she tough-loved my drug-addicted brother: with inexhaustible softness for pain but hard-assed intolerance for progression. Will I ever be ready for her to leave? Will I ever know how to do this on my own?

And I have been buoyed by the other women who have loved me: Dr. White, and my two grandmothers—the schoolteacher and the musician—and the near-perfect composite of the two, my beloved piano teacher, Mrs. Feltman, who taught me and trained me for so many things. Because of her, when the inevitable day comes when I must say good-bye to my mother, I think, I will have rehearsed for it.

Chapter 2

Starting piano at seven gave me a five-year head start on my arthritis. And even after the arthritis showed up at twelve, I had a few years' grace. By the time the pain made unrelenting daily appearances, by the time the disease had written its changes into the very shape of my fingers, around the time I was fifteen or sixteen, I knew nothing better than the piano. I loved nothing—no one—more. I loved myself because of what I could do at the piano. For years, I could override pain or awkwardness with dexterity and coordination. My fingers were extraordinarily good fingers before they were extraordinarily bad fingers.

My first piano lesson with Mrs. Feltman, in second grade, was a lunchtime lesson. My mom picked me up at school and took me to Mrs. Feltman's house on Blossom Drive, a redbrick colonial-style house with slab cement steps and white columns. That first day, I ran up the steps. At the end of my final lesson with her, more than fifteen years later, I inched down them sideways, cursing her for not having a railing.

When I showed up for that first lesson, I'd been begging for piano lessons for a few years, eager to learn how to make sense of the plastic-topped keys of the upright Wurlitzer, desperate to know how my sister deciphered the small black notes in her piano books.

Mrs. Feltman was from another time. I cringed and beamed simultaneously when she boasted that I'd won competitions "and everyone else was *Asian*!" Her house was all wainscoting and chair rails, tea roses and toile, but Mrs. Feltman and her husband, a jazz drummer, seemed always to be shouting angrily at each other over a set of stairs to the basement. She had two sons, and the younger of them, David, was a mysterious and unattainable seventh grader when I began taking lessons. When I was early to my lessons, I would wait in the TV room with David, who silently twirled a hockey stick on its curved foot as he looked at the TV and I looked at him. The time would come when I had, for at least one brief evening, his full attention, but I would have to wait more than ten years for it.

The pages of my sister's hand-me-down method books, already dotted with gold star-shaped stickers, soon had twin gold stars on every page.

Mrs. Feltman said I took to piano "like a fish to water." She said I was "going like a house on fire." I loved her, even if once I drew a nasty caricature of her on the back of a program at a recital. I wasn't careful. I let the program slip down onto the floor and she found it when she was cleaning up the auditorium. She called my mother to tell her how hilarious she'd found the picture—my depiction of her with sagging breasts that showed through the gaping hole in a sloppily buttoned blouse, the crazy-person hair, the cloud of euphemisms that I'd lettered in a halo around her cross-eyed head: *Rob Peter to pay Paul! Put a little oomph in it! It's a doozy!* She wanted to use the picture as the cover for the next recital's program. *No, no, no,* I said, embarrassed that I'd been so mean to someone so huge-hearted, someone who loved me so much, so clearly. But I didn't learn. In fact, I've something of a shameful habit of drawing mean cartoons of the people I love the most.

I played piano whenever I could: before school, between school and dinner, in my coat and gloves, waiting for the rest of the family to be ready to go wherever we were going. I played in Mrs. Feltman's recitals at the community college and won competitions at Peabody Conservatory in Baltimore, solos and duets, duos and trios and quartets. I competed against myself once, performing as one-fourth of one piano quartet, then sitting down in the velvet seat, waiting a few minutes and getting back onstage as one-fourth of a different team. My teams won first and second place and I was disappointed only that I hadn't tied with myself. This episode is darkly funny to me now, as autoimmune infighting spoils my body. On the ride home from Baltimore, I laid my fistfuls of prize ribbons out on the backseat and meticulously filled out the attached cards: *Awarded to: Andrea Serine Avery, On: May 8, 1985, For: "Flamenco" and "Rondino" (solos)*. I can't remember what it was like not being able to read music any more than I can recall when *A-N-D-R-E-A* was a set of glyphs that didn't mean me. In sloppy doctor's cursive, *Andrea* and *arthritis* can look a lot alike. Me, a name I call myself.

The language of music is so deeply ingrained in me that if you tell me to be somewhere at six o'clock sharp, my first understanding is that you mean half past six. If you want me there early, at a quarter till, you should say six o'clock flat.

I figured out how to read music in church, which inclined me to believe in God. I'd had only a couple of lessons and Mrs. Feltman had taught me the basics of the treble and bass staves and the notes that hung on them like beads on a string: *Every Good Boy Does Fine. All Good Boys Deserve Fudge*. Like many kids, I wanted to zoom past this boring homework and start playing already! Then, one Sunday, following along in the Lutheran hymnal—maybe it was "Let Us Break Bread Together on Our Knees"—it simply clicked. Now I can't remember not knowing how to read music. I can hear a piece of music even if I see the score upside down, the same way you can spot your own name on a list even when you're not looking for it. It finds you.

I'd been taking lessons for only a few months when it was time to learn "Over the River and Through the Woods." It was a jazz arrangement that was more complicated than the simple method books I'd played from so far; it had an arpeggiated bass line instead of chunky solid chords for the left hand. Furthermore, the right hand had a syncopated, galloping melody, which meant that my hands were frequently doing very different things but they were expected to make sense together, to make music, and to end up in the same place at the end.

I had a meltdown. I cried; I pouted; I banged my hands on the keys of the piss-stinking piano. And then it happened. I—no, I can't take credit, it wasn't me but my hands—figured it out, and it wasn't hard after that.

If it was so sinfully easy at seven, what kind of musician would I have been if I'd started piano earlier? At five, maybe, or four? Nannerl Mozart, Wolfgang's older sister, also started keyboard lessons as a little girl. She was a musical prodigy in her own right. What if she'd been given the lessons in toddlerhood that her younger brother was given? Would she be more than a grace note in the story of Mozart? If my musical head start on arthritis had been longer, could I have gotten good enough that arthritis, no matter how determined and phenomenal, wouldn't have threatened my playing?

This question, self-inflicted as it is, is troubling. In his book *After the Diagnosis: Transcending Chronic Illness*, Dr. Julian Seifter writes, "Our society is quick to judge people for their illnesses. . . . If you're sick, it's your own fault; your lifestyle, your genes, your fault." This question haunts many sick or disabled people, and I am no different: Is there something I could have done to prevent this destruction, or to transcend it more fully? Could I have loved music more, practiced more seriously?

I torment myself by wondering if a few more years of training at the piano might have made my hands impervious to arthritis, might have made my left temporal lobe more powerful and more musically capable.

In my imaginary RA-themed *Sgt. Pepper* portrait, there would be numerous pianists with arthritis or other serious hand impairments: Leon Fleisher (dystonia), Byron Janis (psoriatic arthritis), John Cage (arthritis), and the composer Robert Schumann (disabling right-hand injury of uncertain origin). But you know them, if you know them, as musicians first, arthritics second. Is this because of the length of their head start on their disease or injury, or is it because they were, or are, more talented than they are sick? It was that latter question that plagued me.

My precocious arthritis and my early accomplishment at the piano were equally improbable, equally mysterious products of perfect conditions. So why is it so tempting for me to see my musical ability as some magical, innate gift that I inherited—perhaps minimizing the amount of sheer hard work I was accomplishing as I sat and "played"—and my arthritis as something I allowed to mess it up?

Though the nature-versus-nurture debate rages on, a compelling 2008 study of an extended Finnish family of musicians posited that musical ability is half-genetic. Of course, a lot of good that half-genetic musical aptitude is if you don't have an instrument in your house, or you aren't offered music lessons, or your public school cuts its music program. Musical ability may be half-genetic, but "neither nature nor nurture can alone make a musician," argued Paul R. Farnsworth in *The Social Psychology of Music*. "Both must be present before musical and other abilities can emerge."

Boy, that sounds familiar. It sounds like the "bad-luck" theory of autoimmune disease.

When people first learn about my having arthritis, they frequently ask if it's genetic. "Do your parents have it?" they ask. "What about your siblings?" The answer is no, no, I'm alone in my family; it's a mystery. Rheumatoid arthritis has some kind of murky genetic component—as do all autoimmune diseases—but it's not as simple as being passed down from parent to child. Like everything associated with rheumatoid arthritis, it's not tidy, it's not easy. I explain all of this to the people who insist that it must be genetic—it must be "passed down," they say. They pause. "What about your grandparents?" they ask, and I want to tell them about all the things that my grandparents did pass down to me. I want to tell them about the music that was entrusted to me.

And in different conversations, people ask just that. "Where do you get your musical ability?" people used to ask me. Grandma Torvik played piano; my mom played piano and plays clarinet, still. It was Grandma Torvik and my parents who later collaborated to buy me a giant, gleaming grand piano when I'd outgrown the little brown Wurlitzer. My dad likes to remind me that he got the highest score on the musical aptitude test in the sixth grade, in 1950. Grandpa Avery was a trumpet and sax player. But the best answer is Grandma Avery, a hold-her-own gal who played in big bands full of men. I come from a family full of music. The question isn't where my music *came* from. The question is where it went.

The tension between my two nature-nurture phenomena is inescapable: The only time I have really loved or approved of my arthritic body is when it has been tucked into the piano. I loved the muscular heat that spread through my hands and arms as I warmed up, the way at the beginning of any practice session my hands were obedient mittens, performing uniformly, but soon started taking individual orders. It was amazing the way my fourth finger would arch and let my thumb pass below, without being told.

How can I be angry at my body for the way it fails me now, when for many thousands of hours at the piano, it did things I hadn't even asked it to do?

My body has frequently surprised—shocked, offended, hurt—me. But the piano is the only place where my body has ever pleasantly surprised me. My hands acted independently of my brain, decoding and executing the tricky bass part to Copland's "Cat and Mouse" before my eyes had scanned the whole measure. In the summertime, they sweated and slipped even more easily between the slick keys, while the edge of the bench dug into the backs of my bare legs.

Before arthritis, I put everything I had into my super-loud, super-rubato version of "I Write the Songs," out-schmaltzing Manilow himself. I binged. I loved Chopin and the songs from *Free to Be . . . You and Me.* I whizzed through "Dr. Gradus ad Parnassum" and Dire Straits. I could sight-read anything. I have perfect pitch.

We had a rule that I couldn't play piano during prime-time TV hours, when my brothers were trying to watch *The A-Team* or my dad was watching *Monday Night Football*. So I'd take a bath and change into my nightgown and sit on the brown tweed couch and watch along, fingering the theme songs on a phantom keyboard on the arm of the couch or my legs, or penning compositions on my manuscript paper, insipid little exercises I labeled "Sonata," ignorant of what makes a sonata a sonata. And then I'd try to squeeze in another half hour before bed, my long, wet hair stuck to my back inside the neck of my nightgown (no time for combing, just spray in some detangler).

I binged on the sheet music we had so much of, pulling out songbooks and folios and anthologies, playing through them cover to cover and moving on. Once, my mother scolded me for leaving my sheet music—much of it hers, or my sister's, or my grandmothers'—in a mess all over the floor. "You wouldn't do that if you really cared about music," she yelled.

I ran to my room and, imitating the cadence of the prose I'd found in my biographies and correspondence of Mozart, scribbled in my diary, "My love for music has been denied."

Somehow my diary was discovered; my brothers and sister had a great time teasing me for my self-serious declaration. "My love for music has been denied" has become a family joke. It was long enough ago now that I can finally be the first to bring it up.

The thought of going a day or two without playing (never "practicing") was unbearable. My mom betrayed me—one of the few times she ever did—at a parent-teacher conference in third grade by blaming my half-assed homework and lack of concentration on the piano. "She can't walk by that thing without playing it," she sighed to Ms. Kalo, and simultaneously I seethed with anger and brimmed with pride.

I just didn't see the point in learning times tables—except twos, fours, and eights, because those are the increments into which beats are often divided.

I wasn't desperate for a driver's license, because I had the piano—and so I already knew the freedom and thrill of feet on pedals, hands moving automatically, eyes scanning the horizon, fleeing.

After arthritis started to invade my body, I found that at the piano I was the puppeteer, not the sloppy puppet I was the rest of the time. At the piano, I was happily shapeless, disembodied, swallowed up in the sounds I made. I was powerful and athletic. My fingers were lean and nimble. And I was in control. I captivated people, amazed them, entertained them. Even later, the piano would be the only place I could be privately, internally arthritic without having to hear about it from anybody.

Playing music is inescapably, inevitably corporeal. But Tobias Picker, a composer who has Tourette's syndrome, has said that as a child, music allowed him a respite from the constant feeling that he was disappointing his parents and anyone else who told him to simply stop the tics that are the hallmark of his disease. Picker is featured in Joseph Straus's *Extraordinary Measures: Disability in Music*, where he is quoted as saying of his Tourette's, "Music saved me. When I played the piano, I didn't have it."

With my head ducked into a score, my tongue hanging out in concentration, my fingers deep in the keys, no one would dare interrupt to call me names or ask if I'd taken my medicine, worn my splints, done my physical therapy exercises. And besides, when I was playing, my arthritis wasn't the most notable thing about me. The music—even if it hurt me to make it—was.

On my list of crushes, circa 1984—right up there with Shaun Cassidy, Ponch from *CHiPs*, the shirtless handyman named Perez who built our screen porch in 1982, and Joe Theismann, #7, quarterback for the champion Washington Redskins—was Mozart. From the very start of my piano lessons, I'd been obsessed with Mozart. I made Mozart out of an ivory soap bottle and a papier-mâché head covered with cotton balls. I dressed as Mozart for some kind of Brownie badge. I watched and rewatched *Amadeus*. I requested booklets of manuscript paper from Santa.

I was a child, and I idolized the child-genius Mozart for the childish and irresistible myth that music came to him so obscenely easily. I was not drawn to stories of overcoming adversity; I was not interested in musicians whose gifts came through struggle or at a cost. Yuck. Of course, the truth is that Mozart's genius, God-given as it may have been, didn't find its way to paper, to keyboard, to concert hall without staggering amounts of grueling work and fastidious revision.

But children do not daydream about hard work or revision. Nor do they dream about poverty, illness, despondency, or early death. So children's books about composers are often sanitized. For example, in *Franz Schubert: The Story of the Boy Who Wrote Beautiful Songs*, Victorian-era children were instructed that Schubert "was born with a spring of melody in his heart and a song on his lips," and that even though he was "quite poor and often hungry, . . . he was always good natured and full of fun." No mention of syphilis; no mention of his failed attempts at opera. The book mentions that Schubert was a schoolteacher, but not that he hated it. Biographies of composers and musicians for children—and some for adults— all seem to hit the same high notes: early aptitude, prolific output, rave reviews. So, for example, you will not find a children's book about the depressive one-armed Austrian pianist Paul Wittgenstein.

Really, there ought to be a children's book about Paul Wittgenstein. Any kid with siblings would get it. Paul Wittgenstein was plenty famous when he was alive, but his own family didn't think much of his playing (his brother Hans was the real pianist, at least before he killed himself), and even before he lost an arm, Paul seems to have been obsessed with the idea that his baby brother Ludwig was constantly judging his playing. It didn't seem to be much consolation to Paul that Ludwig wasn't even a pianist himself (not professionally, anyway—the whole freakily overachieving family played music and they used to have Mahler and Strauss and Brahms over for dinner). It didn't matter that Ludwig Wittgenstein—the genius who went on to solve (and then unsolved) all the major problems of philosophy—wasn't nearly the pianist Paul Wittgenstein was. The reviews and applause for Paul's two-handed piano career, much of it breathless, must have meant nothing to Paul against the knowledge that his baby brother was coolly unimpressed by his key-smashing. According to Alexander Waugh's fantastic *The House of Wittgenstein: A Family at War*, Paul was at times unable to practice the piano because he could feel Ludwig's "skepticism seeping . . . under the door." That off-the-charts insecurity? That was *before* Paul lost his right arm.

For most of my childhood, I believed that my musical ability was the most notable, exceptional, and interesting thing about me, but it didn't especially distinguish me within my family the way it did in the neighborhood or at school. I was not the only musician in the family: Erica had started lessons long before I did, with Mrs. Feltman of course, and even Matthew and Chris had done brief stints at the piano. By the time I began to "hit my stride" at the piano, as my dad would say, Chris was playing first-chair sax in the high school band and squalling classic rock from the basement on his electric guitar in the afternoons after school.

I was no Mozart at home. I may have fantasized about it, but my siblings were never commanded to attend my performances or competitions, they were not forced to sit primly on the living room sofa and listen to me play, they were not ordered to stay library-quiet so I could record a concerto. I never got enough attention from my parents for my musical accomplishments that it incited sibling rivalry. Playing the piano never got me the kind of attention that my arthritis did.

I had—and have—competing sets of feelings about my siblings. As the bratty baby of the family, I need constant reassurance that I stand out *and* that I fit in—that I am original and distinct, but that I also belong to and with them. I had a special family, and I wanted to be special in it.

Erica, eight years older than me, knew the words to every song on the radio. She had bottles of nail polish in every color, including purple. She had things I wanted: a million friends, red hair, curls, a giant jawbreaker that lived under her bed, collecting dust. My dad talked to her like she was an adult. She got a phone for her sixteenth birthday. She was amazing: she wore paperclips as earrings.

She would let me and my friend Janis pick out hairstyles in *Seventeen* magazine and she would braid or tease or curl our hair for us. It never looked anything like the picture, but it didn't matter.

But she could be hard, too: She brought fascinating and frustrating ideas home with her from Rutgers, where she was a philosophy major. "How do you know that what I see as green is the same color you see as green?" she asked me. I grabbed a crayon out of a dinged-up loaf pan.

"What color is this?" I asked her.

"Green," she said.

"See?" I trilled, triumphant.

"Imbecile," she said.

Matthew is six years older than I am. In his room, he had a pyramid-shaped wooden box with a hinged door, where he kept his "treasure." If I caught him on a Sunday afternoon, when he was alone reading on his bed, he would let me open the box and pick out a piece of junk: a rubber ball or a coiled spring. He was always tender toward me, always protective. When I finally got a "preemie" Cabbage Patch doll, Matthew disappeared into his bedroom and came out hours later having made an incubator out of a cardboard box and things from his junk box. He'd referred to the set of encyclopedias; he'd cut circular armholes in the side and attached dust-catching strips of masking tape and computer paper to the open end. Together, we lined it with a nubby old baby blanket.

Chris is closest, just three years older. Chris taught me things, like how you had to rinse your mouth out with water, right from the tap, if you wanted to get the taste of candy or crackers out of there, if you'd eaten a few too many and wanted to get rid of the nagging craving so you'd still have room for dinner. We'd run up to the pantry in the kitchen at the commercial breaks to get more snacks. "These Triscuits are so *addictive*," he'd say. He taught me the word *addiction* and also, later, what it really means.

I was the beneficiary of everything he learned, his pupil: It was because of Chris that in fifth grade I chose Jimi Hendrix for my "Who Am I?" Black History Month project. We had to draw a famous black American's face on a paper plate, glue a Popsicle stick to the back, and then stand on a chair in front of the class to deliver our autobiographies. After two-dozen George Washington Carvers, it was my turn: "I died in London in 1970 of an alcohol and *barbiturate* overdose but I wouldn't have died if they hadn't let me choke on my own vomit, and so I was *asphyxiated*," I said, loyal to Chris and to the facts and vocabulary he had drilled with me. "Who am I?"

Every summer we drove from Maryland to Minnesota in a sticky, three-day trek. The trips always started out tense and late—my dad nervously lingering near the side door, in jeans and T-shirt, his car keys on a silver chain around his neck. "Let's get a move on," he'd say. "I thought the plan was to leave sometime *today*."

We'd hit the road later than planned, always blaming my mother for our late start, and my dad would be steely and silent, still the CIA physicist, for the first few hours. From the backseat, I would look for his eyes in the rearview mirror and I would find them worried, squinting, under the bill of his mesh cap.

But by the time we got to Wheeling, West Virginia, he'd start whistling, and by the time we were in Ohio he'd sing ("'Round on the ends and high in the middle, O-HI-O!'") or play license-plate bingo ("I see Missouri. Do you all have Missouri yet?").

In Minnesota—or on the tent-camping trips to Chincoteague Island we'd take in the summers—my dad would wear cutoff denim shorts and he'd produce magical totems like wooden nickels and pieces of wood from the campfire that could be used to make charcoal drawings. Once, he rode his bicycle backward over a bridge, perched on the handlebars.

On one trip to Chincoteague, long before arthritis, on an afternoon when a thunderstorm had kept us from going to the beach, marooning us at our campsite, my dad and I stood at the fence at the edge of the campground trying to spot one of the fabled wild ponies in the marsh grass as a rainbow striped the sky. "No matter where you stand," my dad said, stepping back so that we were about five feet apart, "you, the center of the arc of the rainbow, and the sun make a perfectly straight line." He gestured with his suntanned arm, flagging a perfectly straight line from his chest to the sun.

Unless you stood in my body, you couldn't see what I saw.

My dad and I had a comedy routine: "Yesterday I could raise my arm this high," he'd say, holding his thin, freckled hand way up above his head, "but today I can only raise it this high." He'd bring his hand down to his waist and then let it float slowly up to his shoulder.

"But you just did, Daddy!" I'd shriek, happy. I don't know if he did this with the others or if it was just for me. I don't want to know.

"No, that was *yesterday*," he'd say, his teeth starting to show through the beginnings of a smile. My dad's front teeth are crooked and they overlap each other right in front. You can only see it when he smiles, not when he talks or shouts or thinks, and so the first glimpse of those teeth peeking through is a rare and exciting treat. "*Yesterday* I could raise my hand this high"—the hand went way up, spastic—"*today* I can only raise it this high."

"But, Daddy!" Oh, it was funny. I swear.

I think my dad surveyed the scenery around 1982—I picture him standing in the middle of our brown-carpeted family room while we tore into our Christmas gifts, I picture him standing there with a black trash bag in one hand and a twist tie between his teeth, vigilant, ensuring that the wrapping paper from our new Lego kits hit the trash without hitting the floor—and decided what each of us was and would always be: Erica, his philosopher and reader, cautious and prudent. Matthew, his tinkerer and engineer, left-brained and self-contained. Chris, his comedian and mathematician, a quick-witted hedonist. And I was—what?—the tagalong, the pest, the ape, the chatterbox, the clotheshorse.

I love a picture from my "before," one that my third-grade teacher, Ms. Kalo, took. It is a dark picture in profile. I am sitting in a window in the classroom. My tangled hair is hanging in my face. I am wearing what I want to wear: an obnoxious black sweater dress with purple handprints all over it. I am sitting at a perfect right angle, legs stretched out in front of me, swathed in horrible plaid stirrup pants, culminating in giant feet stuffed into boy's high-tops with fat, bright blue laces.

"You and your baubles and bangles and beads," my dad would say, laughing as I clanged into the kitchen draped with charm necklaces and gummy bracelets, my sneakers heavy with beaded friendship pins. "You're something else."

Almost as much as I miss that painless body, I miss the joy of dressing it. Before disease, clothing was sheer delight and pure self-expression. It was play; it was not yet costume, camouflage, or cosseting.

A pink tutu. A bright orange Windbreaker with a dollar bill folded into an origami bowtie from my Grandma Avery. White cowgirl boots with silver studs. A baseball-style T-shirt with Joe Cool on it from my cousin Peter, a music composition major at Harvard. I was never a kid who hated getting clothes for Christmas or birthdays.

One Christmas, I received a much-coveted jean skirt. The skirt was an acid-washed A-line, an age-appropriate length, and on the back pocket there was a triangle with a palm tree and florid script, calling to mind another, more expensive name brand. So the jeans skirt was a major score, as was my other standout gift that year, a set of glittery fabric paints in little accordion squeeze tubes, also known by my friends as Sticky Wicky and all the rage at College Gardens Elementary School that year. You see where this is going.

Busily Sticky-Wickying T-shirts in my bedroom sweatshop, wearing my new skirt, it didn't take me long to introduce the seat of the skirt to the permanent paint, leaving a big, butt-shaped blot on the back pocket where it competed for attention with that knockoff brand label with the little tree.

That was the day I learned the word *confiscate*. My mom took the skirt and the paints from me. She did her laundress magic on the back of the skirt and returned it to me and she stowed the paints on a high shelf inside the locked, glass-paned secretary in the kitchen, where they stayed, out of my reach. But my punishment would include more than the confiscation of the *contraband* (another word I learned that day). All afternoon, as my mom worked the stain out of the back of the skirt with repeated washings and the application of good, old-fashioned elbow grease, I was sentenced to wear a pair of Erica's hand-me-down pants: Old. Brown. Corduroy. Bell-bottoms. Death. I hadn't been sent to my room exactly—no, that wasn't my parents' style—but that's where I stayed, horrified at the prospect of venturing out in someone else's skin.

Like this inventive (and effective) punishment, so much of our life in our house on Harvard Court during those happy years—the family meetings, which followed democratic process; my mom's apricot-orange tofu squares, which all of us kids love the way other kids love their mom's mac and cheese; the "paragraph policy," which required that we write short, persuasive essays before we could watch TV (PBS programs excepted, so there was a free-for-all on *Nova* and *Doctor Who* and *The Benny Hill Show* and a wonderful British sketch-comedy show called *The Goodies*); the typed-up room-cleaning contract, which defined a clean room by agreed-upon criteria and laid out a deadline and repercussions, which we signed and posted in our rooms; the fee structure for the use of the word *fuck* (twenty-five cents per utterance, direct quotes, audio recordings, and written transcriptions exempted) was quite different from what was going on in the other houses in our neighborhood. Or America.

As much as I wished to be exceptional, as much as I fantasized about the days when they'd all go off to college or jail and leave me to soak in a concentrated version of my parents' love and attention, as crowded as it sometimes felt, a principle of cohesion was at work when we were all together, some magical principle that was destroyed if any one person was absent. If we had Monopoly or Trivial Pursuit open on the picnic table in the screen porch, my heart would sink when the phone rang. If Chris wanted to go to his friend Alex's to play, or Matthew wanted to go on a solo bike ride, or Erica left with the fascinating, gum-popping, big-haired friend Paula or the boy in a car who brought with him a box of Jell-O Pudding Pops like a suburban bride-price, it would be over. Soon after that, my dad would look at his watch, push his glasses up onto his forehead, and rub his eyes and say, "Let's wrap this up," and we'd play a few more rounds but it wouldn't be fun anymore.

We were a full ensemble cast. We had enough people for any sport or game or skit. We didn't need anyone else. Once, we broke into teams, boys against girls, and made geography pizzas: continents of cheese, oceans of sauce, forests of broccoli. It wasn't the same if even one person was missing.

There was a brief and beautiful before.

There was a point of modulation.

Talent is no safeguard against tragedy. The Wittgenstein home, a gilded and glorious mansion with seven grand pianos, yielded five boys, three girls: all geniuses. Of the Wittgenstein brothers, all five contemplated suicide, two most certainly committed it, and one—Hans, by all accounts the *real* musical genius—disappeared into the Chesapeake Bay forever.

A family is a body and a body is a family: How much joy is it allowed? And how much pain can it bear? We would soon learn.

Chapter 3

When I was diagnosed at the end of sixth grade, I was a fairly healthy kid attached to a sore wrist. On the first day of seventh grade—when I was officially arthritic but the first symptoms had abated—things had changed. But, as usual, I was the last to find out about this radical shift my body had made.

We girls were seated on the floor in the middle school gym with our backs against the sticky plastic gym mats. Our blue-jeaned legs sweated in the new back-to-school clothes we'd been unable to wait to wear. It was impossible to believe that it had officially been summer vacation just yesterday, that the temperature on the thermometer was probably the same as it had been yesterday, that the babies at the public pool were probably even right then splashing happily in a suddenly-less-crowded pool totally ignorant that summer had ended, that school had started, that everything, everything, *everything* had changed.

"You'll change for PE every day," Ms. Babuska said, "and having your period or cramps is no excuse." I paid half attention. I was indifferent to PE, and I still hadn't gotten my period.

Ms. Babuska was slender and plain, with a big nose and bushy brown-gray hair pulled back into a ponytail at the base of her neck. Her everyday tracksuits had some kind of insignia on the breast that I never got close enough to read. She looked like a Romanian gymnastics coach. The rumor, nasty and clichéd as it was, was that she was a lesbian and that she used the annual scoliosis screening to check us out in our bras. "The only way you'll be excused from participation is if you have a valid medical excuse," she said, and here I listened a little more closely.

My mom and I had talked about how I should handle the unpredictable arthritis in my first full school year with it. My mom had sent letters to the school telling them that I would be the one to indicate when I could or couldn't do something. Ms. Babuska went on: ". . . unless you have a valid medical excuse, like Andrea." There it was: the orchestra-hit sound effect, all violins, I have always heard deep inside my ears when I experience mortification. She turned to me. "It's a shame your body is falling apart at such a young age," she said.

My eyes stung and my throat closed and my stomach roiled and I had always been proud of never crying or throwing up in school and I wasn't sure which one was about to happen, so I stood up and crossed the gym and lurched out of the room. I didn't cry and I didn't vomit. Worse: I was silent.

That (first) Ms. Babuska incident—and the meetings that followed—was recorded in the notebooks my mother gave me. I was moved out of Ms. Babuska's class for the remainder of seventh grade, but for some reason not recorded, in eighth grade I was placed back in Ms. Babuska's class "temporarily." One day, we were supposed to run the mile. I changed for PE but I knew I wouldn't be able to do the mile run. My feet hurt. I'd played soccer the weekend before. This is life with RA: sometimes you can, and when you can, you must. I told Ms. Babuska I couldn't do it, and she said I had to. "I can't," I said. She hugged her clipboard to her chest, obscuring the logo on the breast pocket.

"You're disgusting," she said. I turned and I ran toward the building. "You're a liar," she called after me. "See? You can run when you want to! You're disgusting!" Again, I was silent, except for my crying.

There were more meetings, and because there were meetings, there was my mom with her notebook. *March 27, 7:45 A.M.: Babuska excused behavior as not perfect.* In this meeting, my memory and my mom's notes record, Ms. Babuska said my problem wasn't my illness but my behavior. *Right!* I wanted to scream. *My body is misbehaving!* Ms. Babuska thanked my mom for the chance "to vent." Ms. Babuska said she worked with children with "much worse problems" and that she prided herself on her ability to work with the "handicapped." "Handicapped" was not a name I called myself.

This was before the word *handicapped* had fallen nearly entirely out of acceptability; the cutesy *handicapable* wasn't yet in use, at least as far as I knew, though if someone had offered me that term, I would have gagged. Then again, how would I know? I wasn't one of *them*—handicapped people used canes or wheelchairs or sign language. I couldn't be handicapped, could I? Handicapped people *knew* they were handicapped; they *agreed* they were handicapped. It was objective fact: you were either handicapped or you weren't, right?

I can't be too hard on myself for subscribing, at least initially, to this model of disability: coming as I was to this whole question of disability from twelve years of wellness, this black-and-white model seemed inoffensive, if not natural. I was fine, and then I had symptoms, and then I had a blood test, and then I took pills, and then I was a sick person who took pills to try to seem well. It was all very medical.

I think my mother was so angry at Ms. Babuska partly because she was afraid I'd believe what had been said about me. That I'd look down like Wile E. Coyote suspended in midair and discover I'd been fooling myself and that I really was falling apart, disgusting, a liar, handicapped. But I was hurt and scared for the opposite reason: Ms. Babuska was making things up about me. Why was she bringing up handicapped kids? I had bad days and even during the meeting pain radiated through my skin and my custom-made orthotic inserts in the soles of my Keds, but I was still strong.

It wasn't that Ms. Babuska had said something about me that I knew was true, like in fourth grade when Jenny M. discovered that I was the first to wear a training bra and told everyone, forcing me to go to the bathroom and take it off and stuff it into the back of my cubby, vowing never to wear a bra again. (In fifth grade, Jenny M. told everyone I was the only girl who *didn't* wear a bra. There were fifteen Jennys in my class, but I could not win with that Jenny M.) No, Ms. Babuska's words were awful, made-up lies, like when girls at school would start a rumor that you'd kissed the nose-picker fat boy and that you were responsible for the boner he'd gotten in the middle of algebra. I hadn't been exposed; I'd been slandered.

I hadn't yet figured out that it was my body that was the source of all these lies about me, that my body was telling people I was things I knew I was not.

For example: I didn't know my body was falling apart until Ms. Babuska told me it was, and before arthritis, I'd been the last to know that I was fat.

I have always suspected that the stern and angry reaction to my accident with the Sticky Wicky had more than a little to do with the unacceptable body inside the skirt—it wasn't yet arthritic, but it was already breaking family rules: it was wild and ugly and wrong because it was too big; it hogged up more space than was allotted to me. Adding to my confusion about my place in my family—was I really one of them?—was the fact that they were all so thin and I was not.

I didn't know that until everyone in my family made sure I did. Once, as I sat on the floor in the bikini bathing suit I'd insisted on getting, a flounce of purple flowers across my belly, my dad sat on the couch watching Joe Theismann and our Redskins on TV, one leg crossed over the other, his slipper hanging off his foot. He looked at me sitting cross-legged (which they called Indian-style then) on the floor in my bathing suit. "Geez," he said. "Look at your tummy. All you see are rolls, rolls, rolls." It stung, and then it passed. He knew what he saw, but back then and for only a little while longer, I knew who I was: I was Brooke Shields; I was Wonder Woman. They'd see.

I think now I wasn't the kind of fat you really need to worry about, but it doesn't matter if I actually *was* fat. I was too fat for the family of effortless ectomorphs I'd been born into.

When I tried on hand-me-downs of my sister's, my mom would shake her head, mystified. "She wore that in the *eighth* grade and it fits you now, in *second*." There were passing jabs from my brothers—to be expected, I guess—about my being a lard-ass, Andre the Giant. My sister took my plate from me once. "You don't need to eat." She laughed. "You can eat off the fat of the land!" Slowly it crept in, mean noise that obliterated my own voice in the matter.

I heard my mom on the phone with her mother, fretting about me—"What am I going to go about Andrea's weight?" and at the time, I seethed with anger at my mother. What business did she have dragging my grandma into this? Grandma Torvik didn't care if I was fat, or she wouldn't stuff me full of gingerbread cookies and meatballs and pie and lefse and root beer floats and bowlfuls of raspberries and real cream whenever I saw her, would she? But I know now that Grandma told my mom that it would "really be a waste" if I were allowed to go the way I was going, to get fat. I know now that my mom was in a corner, defending herself, and me, against the criticizing inquiries of my grandma, who had taught my mom to hate her too-long legs and high waist because she hated them about herself.

And there was one awful afternoon when my mother slipped and, angry at me for something both of us have forgotten, called me a blimp, the occasion for yet another mean cartoon sketched by me and delivered to its target—in this case, my mother.

I shed the weight problem—temporarily, anyway, and for everyone but me—when I got sick. Arthritis made me skinny and sallow, but even that seemed preferable to most people. If they objected to my too-skinny size, they kept it silent. By the time Ms. Babuska called me handicapped, the problem of poundage had been resolved, at least for everyone else, and I was left with the weightier problem:

This dysmorphic noise inside my head cannot be quieted; the dissonance cannot be resolved.

Every time my body and I work out some private understanding, she goes talking shit behind my back. I live in this body, but I never seem to be the expert on it.

Scars may tell a story, but they never get the last word.

Andrew Solomon, in *Far from the Tree: Parents, Children, and the Search for Identity*, writes eloquently and at length about children with identities they didn't get from their parents and can't share with them—some Deaf children, for example, or musical prodigies, or gay or transgender children. These are horizontal identities, as distinguished from vertical identities, such as race, that are passed down from parents to their children.

I suppose the doctors and the social workers and the guidance counselors all knew that arthritis was sending me away from my friends and family and that I might need a new harbor. As seventh grade, my first full arthritic school year, came to a close, a plan was hatched to take me to Salt Lake City for the 1990 national conference of the American Juvenile Arthritis Organization (AJAO). "Lots of kids your age," the doctors all said, smiling pitiful smiles.

I was ambivalent about associating myself with the Arthritis Foundation, and uncomfortable around anything that stunk of support group. But I was curious. If I couldn't go to Vienna, the elegant, exotic city that had produced my Mozart, or the Duke Ellington School of the Arts, as I'd been begging to do, I'd go to Utah. None of my siblings had been there.

In Salt Lake City, I met kids my age who had me beat: They'd had arthritis since infancy. Many of them had been treated with steroids, and their bodies, arthritic since before puberty and growth spurts, showed the evidence. Many of them were small, with joints fused together. Some of them had chipmunk faces, a combination of the interrupted development of their facial bones and the moon face caused by prednisone. They used walkers and wheelchairs and braces. *These* were handicapped people. I was uncomfortable around the most obviously arthritic of them; I bristled when a pack of us piled into the hotel restaurant and people stared at us—at them, really.

But I discovered that if they were handicapped, I was fit and sporty. I could help someone open a soda can. People would say, "Andrea, slow down, wait up" and I realized I missed hearing that. At the conference's Friday night party, I made a big, cruel show of careening around the room lip-synching and dancing to Aerosmith's "Walk This Way" for the amusement of my arthritis-frozen friends.

There was an unspoken competition: They won because they were seasoned veterans, and I was just a newbie. They could boast of surgeries and scars. But I won because I could take the stairs, because on my own in the hotel lobby, if I took off my Arthritis Foundation name tag, strangers wouldn't necessarily know I was with the group of gimpy kids prowling the halls.

I didn't get kicked off the grand piano in the hotel lobby. I even made a few dollars in tips.

I went to the national conference every year after that until I finished high school—Providence, Columbus, Denver, Philadelphia. As was probably the doctors' intention, I found comfort in being among people to whom I didn't have to explain arthritis. At home, I was the only arthritic kid any of my friends or teachers had ever met. But the principal reason I attended remained this: for a long weekend, my world was recalibrated. At home, I was always too fat or too skinny, too slow, too pale, too sick. At the conference, I was one of the healthier ones. I came home from the conferences having assuaged my guiltiest fear. I came home knowing—or at least thinking—that Ms. Babuska's term *handicapped* did not fit me.

When my mom suggested the second conference, in Providence at the end of eighth grade in 1991, or the third in Columbus in 1992, I didn't need to be persuaded. I had caught on that this whole arthritis business was taking me to new places. At every conference, though, I avoided as many of the official sessions as I could. I quickly figured out which of the other kids with arthritis had older, cute, nonarthritic brothers who had come along. I had good odds with these boys. I didn't have to explain my limp or the pills I took. In Denver in 1993, I latched on to a tall, healthy boy named Clancy, and we roamed the hotel, riding the glass elevator to the top floor of the lobby and throwing paper airplanes into the bowl below, watching our creations swirl and dip into the potted plants, ducking when they hit the tiny people. We got onto the elevator and came face-to-face with Betty White. I got her autograph for my mom.

At that conference, I attended a performance by the arthritic concert pianist Byron Janis. I sat on the floor in the sunny atrium, in the front row with my fingers splayed on the carpet in front of me, certain he'd recognize in me the markings of a concert pianist. He played for us with his fused-solid hands. I wish I could remember what he played. A trick of memory allows me to happily collapse a separate memory into this one and insist that it was Schubert he played.

Before we left the hotel, I left a thank-you note for Byron Janis at the front desk. I told him I was a pianist. I thought he'd write me back. The only other fan letter I'd written had been to Joe Theismann, and it had garnered a quick response. When I left my note for Byron Janis, I still believed that "you've got to send mail to get mail" meant "if you send mail, you'll get mail." I thought Byron Janis was obligated to write me back. But he hasn't, not yet.

My mom says that in these early days of my illness, many of the sessions at these conferences were irrelevant. "I had to figure out how to get your most basic needs met," she says. "You were hurting. I couldn't think about college or occupational concerns or research protocols or what the future held or any of that other stuff quite then. That was all"—she waves her hand above her head—"up here."

Yesterday I could raise my arm this high. Today?

But she knew that we would need to know about all that stuff eventually, and so she went to the meetings with her notepads and she collected names and numbers and pamphlets and research briefs, and she kept it all so we'd have it when we got through those first, disorienting years.

Among the topics that the adults talked about in their sessions— as we kids swam or read from a theoretical script for a Very Special Episode of *The Cosby Show*, in which the Huxtables encounter a Real Disabled Person—was the Americans with Disabilities Act. Signed into law by George H. W. Bush in 1990, the act guaranteed reasonable accommodation in the workplace and public schools for any person with a disability, which it defined as "a physical or mental impairment that substantially limits one or more of the major life activities of [an] individual." Interestingly, the ADA went on to stipulate that a person was eligible for protection under the act if he or she had "a record of such impairment" or was "regarded as having such impairment." Certainly, by those definitions, I was qualified for protection. After all, Ms. Babuska clearly regarded me as having some kind of impairment, and when you are in seventh grade, participating in required PE classes is a major life activity.

I wasn't just a beneficiary of the act; I'd helped to pass the ADA by storming Capitol Hill with a wheelchair brigade—Ms. Stiff Goes to Washington!—personally urging Senator Sarbanes by the power of my "personal narrative," and basking in the attention from the senators but with lots of pouting and sighing and eye-rolling and snarky comments to my mother in Capitol Hill elevators about trotting out the gimpy kids to tug on the congressional heartstrings. The ADA is good legislation, but good legislation can be implemented slowly, badly, or not at all. Quite often, I was the first to tell my teachers about the Americans with Disabilities Act in the first place.

Even after the ADA took effect, and after Ms. Babuska was instructed by a school administrator never to speak to me again (a request made by my mom and recorded in her notes), PE continued to be a problem. In high school, I was allowed to sit out and entertain myself, as long as what I was doing was "related" to the activities of the class. No one checked, so instead of playing scooter hockey, I sat alone in a stairwell and wrote stories about people who played scooter hockey, or drew pictures of people climbing ropes, grateful for the solitude. It was best for everyone if I sat apart. This is not an example of effective accommodation. But at the time, I didn't mind.

I'd become suddenly and chronically sick only a year before, and yet I'd already begun a slow kind of leaving from my family and friends. I felt as though I'd been kicked from my family's nest, warmly feathered with good health, but I didn't have anywhere to land. I was halfhearted at best about belonging to the new community of arthritic children in which I found myself in the summer of 1990 at that first American Juvenile Arthritis Foundation conference.

I enjoyed the weekend—at thirteen, it didn't take much more than a hotel pool, a lobby grand piano, and generous air-conditioning to keep me happy—but I didn't stay in touch with the friends I met at the conference; they were like people you make out with on vacation. In fact, they *were* people I'd made out with on vacation. There wasn't room for them in my real life and when, sitting in the middle of algebra, I had a fleeting memory of how happily I'd traipsed through a hotel lobby with a motley crew of hobbling kids, I was ashamed. But I had taken one thing away from the five AJAO conferences I attended, other than a glimpse of Byron Janis, a crush on Clancy, and Betty White's autograph.

In 1991, at the conference in Providence, Rhode Island, I'd attended an "art therapy" session for us kids with arthritis, which was actually just a stack of construction paper, Elmer's glue, crayons, and tape left in the middle of a folding table in an otherwise empty banquet room where someone in an Arthritis Foundation polo shirt stood nearby and didn't say or do anything. I'm not saying it wasn't therapeutic. I cut and glued and colored silently alongside other arthritic kids. A boom box in the corner was set to a classical music station and a piano piece caught my attention and I boasted, to anyone who was listening, "I can play this."

I'd never heard it before, but I loved it immediately. It began with a far-off melody in a middle register, a major-key melody that sounds like someone absentmindedly humming a snippet of a remembered song. The melody lifts and falls to a pause as the hummer remembers more and more of the song, then there is an ominous rumble from the low end of the piano—a note that doesn't really seem to fit—and the melody returns in a minor key and the rumbling turns into triplets in the left hand against the right hand's eighth notes. I needed to know what this music was and who wrote it. People sometimes say that a pair of shoes in a department store or a puppy at the pound "spoke to them." That's what this was. I needed to get it home and try it on, nuzzle its neck.

I stopped listening after the first movement—the second movement was slow, sad, and boring—but I sat through all four movements huddled next to the boom box like it was a space heater.

At the end of the piece the announcer said it was Schubert's Sonata in B-flat, D. 960, and I committed that all to memory the way I'd committed Tony McComas's phone number to memory when he gave it to me after Sunday school one day, and I made a mental vow to get the music and make good on my boasting.

That was not as preposterous as it looks to me now, committed to paper. By some vicious miracle, even as I got thinner, slower, stiffer, and sicker, I got better at piano. My head start had not yet run out. I was good, and I knew it. Once, I curtsied after performing. The judge wrote, "Don't curtsy unless you're playing for the Queen of England." I thought, Thanks for the tip. I'll remember that when I do. Even two years into arthritis, in eighth grade, I performed the *marche funebre* movement from Chopin's Piano Sonata No. 2 in B-flat minor. One judge gave me a perfect score of ten. The other wrote that I had no business playing that funeral march until I was older, I guess until I knew real sadness or something. *Bah.*

However, the Schubert sonata, as beautiful as it was, had not yet stolen my heart from Mozart. I was still a Mozart girl. I'd crushed on his brash genius from the first plastic-covered school-library biography I'd brought home of the Viennese genius bad boy. Schubert, if I thought of him at all, struck me as boring. The short story on Schubert, at least as far as my piano books had told me, was that he was a penniless, loveless, sickly also-ran. There was another version of Schubert in which he was a guileless natural, just skipping through life accidentally composing music. This version of Schubert had the "natural talent" angle in common with Mozart, but none of the bravado or accomplishment. Over the next several years, as my pursuit of the B-flat sonata became an obsession, I would come to learn how reductive and inaccurate (and pervasive) both versions of Schubert were. But making Schubert's acquaintance in the form of the sonata did give me more fodder for my daydreams of taking off in a time machine for eighteenth- and nineteenth-century Vienna. Escape, to another continent, and another century, was tantalizing: Though I was the only one in our family with an official diagnosed illness, the truth is that 1989 had been a year of modulation for our whole family, and we were not well.

Movement II

ANDANTE ALLA ZOPPA / WALKING, LIMPING

Only I can know if I am really in pain; another person can only surmise it. . . . If we are using the word "know" as it is normally used (and how else are we to use it?), then other people very often know if I'm in pain. Yes, but all the same, not with the certainty with which I know it myself.

—Ludwig Wittgenstein,
Philosophical Investigations

Chapter 4

C hris has said that when I was first diagnosed, he wondered if God was aiming for him and missed. "I felt like it should've been me," he said. "I was already the black sheep. It would have been more . . . efficient." I wanted to know what he meant by *efficient*, that word that sounded so much like something my dad would say. "If you look at it from an economic standpoint," Chris, now an accountant, said, "if you have a fleet of four trucks and one of them already has transmission problems, that's the one you want to get a flat tire."

By that criterion, though, it would have been impossible to select the best Avery to get sick in 1989. The whole family had transmission problems: My parents were fighting. Chris was fifteen, coming home each evening bleary-eyed, smelling like pot. Seventeen-year-old Matthew was arrested for possession of drugs.

Erica, twenty, was still the success story of the family, but she was aggressive and alienating in her visits and phone calls home, shaving her head and daring us to have a problem with it, or giving us all age-inappropriate, condom-themed gifts for Christmas (Chris got a "Tarp Your Load" T-shirt; I got "make your own dental dam" instructions). There was a lot of pain in our house, but I wonder if it seemed to my parents and my siblings that my pain—legitimate, doctor-acknowledged, and blameless—was the only pain our house could accommodate.

Six weeks after my first diagnosis, a couple of weeks after my test of the rheumatoid factor, Matthew was arrested with a pock-etful of *contraband* (there was that word again, which I'd learned in Sticky Wickygate but which now had a more serious meaning that appeared to scare my parents). He spent most of the summer washing buses for community service before taking off for the University of Maryland. My mom says "1989 . . . that was the year everything changed."

In my big, half-empty room, under the bunk beds I no longer had to share with Erica, I kept a huge plastic bin with all the hand-me-down Legos. My brothers no longer wanted to play Legos with me or horseplay with each other in the hallway; the toy guns ended up in the basement with the big, musty box of dress-up outfits and the loaf pan of crayons. We had reshuffled the bedroom assignments when Erica left for college in 1986, with each of the boys finally getting a private bedroom and my sister and I briefly "sharing," at least in name, the big bedroom. Soon, though, her bedroom was moved downstairs. Now, the boys were always behind Matthew's door, whispering, and no password would gain me entry. My parents murmured about the boys' red-rimmed eyes before my mom retreated to her bedroom with pamphlets about tough love and my dad hid out in his shrinking den, a book-lined cave off the laundry room, which had been partitioned to form the downstairs bedroom for Erica when she came home. She was an adult now, on the opposite side of yet another invisible wall, and so my parents decided it was appropriate she have her own space when she was home.

The rumblings of our family's modulation had begun before 1989. Christmas two years earlier, Erica had come home from New Jersey to find that someone had stolen $200 in babysitting money from the change she kept stashed in film cans. Christmas Eve morning, we were awakened for an emergency family meeting. There would be no gifts, my mom said, unless the *culprit* confessed. I was devastated: I had a leather bomber jacket on the line. Chris made a tearful confession—"It's one thing to do it, and quite another thing to lie about it," my parents had always said—and I received my bomber jacket. It was just the one I wanted, with ribbed cotton cuffs and a satin lining printed like an aviator's map, but it hardly offset my growing realization that my house had become impossible to navigate. There were sad and angry people in every room.

By 1989, we'd broken into dissonance. I missed Chris most of all. If he wasn't behind the closed door of his bedroom, he and his new friend Andy Swindells were in the basement, "jamming" on their guitars. I'd come home from school and crash on the couch to the sound of "Paint It Black" from the basement. Andy had long, leonine hair that fell on the shoulders of his jean jacket. My brother had a jean jacket, too, and he'd written "Led Zeppelin" on the back in permanent marker. Sometimes I'd wake up on the couch and Andy would be watching me sleep. "Your little sister's pretty," he'd say to my brother.

"C'mon, dude, let's go," my brother would say, and they'd head out on foot to the shopping center to buy cigarettes or to the park for pot.

Andy's kidneys were failing. He'd been healthy until middle school and then he was dying. When he came over to jam with my brother after school, he kept his kidney dialysis bag in our refrigerator. He had some kind of port in his belly, and he'd tease me by whipping it out and saying, "Want to see my ding-a-ling?"

"You're so gross," I'd say.

"How's your arthritis?"

"Go away."

I didn't think I had anything in common with tender, goofy Andy, besides our shared love for Chris. I didn't mind, however, that a boy (even a sick, chubby friend of my brother's) thought I was pretty enough that he wanted to watch me sleep.

Andy was irritating, but my brother—who'd become so distant from me—was patient with him. They'd taken to hanging out at a town house in our neighborhood everyone called the Hippie House. I'd heard that people gave LSD to kittens at the Hippie House. Sometimes, as I rode the bus home from middle school, I'd see Chris and Andy walking together across the elementary school field in their jean jackets, my brother walking slow, flicking his cigarette to the side as he paused to wait for Andy to catch up—"You all right, man?" I knew he was saying—and Andy using a cane because the immune-suppressing steroids he took to treat his kidney disease caused osteonecrosis of his hip, and now he needed a new hip *and* a new kidney.

Around this time, my parents offered to paint mine and the boys' bedrooms whatever colors we wanted, and we all picked gray. My dad went to Hechinger's to buy three cans of paint, in three different shades of gray.

In the summer of 1989, as Matthew served his community-service sentence, I served my sentence, too: I started going to physical therapy at Holy Cross Hospital right after my May diagnosis, even before, as far as I could see, anything was wrong with me. According to my mom's notes, this plan (physical and occupational therapy twice a month for six months) had been hatched at that July 12 follow-up appointment.

The physical therapy room at Holy Cross was in the basement. The ceilings were low, but the interconnected rooms that made up the PT gym were open and bright. The main room was sparse and clean, with a rug in the middle. Around the edges, always neatly stowed, were foam blocks and big rubber balls and piles of color-coded TheraBands, big swatches of rubber with different amounts of elasticity. I'd come to learn that red and green were doable and that the nasty gray TheraBand was my enemy. In one corner there was a little wooden bridge with railings, the kind you'd put over a creek, maybe, or—now that I think of it—nearly identical to the bridge I crossed symbolically one Saturday afternoon leaving Brownies and becoming a Junior Scout.

Off that room was another room with long tables. I didn't spend as much time in this room. The concern back then was my bigger joints—my hips and knees and feet. This room with the tables was the occupational therapy room for the finer joints, like fingers. On the tables were tubs of pegs and next to them, empty pegboards. This setup resembled the old-timey game we kept in the buffet in our dining room at home, in the drawer above the good silver, where we kept the abacus. The game, the one where you have to leapfrog the pegs over one another so that only one is left, is meant to challenge your brain—your fingers are really supposed to be incidental. But now when I encounter it on the table at Cracker Barrel, as I pass it across the table for someone else to try, I think about the Holy Cross version, and the versions I encountered later, in other physical and occupational therapy rooms. You can figure out the strategy once and know it forever. It's much harder to hold on to those pesky pegs when your fingers start stiffening up. I know that now. I know how to beat that game and also that my fingers won't really let me. My brain can do it; my hands can't.

But back then, I needed the therapy for my larger joints: even by the time I started going to Holy Cross for therapy, I'd had to quit almost all my suburban-kid-in-the-1980s activities. "Had to" isn't really the right phrase. If my parents had let me pawn my flute and my soccer cleats and my Girl Scouts uniform and move to Austria, I would have. Someone—my mom, maybe?—must have been encouraging me to keep doing things other than piano: soccer, ballet, tap, flute, Girl Scouts. At the time, I resented this redirection, this broken focus—"Why can't I enroll in the Duke Ellington School of the Arts?" I begged my mom. "You're crippling my career!" a parallel to Schubert's bristling at his father's insistence that he become something sensible like a schoolteacher instead of a composer—but now I'm glad piano wasn't the only thing I had. If it had been, I wouldn't have had anything to negotiate with, anything to concede to my sickness-god or sell to my body-devil.

These decoy loves were easily traded, but they *were* loves. I was just learning to love running when I got arthritis. Three laps around College Gardens Elementary School field, behind the goalposts and the big fir tree, equaled a mile. Lap one was always a struggle, but somewhere in the middle of lap two I'd hit my stride. I'd stop being able to feel my feet; my knees and hips would churn so quickly, so automatically, I wasn't sure I could command them to stop. My ears closed off to the sounds of traffic on College Parkway or the whistle of my PE teacher. All I could hear was my blood in my ears, my own breath through my nose and mouth. I remember this, so I know that I loved it, and that I miss it.

I used to have flying dreams. In these dreams—they are like everyone's flying dreams; I know that I am terribly ordinary in this way—I'd wave my arms like I was treading water and I'd be aloft. I'd scoop huge handfuls of air and throw them behind me, propelling myself forward.

After arthritis, I didn't dream of flying anymore. I dream now of running. In my recurring dream, I'm running through College Gardens, those same neighborhood streets I know well, or did. In my dream, my eyes are fixed on my feet, which are laced into a pair of athletic shoes I don't own. I watch my feet hop curbs, pound gravel, flatten grass. In my dream, I don't have the sensation of my feet pounding the ground; I don't feel any of the shocks in my knees or hips. The ground whirs by in color. Breathing is easy.

My mom says maybe we don't dream impossible dreams, maybe we dream about those things that are just outside of our reach, the things we can *almost* do.

Which means you're closer to flying than you think. Isn't it agonizing? You're so painfully close to flying, your dreaming mind and your sleeping heart know exactly how to do it, if only the clumsy physics of your waking body would allow you to.

In my waking hours, one by one after my diagnosis, I quit ballet and soccer and tap and running and Girl Scouts and basketball and baritone horn and flute. But I clung tightly to the piano with both hands, and that is not a metaphor. *You can have everything else,* I thought at every concession. *But you cannot have this.*

Still hopeful, still insistent, and still exploiting the five-year head start I had on arthritis, I stretched and tapped my hands through a grueling workout, pushing my average-size hand to reach an octave and then some, training my fingers to crawl nimbly over and yield deftly to one another.

My fingers knew every way up and down a keyboard, in gloves, mittens, even through a piece of fabric (after I read that Mozart could do it).

I needed the strength and balance training at physical therapy for my no-longer-running, no-longer-dancing legs, but I didn't need to go to the finger-therapy room because my hands were still running and dancing every day at the piano.

Much later, the arthritic concert pianist Byron Janis would quip, "Although arthritis is not good for the piano, the piano is good for arthritis." I didn't come across that quote until 2010, when it appeared in the pages of *Arthritis Today* magazine. Still wishing that Byron Janis had written me back, I plucked this axiom of his from the pages of the magazine and—another deliberate trick of memory—delivered it back through time to myself at thirteen, muting the first half ("arthritis is not good for the piano") and emphasizing only the second ("the piano is good for arthritis"). Here, belatedly, was distinct permission to binge at the piano, to obsess and outpace my arthritis, from someone who understood.

I don't remember my physical therapist's name, only that she was kind and soft-spoken and pretty, the way dental hygienists always seem to be, and even in her plain-Jane khakis and pastel-colored polos I could tell she was sporty and strong and had what my mom would call a very nice figure, which means she was thin and well proportioned. She had me walk across the room and back again, and from her small, wheeled stool she'd mark down notes about my gait. She had me stand on one leg and timed me with the digital runner's watch she wore on her slender, tan wrist.

I didn't feel like I needed to be there—at the time, nothing really hurt, and I couldn't see that we had any kind of identifiable goal in all this therapy. Back then, I believed myself to be arthritic only when I had symptoms, when some hot, bratty joint pushed its way to the foreground and demanded attention for a spell.

The notes my mom and the therapist were writing down remained secret from me, but I have them now, and I know this was the most important part of my battle, an attempt to stave off weakness and atrophy, so much more crucial than later bouts of physical therapy when I worked hard on my own behalf, trying hopelessly to restore broken, severed, ruptured, deformed things to some level of function.

After an hour or so, the therapist would walk me back out to the waiting area by the elevators to my mom.

By the end of eighth grade, I was going to physical therapy three times a week at Holy Cross. It was my dad who took me, mostly, and we scheduled the earliest possible appointment so he could get in to work and I'd be only a little bit late for school. It seemed dreadfully early to me, but it was whole hours later than my dad preferred to go to work. He had to slog his way through Beltway traffic to Langley every morning, over the Francis Scott Key Bridge, which he called the "Car-Strangled Spanner." Given the choice, he preferred to hit the road before dawn. Given another choice, my dad prefers being at work over being at home. He always has. I understand why; he likes tidy spaces, predictable schedules, thought-conducive quiet, and immersive projects. Our home, with its cacophony of squalling musics and midnight comings and goings provided none of those things. But I had therapy and he was stuck with me, late, in blinding sun and choking traffic. On the radio in his fastidiously clean car, we listened to the classical music he liked—Mahler—and on my birthday I learned that I shared a birthday with Vivaldi. To a little girl, a thing like that means destiny. Here was yet another permission to believe I would be a real musician.

On one especially memorable morning, it was my mother who took me to therapy. After, instead of exiting the highway at the middle school, and without explanation, she went one exit farther and took me to the Pastry Place Café, where I ate a magical, impractical thing called a Sacher torte. After every physical therapy appointment, then, whether it was my mom or dad driving, I held my breath and wished to be whisked away to the Pastry Place instead of to school. I wished my dad would take me with him to the CIA. I could sit at his desk, draw on typing paper or alphabetize things if he had anything nonclassified I could look at. He could take me to lunch in the cafeteria, or show me off to his work friends. "This is my youngest," he'd say. "The baby." *She's something else.* And I wouldn't roll my eyes or anything.

More and more, I woke up sick and hot and stiff. My hands and feet and arms and legs didn't work until midmorning. Over and over I pieced together Marilyn Monroe's body—thigh, thigh, hair, lips, breast, breast, dress—in the thousand-piece jigsaw puzzle my dad had bought for me for these very sick days. I worked through the paperback copies of *Jane Eyre* and *Pride and Prejudice* that my sister had bought me for my tenth birthday, I read and reread *Little Women*, *Jaws*, and *Helter Skelter*. Sometimes my dad stayed home with me, waiting it out in another room, letting me limber up alone, until I said he could take me to school late.

We didn't spend this time together. I discovered that the TV played old black-and-white movies during the day. The paragraph policy was relaxed or ignored or ditched altogether. I watched everything Shirley Temple. My dad was antsy, dressed for work just in case, his security badge tucked into his breast pocket, hanging on the end of the silver ball chains he liked, the kind you can buy by the yard at the hardware store.

My dad's never been good at wasting time. Stuck at home with me that fall, he took advantage of cool, sunny mornings and set out to paint the exterior of our house. The family joke—maybe true—is that my parents, increasingly unable to have a conversation without arguing, agreed that one of them would pick the house color and the other could pick the trim color and that would be that. No fight, and we'd all just live with it.

The house ended up bright, look-at-me yellow with pine green shutters and trim, which made it easy to give people directions. Our house was the yellow—no, *really yellow*—one.

On Sunday, September 23, 1990, a few weeks into eighth grade, and just weeks after my first AJAO conference in Salt Lake City, my dad and I went to a Washington Redskins/Dallas Cowboys football game with tickets the Arthritis Foundation had given us. My dad liked football in a sedate, intellectual way. He never watches a football game—he "monitors" it. Five years earlier, I had been watching my dad "monitor" the Redskins game on *Monday Night Football* in 1985 when, in the "Hit That No One Who Saw It Can Ever Forget," Joe Theismann so spectacularly broke both the tibia and the fibula in his right leg. "He'll never play football again," my dad said without feeling, but he helped me track down the address of Joe Theismann's restaurant so I could send him a fan letter, and a few weeks later I received a signed picture of Joe, kneeling on the field, pre-career-ending injury.

On a few rare Sundays, I'd even managed to get my dad out in the yard for a stolen half-hour and he'd shown me how to put my hands on the laces to throw a spiral.

As the game ended on that autumn Sunday in 1990—our Redskins won, 19–15—and we came out of RFK Memorial Stadium to walk to the Metro, my legs were leaden and my face hot. I thought I was tired or cranky because my day out with my dad was ending. But when we got home, it was clear that I was sick. I know now that this was a classic arthritis flare-up, and one of the worst I've ever had.

My joints were stuck and swollen. I know that mostly from my mother's notes. What I recall vividly was my fever, the unbearable paradox of weepy-hot eyes and frigorific skin. My head clogged and leaden. The line scumbled between sleep and waking, both states inadequate and uncomfortable, sleep too thin to satisfy, waking too thick to stand. These, too, are symptoms of arthritis in its acute state—a flu-plus, one that strikes during any season, against which there is no vaccine.

For two weeks, no one made me go upstairs to bed; I slept on sheets on the tweed couch where I'd watched the *Challenger* and Joe Theismann's leg explode. I did not play the piano or go to my lessons. I don't remember eating. I became acquainted with my body's new teen smells, the acid armpit odor a child's body doesn't make. I slipped in and out of shallow sleep, plagued by nonsensical, nothing-happens fever dreams, inexplicably horrifying montages: I shut my eyes and watched as two clutches of red thread moved toward each other against a blank background and then violently tangled with each other and I woke up terrified. In another, my head was sinking back into a disconcerting pillow that fluffed up on both sides of my face, and just before I was totally enveloped in the too-soft pillow and suffocated without screaming, I would wake up, sweating.

I never found anyone who could understand these dreams until I found Rainer Maria Rilke's writing about illness and, specifically, fever fear:

> The fear that a little woolen thread sticking out of the blanket might be hard, hard and sharp like a steel needle; the fear that this little button on my nightshirt might be bigger than my head, big and heavy; the fear that this crumb of bread falling off my bed just now could become glass and shatter when it hits the floor, and the oppressive worry that that would mean everything was broken, everything broken forever . . .

Rilke was born nearly fifty years after Schubert died, but it is nonetheless easy for me to imagine that Schubert might have found something in Rilke's work worth setting to song, just as he did Goethe and so many of his poetically talented friends.

I remember these weeks like they were an entire school year. They were a whole separate era to me but only a brief note in my mom's hand, dates and temperatures and names of antibiotics: *Andrea sick from 9/23 to 10/4 Cult neg 9/25 Vicillin 9/29 then Ceclor to 10/6.*

Temp up to 105, swollen glands and tonsils. Then there is a swift, dark underline and her notes revert from the management of this horrible acute illness to our longer-term problems: the management of my chronic illness.

I'd been absent for two weeks and Jenny V. (endless Jennys!) told everyone I had transferred. In a way, I had.

In *Illness as Metaphor*, Susan Sontag declares that "[i]llness is the night-side of life, a more onerous citizenship. Everyone who is born holds dual citizenship, in the kingdom of the well and in the kingdom of the sick. Although we all prefer to use only the good passport, sooner or later each of us is obliged, at least for a spell, to identify ourselves as citizens of that other place."

Flannery O'Connor said it more briefly and bitingly, of course. O'Connor had lupus, a devastating sister disease of rheumatoid arthritis, and therefore knew what it was to be ill with something that was ugly, incurable, and, unlike tuberculosis or cancer, rarely romanticized in art or letters. "Sickness is a place," she wrote, "more instructive than a long trip to Europe." I'd have taken Vienna.

This is my own take on O'Connor: The chronically ill child belongs only partly to her family. She has allegiance elsewhere, she has to be allowed to go there, and no, you can't go with her.

That winter, only months after I recovered from my flare and a year into arthritis, just as my sweet family started to curdle, we went cross-country skiing in Blackwater Falls, West Virginia. Halfway through the trip, both of my ankles were too stiff and sore to walk on, much less ski. My parents couldn't make my brothers and sister stay at the cabin all day because I couldn't ski. I persuaded them to let me stay at the cabin. When my family got back to the lodge we went out to dinner and we played board games and my mom seemed guilty that she'd let me spend all day alone.

But I hadn't felt lonely at all. My day alone had been a sweet, warm interval when no one was asking me how the pain was. Though there was no piano in the cabin, I'd read the strange selection of books my mom had spontaneously, and somewhat uncharacteristically, bought for me at the bookstore one afternoon, inspecting the eclectic but compelling titles I'd pulled from the shelf ("My treat," she'd said): *Geek Love* and *Les Fleurs du Mal*. My mother didn't need to feel guilty about leaving me alone that day; I wanted to tell her that she'd tended to me by proxy, through the gifted books. That I'd been lonely the days before, before I'd admitted that my ankles were killing me, when I'd been trying to keep up with my family on the ski trail as my body reminded me with every tiny turn of the ski that I was different, I was separate, I was unlike them.

Chapter 5

Eighth grade was my year of first love, which primed me for my encounter with the Schubert sonata that undid me—fittingly, in a city called Providence—the following summer. After I recovered from my September flare-up, Jordan Katon finally (and briefly) became my boyfriend. This meant very little Monday through Friday, but on Saturday nights our parents would drop us off at the movies—*Edward Scissorhands* (now *that* guy's handicapped, I thought)—and we'd kiss in the dark, his olive-brown hand in my lap or up my shirt. I could feel the cool metal of the ID bracelet I'd given him against the skin on my belly. I palmed the lump in his jeans with the heel of my hand. It was all surface, happening on our outsides. I was off the hook; I could still keep up with the sex that was expected of me.

Of course, that would change so quickly. By freshman year of high school, people I knew started having sex. For a few years, though, there were enough of us girls who were unabashed in holding our virginal ground for various credible-sounding reasons (God or belief in marriage, fear of AIDS or pregnancy, or a Morrissey-like asexual aloofness) that I was not exceptional or weird in this regard. It was all so daunting that the idea of adopting a monkish celibacy had its appeal. One of the recurring (and apocryphal) stories of Schubert suggests that, after an early heartbreak, he swore off women for the rest of his life, devoting himself instead solely to art and his friends. Then again, he probably died of syphilis. Either way, sex and love seemed treacherous.

Gradually, the end of a date meant more and more was expected (and there's no good way to tell a teenage boy that you're going to have to call it quits on the hand job because your arthritis is flaring up) and less and less was worn. By the time I finished high school and entered college, it seemed that aerobic, generous sex was the expectation after even a handful of dates, and I could not, or would not, comply. It wasn't that my arthritis turned people off right away. In fact, by college, certain boys would find charm in even the few fresh scars I had then, and they would trace their thick thumbs over them and say "beautiful." Susan Sontag again: "It [is] a mark of refinement, of sensibility, to be sad. That is, to be powerless." *Ill* can be substituted for *sad* here, perhaps because people seem to assume that if one is ill, one is sad.

I didn't have trouble attracting boys. The real problem—more problematic than logistical difficulties presented by my body's tender hot spots and lack of flexibility—was the fact that I didn't want to be inside my body and I didn't want to invite anyone else to be.

I didn't like what arthritis was doing to my body, but the things I really needed my body to do, it could do. And so I asked more and more of my body at the piano. In the winter of ninth grade, I tried out for the role of rehearsal pianist for the school musical. I was up against a senior named Stephen who'd been doing the job, and I learned later that no one expected him to be unseated. The show was *The Sound of Music*. After auditions, in which we each sight-read from the score, it was decided that I would get the shorter second act and Stephen would play the longer first act. We received our rehearsal schedules. The first day of rehearsal, I showed up early so I could watch Stephen and see what they'd expect from me. But Stephen was late. "Can you play Act One?" Mr. Frezzo, the music teacher, asked, desperate. I sight-read the act, Stephen never showed, and the play was mine. The whole play was mine.

They were all mine after that. I played for every show, every year: *The Sound of Music, 42nd Street, Guys and Dolls, Sweet Charity*. Even on the bad days, when I woke up stiff and hot and unable to get my fingers out of the curled position they'd worked themselves into as I slept because I'd refused to put on the resting splints that had been prescribed for this reason—"I can't fall asleep with them on!" I whined—I'd soak my hands in the bathroom sink or soak my whole body in the hot tub and I'd get to school just before the halfway point of the day so I'd still be allowed to stay after school and play for rehearsal. Junior year I was rented out to another high school at the last minute because their pianist broke her wrist. "Good thing you're healthy," the musical director said to me when I showed up. This pronouncement—"you're healthy"—would mean more to me than the paltry check I received for my services. It meant that I was still ahead, still outrunning my arthritis.

I played in *Annie Get Your Gun* for the local community theater. I accompanied the saxophonists, flautists, and trombone players from my school in their county and state competitions. I paid for a new metronome with the money I earned. That people would pay money for my playing struck me as a notable threshold in my development as a musician—and other musicians have similarly noted this rite of passage. In fact, a nineteen-year-old Schubert took special note of his own first paid work, writing, "Today I composed for money for the first time."

I spent most of my school day in Mr. Frezzo's room. Mr. Frezzo was closing in on fifty, but he was impish and compact, with a fuzz of curly hair. When he smiled, he looked like he was ten years old, and he smiled almost all the time. Though already older than Schubert would ever live to be, the slight, bespectacled Mr. Frezzo merged with the line drawings and paintings I'd seen of Schubert. He was genial and kind, my very own Schubert, who was once described as "a man full of affection and goodness of heart."

But, like Schubert, he had hot buttons: You didn't want Mr. Frezzo to catch you swearing or he'd cross himself and you'd get a lecture-slash-vocabulary-lesson in elegance, grace, poise, restraint, and decorum. If he caught you breaking concert protocol or demonstrating bad musicianship, he would puff up and his face would turn beet red and you would hear it. *Fortissississimo.* He taught me to love Renaissance choral music. He introduced me to "Erlkönig," possibly Schubert's most famous song, with text by Goethe, about a sick child being ushered off to death on horseback in the middle of the night as he calls desperately for his father.

It was in Mr. Frezzo's room, and under his instruction, that I learned about Schubert in a fashion nearly opposite of the way he is generally known and remembered. Apart from one Schubert duet ("Marche Militaire") I'd played with my sister years before at one of Mrs. Feltman's recitals, the only Schubert piece I knew well was that compelling sonata—and just the first movement at that. Immediately upon returning from the Providence conference, probably at Waxie Maxie's in Congressional Plaza, I'd found *Horowitz the Poet*, a tape-recording of the legendary Vladimir Horowitz playing the Schubert sonata. Also on the tape was Schumann's *Kinderszenen*, or "Scenes from Childhood," much of which I'd already performed in competition. I listened to the tape until it wore out, and then I ordered it on CD from Columbia House.

I'd bought the sheet music for the sonata as soon as I got back from the AJAO conference in Providence. Ever since, I'd been working on the first movement of that sonata, albeit only in private. I hadn't brought it to Mrs. Feltman, hadn't lobbied to get it on my competition repertoire. I kept it to myself like a first love, stoking that happy interval when it was all my own.

The sonata was so captivating, I found it impossible to believe that Schubert was not known as a sonata-composer most of all. During his lifetime, though, Schubert was known nearly exclusively as a great and prolific songwriter, the Prince of Song. His longer, more serious instrumental works were virtually unknown until well after his death, in 1828. According to Christopher Gibbs, author of *The Life of Schubert*, even one of his best friends and advocates, writing in 1839, reinforced this song-centric view of Schubert: "We shall never make a Mozart or a Haydn of him in instrumental and church compositions, whereas in song he is unsurpassed."

It was easy to make myself at home in Mr. Frezzo's room, anchored as it was by a grand piano and every cabinet filled with stacks of books and sheet music. I co-opted his music encyclopedias, flipping first to the sections on Schubert's final sonatas—my sonata—and then starting at the beginning and working my way through his thirty-one years. These books would be my first primer in Schubert, providing me with a sketch I would flesh out for decades to come, relying first on *Grove* volumes and eventually on Gibbs's *The Life of Schubert*. After the Internet became available, from a succession of dorm rooms, apartments, and houses, I would click my way through the growing body of Schubert analysis and biography.

In Mr. Frezzo's class, I got a nourishing musical diet; in addition to my self-assigned study of Schubert, I transcribed the potlatch songs of the Kwakiutl Indians and feasted on Puccini. The cyclical structure of opera—with its talky recitatives to advance the plot, and its mellifluous arias for characters to have feelings about what had happened—made an intrinsic kind of sense to me.

Mr. Frezzo had learned to play the accordion growing up in Mount Vernon, New York. It was there too, just north of the Bronx, that he learned that you should hang up your clothes in the closet with all the hangers facing the same way. "If there's a fire, you need to grab and go!" he said. I think of him every time I hang up my jacket.

He was generous—with his time, and with praise. "Boy," he'd call to me, from his office in the back of the music room as I practiced during lunch on the grand piano, "that is really sounding good." I was his accompanist not just for the musicals but for the choir and the madrigal singers. He prepped me for a master class with the pianist Thomas Mastroianni. Sometimes he'd let me warm up the choir or lead them through their parts. On the rare occasion he was absent, he left notes for the substitute that read, "Andrea will lead—she knows what to do." This delighted me even more when I read that Schubert, the composer who was slowly inching out Mozart in my affections, had been extended the same privilege and responsibility as a student at Vienna's Imperial and Royal City College.

And so I built my days around the piano, shuttling straight from school to musical rehearsal with Mr. Frezzo to late-evening practices or lessons at Mrs. Feltman's, going home only to sulk and to sleep. Mr. Frezzo and Mrs. Feltman became ersatz parents, and I was kinder to them than I was to my real, dueling parents.

My only real rival in piano—or for Mr. Frezzo's affections, which I craved furiously and possessed assuredly—was Randy Cohen. Randy was a year older than me, smug, red-haired, and a piano phenom. The other kids would go between us—"Randy can play 'Rhapsody in Blue.' Can you?"—or take sides. "Randy's good and all," one boy told me. "But he's like a robot, and plus he doesn't have arthritis." If this was a pickup line, it eluded me. I knew Randy was better than I was, arthritis or not. He knew he was better than I was, too, and he didn't need to prove it the way I did. He could easily have snatched the rehearsal pianist role from me, but he was more interested in conducting. So for three years, we worked together contentiously in the orchestra pit for the musicals, Randy with his conductor's baton and me with my piano. Then Randy went off to Oberlin and I retained my nearly uncontested claim to the piano and to Mr. Frezzo.

I had no real rival for Mrs. Feltman's affections. Though I grudgingly accepted that she had other students, I insisted on believing that she didn't tell them that they were the daughter she never had.

I paced between my two beloved teachers, and I tried to keep up with them, and I tried to please them. I felt as sure and regal as a child does who holds the hands of her parents and tells them, "Swing me!" and they do, each of them doing their part to lift her up and let her soar for an instant without fear, to let her believe she is flying, and then see her safely back down to the ground.

The summer after ninth grade, I spent a week in California with my dad's cousin Susan and her husband, Jim. "They have a kid about your age!" my parents told me. "Your second cousin Kevin! And his older sister, Erin!" We'd never been an exorbitant-vacation family, not a big-gift-for-no-reason family, so I was suspicious that my parents were trying to get rid of me to try some kind of miracle sunshine cure on me, like in *Heidi* or *Little Women*. It was an echo of an old fear of being sent off to fat camp even though arthritis had now made me thin and almost waiflike. Susan and Jim took me to Catalina Island with them. Their kids—busy with exotic California things I'd never heard of, like junior lifeguards and Chinese chicken salad and friends named Cody—stayed back in Orange County.

There were no kids in Catalina Island to speak of, apart from the gawky, maladjusted only child of friends of Susan and Jim's. The girl, who insisted on calling me "kid," even though she was two years younger than I, had grown up on a boat. She showed me her triangular bedroom in the boat, nearly filled by her triangular bed. "Do you go to *malls*?" she asked me when I got set up on an afternoon playdate with her. "Can I play with your *Game Boy*?"

We stayed in cabins on a sparkling inlet. I had a small cabin to myself. I'd given the weirdo the Game Boy, which I'd borrowed from a friend back home anyway, to keep her busy in her berth room. In the evenings, Susan and Jim took me on the "cocktail hour" rounds of yachts anchored in the cove. They let me drive the dinghy, even though I couldn't even drive a car yet.

When we tied up the dinghy at the dock, they disappeared into their cabin and I hung out by myself. There was a swing set with a single swing that arced out over the placid water. I pumped hard with my pale legs; I swung until I was tired, I wished I felt like singing, and then I went to my little cabin with its white sheets made crispy by the salt water and sand from my skin.

All week long, I wore bathing suits and shorts and let the sun soak into all the parts of my body I'd kept covered during the school year, the parts that I knew I would cover up again when I got home.

In the afternoons, we took a boat around the island to snorkel, which I'd never done before. At first I was panicked; I put the snorkel in my mouth and ducked underwater and started hyperventilating, flailing—*We can't breathe underwater!* my lungs insisted. *This tube terminates* above *the surface of the water,* I told my stupid lungs, *and you're breathing just fine.*

On one perfect day we snorkeled into the gaping mouth of a U-shaped cave. I held onto Jim's ankle as we entered the dark middle of the curved cave. He pulled me through and we emerged into the open water again, light pouring through the open end of the cave and slicing the water so that the seals and rays and Garibaldi fish below—things I'd never seen—were illuminated. Floating facedown on the surface of the water, I realized there was more life—and more beautiful life—above me than below. Less behind me than where I faced.

Water has inspired and soothed countless people, including Schubert. His famous Trout Quintet was, according to Gibbs and others, composed during a joyful summer trip in 1819 to the lush and lovely countryside of Steyr with his friend. Always able to depict visuals evocatively in his music—and indeed to go well beyond mere tone painting into the realm of depicting metaphors and abstract emotional states—many people believe that the ebullient Trout Quintet is meant to evoke darting fish and shimmering waves. Schubert wrote numerous songs about or evocative of water, but perhaps never again so happily as he did in the Trout.

I was healthier in water. Weightless, "like spaghetti instead of Popsicle sticks stuck together with Play-Doh," as I'd once told my mother, and which she recorded in her notebook. When I am painless, I am harmonious, homogenous. When I hurt, I am made of parts that don't go together. The fission, the discord, hurts as much as my joints do.

But my body peace was not to last: after snorkeling, I took a shower in the wood-slatted stall of the bathhouse. When I looked down, I spotted a dime-size, dark brown patch about six inches below my belly button. It stood out starkly against the light covering of hair. I scraped at it with my fingernail and it wouldn't come off. Completely virginal, but fully indoctrinated by scare-tactic public-school assemblies, I was sure I had contracted an STD. Either that or I'd gone and gotten skin cancer, some quick-setting variety they hadn't discovered yet (would they name it after me?) in California. Either way, it wasn't good. I used the pay phone behind the bathhouse to call my mother collect. "I have a brown patch that's not supposed to be there," I cried. "It's—down there."

"If you're worried about it, or if it changes," my mom said, ever calm, "I want you to tell Susan. She can take you to a doctor."

I didn't tell Susan. I waited it out and went home, the disgusting brown deformity eclipsing the sun from the mouth of that cave.

At home, the dermatologist tried to scrape at the barnacle, too. When it wouldn't come off, he ordered a punch biopsy. When the results came back, they called it a seborrheic keratosis—a common, painless, noncancerous skin growth. The website of the American Academy of Dermatology is nearly poetic in describing the appearance of these growths: "Some look like a dab of warm, brown candle wax on the skin. Others may resemble a barnacle sticking to a ship."

It's really nothing, my own less-than-poetic doctors assured me. Benign. But to me it's a note left by my terrorist body: *Don't get too comfortable*, it says. *There's more where this came from. I can do anything I want.*

There are no notes in my mom's notebook from January 25, 1993, so I don't know how I was feeling on the day a gunman got out of his car at the entrance to CIA headquarters and started shooting people as they sat in their cars waiting to turn in. I learned about the shooting when I walked alone to the 7-Eleven to buy a hot dog at lunchtime. I heard it from the small TV the cashier had next to the cash register. I wasn't worried about my dad. I knew that by 8:00 A.M., when the shooter first leveled his gun through the driver's side window of a CIA employee's car, my dad had probably been at his desk for three or four hours. It was a good thing, I thought, that my dad wasn't still taking me to therapy in the mornings. When I began high school, my physical-therapy sentence had been commuted. I interpreted this as a good sign (I don't need it anymore!), but in retrospect I wonder if it was decided that I was a lost cause.

Sophomore year, after four years of arthritis and nine years of piano, as my classmates dreamed of being surprised with cars topped with big red bows, we shopped for pianos. Mrs. Feltman had been saying that I needed a better instrument to improve my playing, that I needed an instrument that had better action, better dynamic response. Though I expected my parents to balk—we didn't have several thousand dollars to spend on this, and anyway, weren't my hands an incredibly bad investment?—they didn't. My mom started a new notebook for her research into grand pianos. Grandma Torvik had given my mom $10,000, and my mom and dad would find the rest.

We looked at refurbished pianos first. My mom and I went to a piano shop where I fell in love with a brown Mason & Hamlin, only to learn from the smarmy shop owner that he was selling it to a woman who was going to put a Disklavier in it so it would play itself. Another piano seemed like the one until my mother had an appraiser look at it. "No," the appraiser said. "The soundboard is warped. I can fit my business card in there."

It was hard to believe that a thing so beautiful could be worthless.

We looked at new pianos then. In a bright showroom, I found the five-foot-ten satin-finish Kawai KG-2A. I don't remember what I played on it in the showroom, or even falling in love with it, because I think I didn't allow myself to fall in love until the adoption was final, until the papers had been signed, until the piano came home. But I do remember *that* day, and I remember falling completely in love with my piano. It was such an extraordinarily beautiful and well-made thing, and it was all mine. Why me? indeed. In this fortune, I was right in pace with (ahead of!) Schubert. His family didn't get their own piano until Schubert was seventeen, and it couldn't have been as fine an instrument as I now had. It was during Schubert's lifetime that the piano evolved in many ways to become the instrument we know today, though the standard-bearer Steinway grand would not premiere until forty years after Schubert's death. Nevertheless, the piano's being in a nascent state served Schubert well. According to Gibbs, the improvements in piano design and construction allowed the composer to create "thrilling keyboard parts of unprecedented intensity, extraordinary difficulty, and unifying power."

We don't know what Schubert felt, if anything, upon the delivery of his family's first piano. Schubert was not a diarist. He left only a few letters and diaries. His work tells his story. As Schumann said, "What a diary is to others, in which their momentary emotions and so forth are recorded, so to Schubert was music paper, to which he entrusted all his moods. His thoroughly musical soul wrote notes where others used words." If we want to know how Schubert felt about his piano, or pianos generally, we need only listen to his piano music.

My grand piano was delivered June 29, 1993. I was sixteen. In my journal, I wrote, "I want to remember every detail—including the fact that there's buzzing on the A one octave above middle C." The buzzing was probably from the piano's move and must have worked itself out, or maybe the piano continued to buzz and my memory, insistent on being happy, has edited it out.

We'd made room in the living room for the piano. That old brown Wurlitzer went, on indefinite loan, to the family next door and their two little girls. The deliverymen brought in the new piano bundled in blankets, its legs in a separate package, deftly dodging our cat and dog. The men were wordless, a team of expert surgeons: They rested the piano on its side and screwed the legs in and turned it upright and then there it was. The movers left with their blue quilted blankets in deflated bundles hugged to their chests.

I missed our two dead cats, Shadow and Tinkerbelle, but I was glad, for my new piano's sake, that our new cat, Pandora, was not a sprayer like those two. Days ahead of its arrival, I made plans for my piano: No one would be permitted to play crap as crass as "Heart and Soul" or as overdone as "Für Elise" on my piano. My piano's first words would be the first movement of Schubert's Sonata in B-flat, the sonata that had infected me as I sat coloring with the other arthritic kids in Providence two years earlier.

I'd been practicing the sonata on our old brown upright and on Mr. Frezzo's piano at school, conveying the increasingly dog-eared red-covered book of Schubert sonatas back and forth to school in my backpack. I hadn't yet mastered the sonata's first movement, but I had my hands capably around it. I couldn't wait to hear if my playing of it was improved, or transformed, by an instrument more deserving. It seemed important, too, to christen the piano with the right piece, as if the wood and felt and lacquer and metal would calibrate themselves to that first utterance.

On the day the piano was delivered, the opening notes of the Schubert sonata fit in my still-strong hands, and it did sound different on this new instrument, but not better. The grand piano was a more subtle and sensitive instrument, and it allowed me to hear the holes in my playing, the places where strings of notes that were supposed to be legato were not as sinuous as they needed to be, where I was manhandling fortes too hard, muddling trills and being timid and noncommittal instead of soft. The new piano allowed me to hear my playing in high definition. My Schubert sonata was not ready for prime time, but I was overjoyed: I had work to do, and an instrument to do it on, and hands to do it with.

Even though arthritis was already scribbling its graffiti on my swollen hands and wrists, I could play this piece—technically. I could capture most of the notes of this first movement in my hands. It was my favorite piece to play on my new piano. It was the first piece I ever wanted to really work on, not just sight-read and move on. I wanted to know it, to transcend the mechanics of this note, that note, and figure out what it was saying.

As intensely possessive as I felt about the sonata, I soon learned that it was not musical kismet or my own extraordinarily perceptive listening that had made the sonata speak to me the way it did. I'd looked it up—probably in one of the *Grove* dictionaries I'd found in Mr. Frezzo's room or at the used bookstore—and learned that this sonata was considered by some to be Schubert's true masterpiece.

The B-flat sonata was the last sonata, nearly the last instrumental work, Schubert wrote. It was composed sometime in the late summer or early fall, probably September, of 1828. Having now read everything about the sonata I can find, I see that the effusiveness in the *Grove* volumes is no fluke. When people write about this sonata and the two others that precede it and form a trilogy, they swoon. They drop phrases like "wonderment, terror and awe"; "sublime theme of utmost calmness and breadth"; and "sinister beauty." The romanticism is irresistible. In some versions of the story, Schubert finished the sonata while ailing from syphilis; he performed it at a party the day after finishing it, and he dropped dead two months later at age thirty-one. I'd matured since my Mozart-crush days; I was now a sullen teenager in love with Kurt Cobain and this— *this!*—was a composer I could get behind.

But it wasn't just the dashing, tragic romanticism of Schubert that captivated me. I was maturing, and I was discovering the focused pleasure of truly studying a piece of work. I opened the score to the sonata and read it over during any spare moment—in a doctor's office waiting room, in front of the TV, even brazenly in the middle of chemistry class. Reflective, disciplined study of the work of others doesn't get romanticized as easily as Mozartean bullishness, but this is what Schubert was teaching me—and this is what Schubert himself did. Gibbs describes a scene in which one of Schubert's friends comes upon the young composer, just a teenager, with the songs of a master lied composer spread in front of him, intent on unlocking the mystery of why they moved him so.

"The piano is yours," my mom said, "but it stays here until you're grown up and settled somewhere for good, when you're responsible enough to care for it." I would start immediately. I would wipe down the keys after every session. I would always keep the strip of bright red felt over the keys under the fallboard. I would earn this $13,786.23 endorsement.

On that day, the idea of the piano's sitting alone, mute and inert and untouched, for months on end, was unimaginable.

Chapter 6

By the time the piano moved in, the yellow house on Harvard Court, already empty-feeling, was nearly empty: My philosopher sister was in Seattle or Brooklyn or Africa or Ecuador. Matthew had gone to the University of Maryland in the fall of 1989, scared straight after his arrest for *contraband*, a math major.

Chris was gone most of the time then, too: He snuck out in the middle of the night or didn't come home at all. "Your brother's a stoner," the kids at the bus stop would tell me. When I entered high school in 1991, Chris should have been a senior at the same school—technically, he was—but he was enrolled simultaneously in an alternative school where he got pee tests and they went on river-rafting trips as a metaphor for recovery. My mom kept a stock of Breathalyzers and urinalysis kits in our foyer coat closet, too, and if Chris came home odorous or out of it, he had to puff on the clear plastic tube filled with color-changing crystals, or piss in the cup while my dad stood watch. "Hey, hey," my mom would say, clutching Chris by the lapels of his jean jacket, her chin inclined to his, her nose to his mouth, "you been drinking?"

My mom sent the tests off to a lab and paid a $15 processing fee; the rule was that if it came back positive, Chris was to reimburse my mom the $15 and that money would go into a college fund for him. In 1992, he graduated twice—once, alongside five hundred other kids, wearing the black robe and gold tassel of our high school, and a second time in a small auditorium where drug counselors played a bongo-and-guitar version of "I Can See Clearly Now." And then in 1992, he was gone, too, off at a small college in Virginia, and I was an only child.

Our house was loneliest when the few people who lived there— me, my mom, and my dad—were all home together. I was sorry for all those times I'd wished my siblings away, desperate for the undivided attention of each of my parents. I loved our house most when I was the only one in it.

Happily alone, I pigged out on cookies that no one was counting as I ate and I chased them with milk and ibuprofen and I read *Sassy* magazine and I wrote Nirvana lyrics on my shoes and I modified sweet old dresses to make them fuck-you ugly, and I left the lights off as leafy-green dusk descended through the back door and the windows to the screen porch; I played the piano in the living room with only the piano lamp on. I'd sing if no one was home to hear me: "Killing Me Softly."

In the evenings, my dad and I sat in the dark of the family room and watched *Law & Order* in silence—him in the rocking chair because my mom had swapped the old tweed couch for a cool and slippery white leather sectional that would accommodate more of us at once even though nearly everyone was gone and he vowed never to sit in it. My mom was in the kitchen reading the paper, or up in the bedroom, lying on the made bed, her face smeary with tears and her glasses on the nightstand.

Maybe they fought more then, or maybe there were just fewer people around to absorb the tension. We three made stabbing, sulking attempts to eat together. "This is pretty good chicken," my dad would say, and I would puff up with hope. "What's in the formula for this?" he'd ask.

"I'm sorry, I don't know what you mean by *formula*," my mom would say, leaning across the table with her head cocked, resting her fork on her plate of bean curd patties, as if eager to know what he was trying to say.

"The goddamn *formula*," my dad would say. "For the chicken."

"Oh, if you mean the *recipe* . . ." my mom would say, pretend-trying, mock-epiphanic.

She'd been vegetarian for years but she would make chicken for him and me, and yet he found it impossible to compliment her in language she'd understand. And she—he was trying to pay a sincere compliment, and she refused to hear it. I sat between them, trapped in their marital dissonance, with no one to roll my eyes at.

I wrote a song to amuse my siblings when they called or came home:

> *They're fun-da-men-tal-ly in-com-pat-ib-le*
> *but they both watch* Dal-las.
> *They're fun-da-men-tal-ly in-com-pat-ib-le*
> *but they both like ten-nis.*
> *Mom says, "Let's talk, let's go take a walk,"*
> *but Dad says, "What's the point?"*
> *Mom says, "Let's eat, but I don't eat meat,"*
> *and Dad says, "Horse hoc-key!"*

And so on. It was cruelly funny, painfully necessary.

Lucky for me, sick was the new black. Just as "Chopin was tubercular at a time when good health was not chic," according to Camille Saint-Saëns, I was anemic at the height of grunge and I was, after Randy Cohen's departure, no longer the second-best pianist at school. I was the Chopin of Richard Montgomery High

School. People who looked sick like me weren't exactly in the halls of my school, but they were on the covers of *Rolling Stone*, just the way that nineteenth-century painters chose as their models big-eyed, sickly girls with diaphanous skin. Real-life Victorian wannabes used arsenic to pale their skin; twentieth-century grunge wannabes bought special hair goop that made it look like they hadn't washed it. I had them all beat. I was 100 percent naturally anemic, with skin the color of cataracts, and some mornings I couldn't raise my arms high enough to wash my hair.

Whereas the Victorian woman tied her midsection down to twenty inches in an organ-mangling corset that exerted fifty pounds of torque on her body and hauled around fifteen pounds of petticoats to have "the look," arthritis made me skinny and the "Seattle look" allowed me to cover what I needed to cover and coddle what I needed to coddle in a very comfortable fashion. Oversize flannel shirts hid my rigid, crooked elbows. Doc Martens, with a custom orthotic slipped inside, meant my troubled feet were reasonably comfortable and the shoes were roomy enough to not crowd my swollen feet. And so I threw myself into this "look." I'm desperately—probably inordinately—grateful that the nineties were the backdrop for this period of my life in my body. After all, it was important to me that I look "good." It just worked out nicely for me that what looked "good" in 1993 was consumptive chic.

From the outside, it probably appeared that I was simply a taller, thinner, weirder version of the little girl who liked playing dress-up so much. Teachers and classmates thought I was a gutsy, she'll-wear-anything girl. But my dressing-up now was joyless, and I was a hypocrite. My dressing up was strategic. Though I'd wear an antique floor-length lace dress to school, and I'd dye my hair in the bathroom sink with Kool-Aid, I would not—I could not—wear sleeveless shirts or shorts. My clothes screamed, "Yeah, so what? I don't care what you think of me!" but the truth was my clothing was a diversion tactic, something for people to look at so they wouldn't see my body. So they wouldn't see me.

My efforts in concealment (hiding what was wrong with my body) and deflection (redirecting the inevitable gaze away from my body itself and toward the bizarre clothes I hung on it) are, though I wasn't aware of it then, classic tactics used by women (both with disabilities and without) in response to the immense pressure to conform to body norms. A third tactic, normalization, in which the disabled person highlights, or at least acknowledges, her bodily difference in an effort to educate others or recalibrate their expectation of what a "normal" body might be, is also classic, but this was not a tactic I yet used. I didn't think I had any right to argue that my body, this changed body, this ugly body, should be considered "normal." I'd had a normal body *before*, and now it was gone.

My dad could not any longer hide the momentary grimace that flashed across his face when he noted my gnarled fingers or limping gait. When he said, "Hi, there, honeybunch," it was hollow-sounding. He was looking for Goldilocks, and I disappointed him.

And he disappointed me, too: I wanted my dad to call me kiddo; I wanted him to pass by me on the couch and dig a noogie into my scalp; I wanted him to put me on his narrowing shoulders or carry me up the stairs by my steaming ankles, pretending to sweep the kitchen floor with my long hair; I wanted him to fake me out with the foam-rubber rock he kept in his den that was painted to look like a heavy stone or show me the fossil rock he had; I wanted him to give me a wooden nickel and tell me not to spend it all in one place; I wanted him to watch me play the piano; I wanted to watch him monitor the football game; I wanted him to smack my mom on the ass like I'd seen—maybe—once, or kiss her neck like I'm not sure I have ever seen. He had so few words to spend on us then, and it seemed all I got was "Did you take your pills? Did you do your exercises? Are you wearing your splints? How do the joints feel today?"

These questions were a sickly imitation of the game he used to play with me, in happier, healthier days, when he'd shoot his freckled arm high into the air and tease, "Yesterday I could raise my arm this high," and then, feebly waving it only ear-high, "Today I can only raise it this high."

One of the requirements of my piano study as a high school student was participation in the Maryland State Music Teachers Association's annual piano exam. There were grades on the exam, I suppose, or scores—who knows?—it was another thing you could write on your application to conservatories. The exam would prepare us well for studying piano at a college or conservatory, for our end-of-semester juries. For the piano exam, and for college juries, the pianist prepares her repertoire and several octaves of scales and arpeggios and then plays until someone with a clipboard tells her to stop.

The piano exam in May 1994, my junior year of high school, came the week before our spring musical, *Guys and Dolls*. It was held at the home of one of the association's piano teachers. Mrs. Feltman would meet me there, though she wouldn't be permitted to be in the room. She'd have to wait outside and listen through the door to my playing. I was allowed to stay home from school in the morning and drive myself to the exam. It was not a bad day; I woke up and practiced. I practiced and practiced. I ran scales and arpeggios, I played through my repertoire time after time. I was ready.

When I got to the teacher's house, I waited in her living room until it was my turn to go downstairs to the finished basement where she had a piano studio. As I waited, I tapped out my music on my lap. My fingers were stretched and warm and fluid and strong and ready. I'd practiced for hours. When you can, you must.

When my name was called, I went downstairs. I sat at the piano. I placed my hands on the keys and waited for the cue to begin. The judges looked at me over their half-glasses and smiled warmly. "You may begin," the first judge said.

I started with Chopin's Étude No. 3 in E Major. It was a serene, comfortable, easy-on-the-hands, hard-on-the-brain piece. I hated it. It was easy to play, at least as far as my hands were concerned. The difficult part was making it musical, making it lyrical, giving the inner harmonies voice but keeping them under the singing top notes even though the big fat thumb on my dominant right hand was responsible for sounding some of those inner notes and the relatively delicate pinkie was in charge of the melody. *Keep the blowhard thumb under control. Not too much. Don't manhandle it.*

I didn't like pieces like this or the second movement of the Schubert sonata, which I'd barely glanced at before dismissing it. I'd taken one look of the "andante sostenuto" tempo marking—slow, sustained—at the top of that second movement and decided that it held no promise for me. As captivated as I was by the first movement of the Schubert sonata, and as eager as I was to truly study it, there was still a little Mozart in me: I foolishly ignored the likelihood that the second movement would also be transcendent. It was slow, so it was not for me. I liked flashy, fast-moving pieces. To play a piece like this étude well, I had to think both horizontally and vertically. I had to hear the harmonies that came when the notes stacked up on top of one another, and I had to sculpt the long phrases that were created when I moved just one note or left a note sustaining even as everything else moved beneath it. I liked the pieces that moved in such quick-fingered perpetual motion I didn't have to think and an undiscerning audience didn't have time to consider whether it sounded like music. They would simply be wowed. For the étude, I had to use my brain, and I considered that a waste of the dazzling machinery of my hands. I liked to set my hands loose at the beginning of Beethoven's "Rage over a Lost Penny" and then catch up with them at the end.

It wasn't that I thought I had the piano exam in the bag. I wasn't at all sure what score I would receive, but I was certain my *hands* would come through. I thought the variable of a good performance was my ears or my heart. I thought I could count on my hands to do their relatively easy job. Back then, willing to forgive my body, insistent that its transgressions were fleeting, I believed my body was a sure thing, the surest thing. I was happy to let my hands surprise me by executing trills and mordents before my brain even processed the work order. Though I had mounting evidence to the contrary, I insisted on believing that only my mind or heart could betray me.

Brief, beautiful, before: I fit my hands into the E major chord that opened the piece.

Brief, beautiful, before: I stretched my hands for the series of close-clustered, near-dissonant chords that climbed the keyboard like a cat—Shadow or Tinkerbelle—jumping across the keys.

Suddenly, everything went wrong.

Suddenly, the top of my right hand felt bruised, flattened, like a poltergeist had whacked it with an invisible ball-peen hammer. My hands lost their pert, wrist-up piano posture and collapsed onto the keys. My right elbow swung out and banged the edge of the keys. My right hand dived and tried to burrow into the hot, safe nook under my left arm, a scared kitten at the vet.

Voiceless, sick and betrayed, I fled. I said nothing to the judges. I bolted up the stairs and pushed past Mrs. Feltman and went straight to the car and drove home, the road blurring in front of me, the wheel of the car nearly unmanageable in my aching right hand.

Half an hour later, Mrs. Feltman's giant sedan lumbered up the driveway. She seemed strange and out of place at our house, too big or too glamorous; our relationship took place at her house and in concert halls and practice rooms. Though she'd served me a million lunches of peanut butter and jelly, I never once fed her. On the days in elementary school that I'd been permitted to leave school at lunchtime for my lessons, I couldn't have been more proud if I'd been Schubert himself, leaving school early for his lesson with the great Salieri. Though I considered Mrs. Feltman a second mother, she'd only been to our house once before, to check out the Kawai when we got it, to approve it, to bless it, to pronounce me a lucky, lucky girl. Did I know how lucky I was?

She had my sheet music. She'd collected it from the judges.

I waited for her to tell me what had happened. Was it all over? Were we finally going to sit down at the kitchen table and sketch out every young artist's worst nightmare, the plan B?

"They'll let you take the exam again," she said. So I hadn't blown it after all. This was a fluke. "Rest for a while and you can come back for the last time slot of the day. I told them all about your arthritis and they think you're a real trouper."

I knew then my score on the piano exam would be spectacular, no matter how I played, whether I showed up or not. I was embarrassed, of course, but my sadness and shame went deeper than that. For the first time, arthritis had lapped me. It had beaten me, and instead of being amazed at how I played *despite* arthritis, these teachers were now factoring my arthritis into my score, which would itself swell. I would feel, really for the first time, the acute devastation of pity. I was fine with having arthritis myself, but for the first time I had infected the music. Now it was arthritic, too.

I was late to class most days, not because I was walking slow but because I'd duck into my guidance counselor's office, where she'd let me sit in a chair, silent, hug my backpack on my lap, and cry while her three hundred Garfield figurines stared at me. She didn't make me talk. "You should go to Pomona College," she told me, scribbling out a hall pass for me, flinging it at me from under her purple serape. "I think you have seasonal affective disorder." I didn't have the grades for Pomona. I'd barely passed Algebra II. I'd managed to get a senior-year schedule that had two English classes and five music classes. I had piano. That's it. When Schubert was a teenager, even though he was a bright and good student, he committed himself so fully to composing that all his other academic subjects suffered (especially math). And so he leaped—he opted not to pursue the university track and, to his father's dismay, chose instead to devote himself to music. I wanted to leap, too. Even with painful feet and knees and hands, I wanted to leap toward the piano.

I visited and toured Juilliard with my mom, and we both took it seriously enough that she bought me a $50 sweatshirt.

Or maybe, by then, six years into arthritis, wise with adulthood, motherhood, nursehood, she bought me the sweatshirt because she knew she couldn't get me into Juilliard. After all, I came home with a sweatshirt but no glossy pamphlets, no business cards from the admissions office.

Or maybe Juilliard was just a side trip because we were in New York to visit Erica in Brooklyn.

Maybe the great beautiful piano wasn't endorsement at all. Maybe it was my consolation prize. My parents must have known my hands were a bad investment, but thank God they thought my heart—my happiness—was not.

In June, my parents came home from their thirty-second anniversary dinner to find me curled on the floor of the bathroom. Everything between my sternum and my ilium was clenching in rhythmic spasms of pain. They took me to the ER, where the doctors found an inflamed appendix and a grapefruit-size cyst on my right ovary. The next morning, the doctor on rounds came to report his findings, to itemize what he'd removed from my body. "Do you feel any better?" he asked. "Sort of," I said. Later in my hospital stay, they found I had colitis. "Wow, when you get sick, you really go all the way," the doctor joked.

After a year and a half away at school, Chris came home. Andy Swindells, of course, hadn't been able to go away to school. He couldn't work, either, so as far as I know he doodled and played guitar and wandered around Rockville alone. With Chris away, Andy called me. "Heyyyy, man," he breathed into the phone.

"What do you want?"

"You know your brother's still doing drugs," he told me.

"Shut up," I said. "I have to go." I did not know whether to believe him. Was this just a diversion for him? Was he baiting me like all older brothers do to kid sisters, as if serving as Chris's understudy? Was he flirting? Or was it true? Was this a secondhand call for help?

And then he showed up at the music store where I was working, with details. Andy was counting on my being a bratty, tattletale little sister and I played the role. I told my parents what Andy had told me. "We're not paying thousands of dollars so you can sleep your way through life *stoned*," my dad told Chris, and the tacit suggestion was that Chris could just as well do that at home. So that's what he did.

As I recovered from the surgery that took my appendix and the cyst on my ovary, Chris took the pain pills I'd been prescribed and replaced them with vitamins.

Great siblings do less-great things to each other: Schubert's brother Ferdinand, a credible musician in his own right, passed off several of Franz's compositions as his own to bolster his reputation. It must have seemed to Ferdinand that Franz had genius to spare and that Ferdinand had a legitimate claim to some of its product, just as it must have seemed to Chris that I had opiates to spare and that he had legitimate pain, too.

And siblings forgive each other. Schubert forgave his most beloved brother—even permitted the theft. I forgave Chris, and Chris forgave me for my part in derailing his college education. I was briefly allowed into his room again. His friend Will, who claimed to be a reincarnation of Jim Morrison, had taken a liking to me. Will had a car and Will liked me, so I went to the parties my brother went to. I was happily at the center of a ring of long-haired, music-playing Bohemian boys, just like my beloved Schubert.

That November, in the parking lot of Tower Records with Chris and Will and Andy, Andy scooted the front seat back so quickly and so far that he pinned my right knee between his seat and the door. "You big fucking idiot," I yelled at him.

"Geez, Andy," Chris said, "Watch out for my sister."

Later, at the party, Chris watched the bong go around the room, and when it got to me, even though I would pass it and he knew it, he growled protectively, "Don't give any of that shit to my little sister." My heart swelled; my knee swelled.

I broke up with Will because he smoked too much pot. "I'd like to quit," he said, "but what if I'm not interesting without it? I only like myself high," he cried. I told Will he was fucking crazy, but I understood, perfectly:

I have never smoked pot because I'm afraid I will really like it, that it will help, that it will make my pain go away. And then what? I can choose between a sharp mind and a painless body? I was incubating a suspicion—which has hatched into truth—that my brain would be the only thing I could use to apologize for my body. Better to get used to the pain.

The piano exam episode was forgotten, quickly. Mrs. Feltman and I never spoke of it. Days or weeks later, my hands were fine again: I played for the shows, that year and the next. I went to the cast parties. I finished high school with the Most Valued Musician medal, a little heavy coin on a swatch of ribbon with a safety pin. Mr. Frezzo bestowed it on me, and it is my purple heart. The only picture of me in the yearbook apart from my stock black-drape-and-pearls headshot is of me at the piano. The caption says I am performing for the piano club, which is not true. But I am so glad for the photographic evidence of me at the piano in Mr. Frezzo's room, in a scarf I pilfered from the dress-up box in the basement and the grungy outfit concocted to cover as much of my body as possible. I turn to that page sometimes now to reassure myself: *It was true. You were not a fool to believe it.*

Even Schubert's leap toward music was tempered with practicality, backup plans. He became, for a while at least, a schoolteacher, just like his father. My leap would not be to Juilliard or any other conservatory. It would be more of a stumble than a leap—I would pursue music but in a bland, noncompetitive place. There would be no New York—the American Vienna?—for me. I sent audition tapes off to the music departments of the big state schools. Mrs. Feltman enlisted her cranky husband to help me record a Mozart concerto on his eight-track recorder. I played both parts, the soloist part and the condensed orchestra part. My parents urged me to consider the flat campus and dry climate of Arizona State. I convinced myself I wanted to go there and my arthritis was not making this decision for me. My tape got me accepted to ASU and I went.

The day I left for college I wore: a gray Army T-shirt, a hoodie, a crinkly blue-and-purple broomstick skirt, argyle knee socks, brown Chuck Taylors with orthopedic inserts. I was covered, head to toe.

It wasn't scars I was covering, not yet—the only scars I had were the fresh itty-bitty marks on my belly from the appendicitis and ovarian cyst. My waxy barnacle spot was still there, but I had learned to ignore it. Other changes were more pressing. My limbs had begun to atrophy: I was too thin, and I was pale and angular, and my knees and elbows had started to scream when I tried to extend them completely. So I kept them comfortable, ever so slightly bent inside my sleeves and jeans.

In Arizona, I forgot the piano exam and I chose to remember all the applause I received. I tucked away the secret that by now I couldn't clap for other people's music because hand against raw hand hurt too much. I'd pat my palm against my thigh to substitute for clapping. I carried skiers' hand-warmer packets in my backpack, cracking them open for chemical heat during my English 101 taught by a poet named Catherine Hammond, even though it was 120 degrees outside, trying to re-create the sweaty, finger-freeing heat of those summer nights from my childhood I once was so desperate to escape.

The only window in my dorm room faced west, so if I wanted to look at anything other than the claustrophobic beige of my room, or the keening face of my intrusive roommate, I had to stand with my back to Maryland, my family, my grand piano. I stood there at night, at that barred, unopenable window, taking in great gulps of strange orange sky, and I tried to reassure myself that the disintegration I'd left behind—my family, my piano career—was suturing itself together in my absence, fortifying, recovering to receive me back after this interval away. I'd return in four years, I thought, tan and prodigal and healthy, to my intact family encircling my piano, and I'd play for them.

For two summers during his short life, Schubert worked for the family of Count Esterhazy, serving as live-in music master to the count's daughters, Marie and Caroline. The post took him out of Vienna, where he was working miserably as a schoolteacher, to Zseliz, in the Hungarian countryside. At first, during the summer of 1818, twenty-one-year-old Schubert was very happy there, writing that he "lived and composed like a god."

But he eventually came to feel alone in Zseliz, cut off from his adoring circle of like-minded friends, no doubt missing the convivial Schubertiades, musical gatherings featuring Schubert's compositions and, often, the man himself at the piano. As Gibbs describes in *The Life of Schubert*, a good friend of Schubert's, Moritz von Schwind, once captured a Schubertiade in a sepia drawing, grouping together the distinct artists and musicians and writers that made up Schubert's fluid circle of friends. The drawing reminds me of a Schubertian *Sgt. Pepper* cover.

The second summer he went to Zseliz, in 1824, he was motivated not by an escape from his dreaded teaching job but rather unofficially exiled from Vienna by his deteriorating health and need to make money as music master to the Esterhazy family. Writing from Zseliz that second summer, in the "depths of the Hungarian countryside," twenty-four-year-old Schubert wrote to his friend Franz von Schober of his aching longing for his friends and music in Vienna: "I want to exclaim with Goethe: 'Who will bring me back an hour of that sweet time?'"

I want to exclaim with Schubert.

Movement III
LARGO AFFANNATO /
SLOW, ANGUISHED

We surely do not invariably say that someone is complaining because he says he is in pain; so the words "I am in pain" may be a cry of complaint, and may be something else.

—Ludwig Wittgenstein,
Philosophical Investigations

Chapter 7

It's a different kind of hot in Arizona—dry and constant and all wrong for grunge, it turns out. And anyway, Courtney Love was out; Courteney Cox was in. Everyone was wearing belly-baring ringer tees and getting their hair cut into the high-maintenance "Rachel." I couldn't keep up, so I morphed into a more attainable mid-nineties cliché, the poseur raver/skate Betty. I wore OshKosh overalls and men's T-shirts with skateboard logos on them. I wore gold star stickers on my face, the same ubiquitous kind Mrs. Feltman used to put on my piano music. On Halloween, the sorority girls on my dorm floor raided my closet for costumes. Three of them went as "hillbillies" wearing my flannel and overalls.

"You'll wear anything, won't you?" the sorority girls said as they flipped through my tiny closet. Their tone of voice was half-admiring, half-ridiculing. "I guess," I said. But what I wanted to wear was shorts. I wanted to wear cute T-shirts that fit. I wanted to wear a skin I could like, arms and legs I could claim as my own. These girls had taut, sun-browned arms and legs that unspooled easily from their cropped tank tops and miniskirts. The combination of admiration and ridicule worked both ways. One of them was just *dyyyyyying* to get a second interview at Hooters. I scoffed, and I sneered, and I was consumed with envy. The same girls picked out something for me to wear on the one real "date" I had first semester, when a tall, redheaded athletic type in my English 101 class asked me out.

One magical day, David Feltman appeared in my dorm room. He had traded the hockey stick for a golf club and he was also attending Arizona State. I'm sure his mother insisted he call me to be polite, but I doubt she insisted he sleep over. He stayed that night in my tiny twin bed, and I clung to him chastely, enjoying kissing him almost as much as I enjoyed the idea of telling Mrs. Feltman about it someday. In the morning, he left with $20 of mine, promising to buy me a ticket to the Phish concert and to take me. He didn't do either one.

I saw David only more time, about two years later, in the parking lot of Safeway. "Hey, Andrea Avery," he said, "you old enough for me to take you for a beer yet?" He had a six-pack under his arm; I had the prescription for painkillers I'd been issued just minutes earlier, upon my discharge from the emergency room. We could have had quite a party. My knee, the same one Andy Swindells had smashed in the car all those years ago, was now the size of a pumpkin, leaking fluid down inside my calf, so for once, my calf looked sort of thick and muscled. "Not yet," I said, trying to smile. I added this run-in to the funny story I would tell Mrs. Feltman.

During those first happy months in Arizona, the painful failure of my hands at the piano exam was the furthest thing from my mind. It was as if I'd left it back home in Maryland, along with my teddy bear and my winter coat and my friends. My grandmothers and Mrs. Feltman were alive and, as far as I knew, well. My hands frequently hurt but they did the job, hour after hour in the practice rooms. I won third place in a piano competition at school playing three contemporary pieces composed by my cousin Peter at Harvard. I could ignore the pain, and I did not think to wonder if the tendons in my right hand were thinning, shredding on the craggy knob at the head of my ulna.

Even though it stung that arthritis had chosen my college, I couldn't dispute that Arizona was good for me. I biked everywhere; I swam most days. I don't remember being in a lot of pain, but that doesn't mean much: Intellectually, I know I've been in pain since 1989. But if I pinpoint a day when I know I struggled, or I select a page from my journal where I've written about being in pain, I can't summon the pain.

It's like being able to remember some thrilling transgression but not the punishment you earned transgressing—skipping class but not detention. And, in fact, the word *pain* comes from the Latin root *poena*: punishment. Penalty.

In the 1940s, researchers tried to create a unit of pain measurement—the *dol*, from the Latin *dolor*. They went about this in a barbaric-sounding and probably unethical way, by burning the foreheads of volunteer medical students and the hands of women in labor. The *dol* didn't catch on.

Numerous pain reporting and quantification scales exist. In my experience doctors use mostly the Wong-Baker FACES pain-rating scale (in which you match your pain with one of a range of smiley/not-smiley faces) or a simple numerical scale of zero to ten, where zero means you have "no pain at all" and ten represents "the worst possible pain you can imagine."

This pain scale is faulty: Does anyone, ever, have "no pain at all"? And do these people know what kind of *imagination* I have?

The pain scale might as well be a musical scale. I might as well say to a doctor that my pain is at about, hmmm, let's see, A-flat. *Dol* sounds to me like a solfège syllable, a note Maria von Trapp as nurse, not nun, might sing: dol, RA, me.

Pain is personal and superverbal. I will never know if my "six" on the pain scale is comparable to anyone else's. My six could be your two. This is the same troubling concept Erica brought home from college that day: "How do you know that what I see as green is the same color you see as green?"

Schubert was preoccupied with the idea, too. According to Gibbs, he is said to have written that "there is no one who understands the pain or the joy of others! We always imagine we are coming together, and we always merely go side by side. Oh, what torture for those who recognize this!"

This is, in fact, the problem of private language, a philosophical problem introduced by one-handed pianist Paul Wittgenstein's genius-philosopher (baby) brother Ludwig. Philosophically, a private language is a language that is understandable only by a single person. It isn't simply an undiscovered language or a privately invented, codified version of another language, both of which could, theoretically, be deciphered, even if they never are; a private language must be untranslatable and unlearnable by another, inherently individual. Language, according to Wittgenstein the younger, is essentially and inevitably public, shared.

Pain, on the other hand, is inherently private, personal. Pain is one of the things we each keep in a tiny box. We never see anyone else's. We must all agree that, without my seeing your pain or your seeing mine, we will call *that* sensation which causes us to behave *this* way (grimace, double over, gasp, compose a sonata, write a book) "pain."

Did Paul and Ludwig ever compare notes? I wonder. Did Ludwig ever concede that Paul, a pianist robbed of a hand, might possibly have some expertise in this topic of "private language"?

That summer, I went back home for the first of two summers where I went to work with my dad. I had always known that children of CIA employees were eligible for a summer internship program, though none of my siblings had taken advantage of it. It seemed like the perfect job: the pay was good, the sedentary work was arthritis-friendly, and I didn't have to worry about transportation. I could carpool to Langley with my dad. It was an extended take-your-daughter-to-work day. I was worried we wouldn't survive a summer of late starts that were my fault and tense car rides in Beltway traffic. But I was desperately curious about what he did all day—and I thought the forced togetherness would be a delicious punishment to inflict on my dad for never taking me to work with him on any of those mornings after physical therapy.

On the first day, I went alone to my Entrance on Duty orientation. It was held at a bland conference room in a nondescript building in Tyson's Corner, and I was the only non–political science/foreign language/international relations major in the khaki-clad bunch. They showed us a video about the kinds of weaknesses bad Russian spies exploit when they turn good American spies into moles, none of which turned out to be relevant in my post in the CIA's Equal Employment Opportunity (EEO) office, where I would shred sexual harassment depositions into eight pieces (by hand), stuff them into big paper bags marked "soluble/classified" and push them down a chute at the end of the hall.

Once again, my dad had had to rearrange his work hours to accommodate me and our daddy-daughter carpool. He wanted to go to work at 4:00 A.M.; I wanted to go to work at ten. We settled on eight. On the ride to work I was sleepy and cranky; my hair was wet, and I delayed putting my shoes on till the last possible minute; I flitted in and out of sleep as my dad navigated the Car-Strangled Spanner and the George Washington Parkway. A block before we got to the intersection where the shooting had taken place, he'd wake me up, poking me in the thigh—"Honeybunch, hey, hey"—and tell me to sit up. At the booth, we held our photo badges up wordlessly—his blue, mine gray, but with the same name and the same giant forehead—as the armed SPOs peered through the windows.

When I forgot my badge (which I inevitably discovered only as we pulled up to the guard gate, even though my dad had probably asked me as we pulled out of the driveway whether I had it), my dad would sigh. "Dammitallanyhow," he'd grumble. "I've forgotten my badge only twice in twenty-nine years, and I know exactly what dates they were, too. One was the day your brother was born." If you forgot your badge, you were assigned a red temporary badge, and all the other summer employees—"gray badgers"—and legitimate, full-time employees—"blue badgers"—would laugh at you.

In the EEO office, I got my first exposure to adaptive office technology like voice-command software, though it would be many more years before I ever required such technology for myself. These are the kinds of adaptive efforts the ADA had mandated. Was it some kind of sign that I'd been randomly assigned to this office? *Had* I been randomly assigned? And as long as we're looking for signs, what's the significance that another worker in that office was the brother of the famous twentieth-century composer George Crumb?

The EEO office and the public relations office, where my friend Lauren worked, were in two different parts of the building. So when we finished our morning work, we'd fetch each other or we'd meet up by the great seal on the floor and make window-shopping trips to the map room, or troll the hallways looking for boys. One of the agency photographers (a blue badger) had a crush on Lauren. We took advantage of that during our second summer there to get a photo appointment on the seventh floor with George Tenet.

When the starry-eyed photographer gave us our prints, we autographed them and dropped them off with George Tenet's secretary.

I'd known and gone to school with Lauren since kindergarten, and she'd been in all the high school musicals with me, usually as the star, and so at the CIA we got the band back together: Both summers, Lauren and I prepared a routine for the agency's "All-American Days Celebration," a day in July when agency employees of all stripes demonstrated their absurd skills and talents in the courtyard of the cafeteria—as in, "Who knew that Lois, the linguistics expert from counterintelligence–Latin America, could yodel?" Lauren and I procured an electric keyboard; dressed in red, white, and blue; and presented a medley of American show tunes. In between songs, as I vamped on the keyboard, Lauren would read the "Great Moments in United States Intelligence" that we'd prepared on note cards: "In 1946, when Truman abolished the OSS and then formed the CIA," she chirped, "the musical *Carousel* was on Broadway. Next up, 'You'll Never Walk Alone'!" We reprised our performance the second summer.

Preparing for our performances meant many evenings together at either my house or Lauren's, which was only a few streets over, in the neighborhood we'd both grown up in. To prepare our revue, we huddled together on a piano bench, faces pinked by a golden lamp, choosing songs and playing and singing and laughing together. Schubert's friends were the center of his life. Many famous artistic depictions of Schubert show him just like this—sharing the piano bench with someone he loved, singing and playing. Schubert knew, and I know, that moments together with beloved friends, spontaneously and joyfully making music, can be more powerfully gratifying than applause or acclaim.

At the end of each summer, I received a fancy plaque (and a cash bonus) recognizing my "outstanding service and valuable dedication to the Central Intelligence Agency."

"Geez," my dad said, holding the framed plaque in front of him. "It took me twenty years to get one of these! You've got more of these than I do!"

I think my father enjoyed my working there with him, and I think I also ruined the place for him. My very presence made it impossible for him to keep his two worlds separate, especially when he heard through the grapevine that I'd been spotted chatting up John Deutch in the hallway. Or when my boss said, "How come we've never seen you at Family Day?" and I marched straight to my dad's office to ask him why I'd never even *heard* of Family Day.

"We went one year," my dad said. "Don't you remember?"

When I checked with my mom I learned that the family had gone to Family Day just the one time, and long before I was born. "Matthew drew pictures of locks and vaults and keypads for weeks," she said.

During the school year in Arizona, I was living out all those long-held youngest-child fantasies of leaving my siblings behind—but I still flared with envy at any mention of the family's life before I was born. These anecdotes—about the old house on Wick Lane, or when Uncle Steve came over and played "Little Bunny Foo Foo" in drag—reminded me that for all of them, there were earlier iterations of our family that were whole without me; for me, there is no version of our family that is complete without every single one of them.

Until those summer internships, the most time I'd spent alone with my dad had been all those early mornings when he took me to physical therapy. Back then, I'd been sullen and inflamed, more interested in my Rod Stewart tape than in conversation with my dad. In the morning commutes to the CIA, I was again that grumpy, wet-haired girl. But in the afternoons on the ride home from Langley, I softened and he did, too. I could get him to tell me a story simply by asking him: He told me how he'd gotten his job at the CIA after he spotted an advertisement in the back of *Scientific American* magazine—"It was the September 1963 issue"—called the number, and scored an interview in the lobby of the Leamington Hotel in Minneapolis.

"How will I know who you are?" he'd asked the person he was supposed to meet.

"We'll know who you are," they told him, without a hint of irony.

Stuck in snarling Beltway traffic, we invented a game. We picked out the license plates that shared acronyms with offices in the agency: DCI = Directorate of Central Intelligence. WTP = Weapons, Technology and Proliferation. OTI = Office of Transnational Issues. It was our new private game, our new "Yesterday I could raise my arm this high; today I can only raise it this high."

In the car, he told me about his score on the sixth-grade musical aptitude test and that he dreams in black and white, except for a red barn, which he attributes to the memory of a childhood friend who died when he fell out of the loft.

In the car, I finally learned to stop waiting for my dad to say what I wanted him to say and to hear it in what he *did* say. I learned that he speaks with an accent: science. He is clumsily literal, awkwardly specific. He uses negation where other people are affirmative; when I dazzled him by parallel-parking effortlessly, he said, "Ah, you are good at something," when I know he meant to say "Ah, another thing you're good at!" I got that after my two-summer immersion program in Dad-ese. I am nearly fluent in his language, and I know now that my dad will tell me—in his unique way—whatever I want to know, if I ask for it explicitly.

"Used to be, I could get some work done at lunchtime," he'd tell the people in my office at the CIA when he came to pick me up for the drive home. "Now I've got this one waltzing into my office—'Da-ad, I forgot my lunch money, Da-ad!'"

"She's wonderful," they'd tell him. "She's a good worker."

"Yeah, well, don't tell her that, she'll get a big head," he'd say.

But his teeth were showing.

Midway through my sophomore year of college, just before I flew home for Christmas of 1996, I was standing in the lobby of the Music Building at Arizona State, talking with friends. A boy, a jazz saxophone player from Romania who'd confided to me the first day I met him that he'd been circumcised at twelve, came dashing through the lobby.

Radu and I had been on one date that semester. In October, he'd picked me up at my dorm in his beat-up red pickup and driven me out to Fountain Hills to see some of our classmates and teachers play in a jazz combo at a church. The weather that night was typical Arizona autumn: we were happily sandwiched between earth and sky, the day's afternoon heat radiating up toward us as the nighttime cool descended on us like a silk scarf. As we cut a speeding swath through the desert, past where the lights of Phoenix fell away, I went to lift my right hand from my lap and rest it on the open window. As soon as I did, something shifted in my wrist, sending flames of agony in contrary motion, up to my elbow and down to my fingertips. It felt like something had broken or fallen out of place in my wrist and no matter how hard I tried I couldn't rotate my wrist at all to try to shake things back into place. I bit my lip. Any movement made me dizzy with pain. I had no choice but to leave my arm where it was. I was grateful that Fountain Hills was so far away, but I knew at some point I would need to scrape my limp, screaming arm off the door of Radu's truck.

By the time we got to the jazz church, my wrist was throbbing dully. I could keep it under control by gripping it tightly with my other hand. I don't think Radu wanted to hold my hand that night, but neither hand would have been available to him anyway: One hand was out of commission and the other one was busy tending to it. Story of my body, story of my life.

At the jazz church, Radu grinned and tapped his toe on two and four; I gripped my right wrist, massaging it in time with the chords the pianist greedily grabbed out of the piano with his fat, red-freckled hands. We ate cookies and drank coffee provided by the old ladies of the church, and we headed back to Tempe. I never told Radu about the crisis that was the most memorable part of our only date, though if I had, I might have averted the injury that came weeks later.

Radu was unaware that I tended to go to pieces—literally—when he was around and so, in December, in the lobby of the music building that day, Radu passed behind me and grabbed my left hand, intending to twirl me. He didn't pull hard—I tried to tell him that later, consoling him—but it didn't matter: A hot-pink streak of pain shot through my upper arm and shoulder and I screamed as my rotator cuff tore away from the bone.

I didn't know that's what had happened, of course. I knew only that my backpack had to be hoisted on my right shoulder for the flight home, that I couldn't put my hair in a ponytail, that I'd wake up if, in the night, I rolled onto my left side. Seven years into arthritis, I thought it was simply my lot that body parts would stop working without warning. I trusted that, given a few days' rest and an ice pack, they'd come back to me. I was ignorant of the tearing, ripping, permanent damage that was going on beneath the surface. Days after the jazz church date in October, after all, my right wrist had felt fine and so I had no memory. I had greedily accepted its return to me like a mother so glad her child is home safe she forgets to yell at him for wandering off. If I have made mistakes in managing my arthritis, the biggest is probably this: I have been too willing to forgive and forget.

Days after Radu's ill-fated hug, I flew home with my left shoulder aching and then immediately my parents and my sister and I packed into a rented minivan to drive to Minnesota to see my grandmother die.

I had never been to Minnesota in the winter. We'd made a pilgrimage every summer and we kids would come home lake-tanned and dotted with mosquito bites, our bellies full of sugar cubes snuck from the fancy glass dish on the counter, and the soda we were allowed to have only on special occasions. For weeks we tanked up on root beer floats and Coca-Cola because grandparents, like school field trips and sick days, are special occasions.

My parents are both Minnesotans, and my dad says he forgets that we kids, all of us born and raised in Maryland, aren't. I'm a Marylander, I suppose, but even by then I'd started to think of myself as an Arizonan. In December 1996 I was three semesters into my college life in Arizona, where the hot, dry air and constant sunshine made me feel solid, galvanized, expansive. When I inhaled the Minnesota winter, my lungs clenched and stabbed. The cold was powerful and awful.

But it was a permanent ice pack around my shoulder where Radu had ripped it. At night, in the freezing cabin, my shoulder was so numb it didn't keep me awake, even if the cold did.

It's not that we were ignoring my painful shoulder. The truth as far as I can see it is that the pain receded. Pain is smart that way; it knows we can handle only so much and it will quiet itself when there is something else you need to pay attention to. Got a headache? You won't, if you slam your finger in a door. The magical thing I know now is that pain will quiet itself even in deference to someone else's pain.

God only knows how many of her own pains—or my brother's pains—my mother, like all mothers, ignored all those mornings I called for her from my bed. In the doctor's transcribed notes from that first visit to Children's, as we tried to get to the bottom of the mystery my body had become, there is this dispassionate sentence: *The mother has pain in the hands, but has not been formally diagnosed.* This is a truth about pain: There is only room for so much in one body, one room, one family. There is always a process of triage. My body let me be painless that Christmas when my grandma was dying, because there was more profound pain to contend with, because my body simply was not the sickest in the room.

These were cold, sweet days. We commandeered the kitchen in the nursing home and we prepared a feast on Christmas Day. We should have realized Grandma was dying when, completely out of character, she stuck her fingers in the mashed potatoes and licked them greedily, happily, even before we said grace.

The next day, we packed up our cabin and headed into town to say good-bye before driving back to Maryland. We lingered all morning, standing around her room. My sister disappeared to bake blueberry muffins in the kitchen. The nurses brought my grandma's lunch. My mom tried to encourage her to eat. My grandma babbled about a call she'd received from Medicine Lake. Her ninety-three-year-old sister, Elsie, had died. "No, no," my mom said, thinking that Grandma was confused. "*Ella.*" Grandma's 104-year-old sister, Ella, had died that October.

At some point, everyone left the room except for me and Grandma. I stood by her bed and I held her hand. She couldn't speak clearly—her breathing was labored and rattling. Our shared language of sweets and Chinese checkers and yarn crafts was useless to us. But we still had music. I held her hand and I opened my mouth and the Beatles came out. Songs, songs. Schubert knew—sometimes only a song will do.

I don't know why I sang "The Long and Winding Road." Probably I had borrowed a Beatles tape from the bookshelf in Chris's room for the long drive. Grandma, as far as I know, was no Beatles fan. But it was now the sound track of all those summer visits to Minnesota coming to an end;

of all of us standing on the blacktop driveway;

of the station wagon packed up and humming; of my mother saying good-bye to her mother, both of them teary-eyed;

of my siblings and me scratching our bug bites and shifting our weight, eager to leave, dying to get to the next thing!, not understanding why it was so hard for our mother to leave her parents, unable to see how old they all were getting—her parents and ours, too—in front of our eyes, and unable to understand how far away they lived, in Minnesota and in old age and encroaching illness;

of the station wagon dusting down the highway, our parents' marriage disintegrating invisibly in the front seat, us kids oblivious and plastered to the back window and waving gleefully to our old, shrinking grandparents standing in their driveway, waving to us until they were finally, completely, gone.

I sang to her and then everyone was back in the room and then she signaled she had to go to the bathroom and the nurses herded us out of there and when they got her up to go she died.

We brought Grandpa in. We didn't tell him she was dead. He sat with her, holding her still-warm hand, unable to see and barely able to hear, until my Mom told him Grandma was gone.

We learned later that a call had come from Medicine Lake after all. Elsie *had* died. We learned that being sick—nearly dead, even—doesn't mean not knowing what the hell's going on.

Later, my dad drove me into town to pick out some sheet music to play for the funeral. I wanted to play "The Long and Winding Road." I wondered if I should play the Schubert—I knew it by heart; I wouldn't even need the sheet music!—and then decided that the movement that had me by the heart, the one I would have liked to dedicate to my grandmother, was too long and not funereal enough. And still, despite years of studying it and playing it, I did not think it was good enough. I was not doing Schubert justice. In a nod to our Norwegian heritage, I settled for Grieg.

When we finally went back to Maryland afterward, my shoulder was hurting where Radu had yanked it and my mom took me to the doctor, who said the rotator cuff was torn. And that it couldn't be fixed. "We'll just clean it up as best we can," he said. "The bone is too squishy and unhealthy for us to fix it." It didn't matter that I'd delayed getting my shoulder looked at; the rip in my rotator cuff wasn't the real problem. The problem was the body the rotator cuff had torn itself from, as if bailing from a sinking ship. I was a lost cause, then. A bad bet. I stayed an extra week back home. I had surgery and did some physical therapy. I learned that an immobile, uncooperative shoulder could be moved if I stood next to a wall and walked my fingertips up, up, up. I learned that what a shoulder cannot do, fingertips can.

Back in Arizona in January, I continued my physical therapy alongside Sun Devil athletes at the Student Recreation Complex. The therapy room was a little glass box at the end of the gleaming main hallway. It was right next to the state-of-the-art gym and directly across from the towel counter. To get to the PT room, I had to pass through the turnstiles and swipe my student ID, bottlenecked between muscled boys in tank tops, their little nylon drawstring backpacks with the school logo hanging between their scapulae. The girls at the SRC were the kinds of girls people pictured when they pictured ASU: blond and bouncy, in sports bras and full makeup, with horse-strong cheerleader legs coming out of tiny cotton gym shorts rolled over at the waist to show their flat, brown bellies and navel piercings. For the most part, my music major (and my hours of practice) kept me segregated from these people. Even at a giant, football-fueled party school in the Valley of the Sun, the music school promised an enclave of my kind of people: pale people in corduroy pants and Chuck Taylors, people whose darkest hickeys were left by the chin rests of their violas.

The tough, sporty girls in high school, the field-hockey players or the softball pitchers, would show up at school from time to time on crutches or with ACE bandages. They'd boast about how they had to have their ankles taped before the game. They made a big show of getting out of class to go to the nurse's office for ice packs or to have their ibuprofen dispensed. They worked out in the weight room with the boys. They were our heroes.

As I lay on the therapy table in the SRC, on display for the healthy people coming and going from the state-of-the-art gym, I felt the same way I'd felt in high school, sitting out from PE because of a throbbing ankle. Was I really so different from these champs? I had gear, and ice, and pills, and splints, and tape. I had a regimen of drills, I had sets and reps. I was quarterbacking my fight with arthritis. I was in a scrimmage every day and for a long time I'd been winning. If I started at the bottom of my body, with my feet, I could pretend I had nothing more than a worship-worthy sports injury. So I moved up my legs to my knees, trying to label all my swelling and stiffness and immobility sports injuries. It worked for a while but there was always a point when I realized that I wasn't fooling anyone, least of all myself.

It is one thing to be injured and a very different thing to be sick. To be injured is to visit the night-side of life; to be chronically, incurably ill is to be *Locked Up Abroad* there.

As I struggled to grip a two-foot broomstick in two hands and raise it above my head, I pretended I was a hard-core Sun Devil discus thrower and not a fragile music major. I dreaded and yearned for the moment any of those meatheads asked me what my injury was. Luckily—and not surprisingly, given my pallid, fragile, decidedly un-sporty look—they never did.

My course of therapy also included ultrasound on my shoulder. In the bathroom, I'd change from my T-shirt into a gown, open in the back, leaving my cargo pants on. I'd bundle my bra inside my T-shirt and stuff it deep into one of the cubbies, just like in fifth grade. I'd come back to the table and pull the neck of the gown down so Jan, the therapist, could see my naked shoulder, the impression my bra strap had left. Jan would slather it with clear, cold jelly. Then he'd turn his back to turn on the ultrasound machine. Once, I asked him what the jelly was made of. "Mostly sugar," he said casually. So when he wasn't looking, I turned my head slightly and took a swipe at the jelly with my tongue. He turned back around and, seeing my puckered face, knew what I'd done. "Did you eat it?" He sighed, disgusted, as he handed me a towel and shook his head. It may be sugar, that gel, but it's not sweet like a purloined sugar cube.

I will likely never have a pregnancy ultrasound. And yet I know the blurt of the gel, the sudden coldness of gel on flesh, the smoothness of the transducer head, the *puck-puck-puck* of the monitor that most mothers know. I know wanting to see inside to see what the hell is going on in there.

They did the best they could with my shoulder, and at the end of several weeks, Jan told me there was no way to fix it but if I built up the muscles around the rotator cuff by swimming, it could sort of fix itself. It sounded like bullshit to me. I didn't live in a body that healed itself. I lived in a body that attacked itself. But I still had so much to learn then about what a body will do on its own behalf, how protective and nurturing a body, even my body, could be.

And then I was healthy again. My life had taken on the operatic structure I'd learned about with Mr. Frezzo: I had fast-moving periods of advancement and relative health (recitative) in which it was crucial that I cover as much ground as possible, followed by surgical intervals (arias) in which I could make no forward progress but I turned inward and indulged in swooning, aching romance and woebegone heartbreak for my body.

By spring break of 1997, just a few months later, I had forgotten about my shoulder. My mom came to visit. We went to the Grand Canyon. She took a picture of me on its rim, my arms stretched out in an "I love you this much" wingspan. When the pictures came back, I realized my arms didn't straighten. My smile is authentic and unpained, but the shape of my arms is a crimped W and, invisibly, the head of my right ulna is getting craggy, and two extensor tendons that run over that jagged bulge with every infinitesimal motion I make in my daily four hours of piano practice are becoming frayed like rope over a canyon ledge and preparing to snap.

That July, I went back to Maryland for a second summer job at the CIA. Most of my belongings went into storage in Arizona; I packed some clothes and my Schubert recording and score. That summer, happy news bubbled through the hallways of CIA headquarters:

Mir Aimal Kansi, the gunman who'd shot up those people at the intersection years before, had been caught. I took the news home like it was my own—better yet, like it was ours, mine and my dad's.

My dad's mom, Grandma Avery, died in June of that second summer, and we went to Minnesota again. The night before the funeral, my dad and uncles had sorted through most of her stuff. The organ, which she had left to me and my sister, was given to a lady at church. "You don't really have room for it," my dad said. "You live in a dorm."

"Can you tell that lady to leave it back to me when she dies?" I asked. He didn't answer.

I hoped I might get a pair of Grandma's wild, rhinestone cat-eye glasses, her accordion, or the hot-pink satin baseball jacket I'd seen hanging in her closet for as long as I could remember. In the hotel room, my dad brought out a small box of objects with tags on them. "This is for you," he said, and gave me a tiny Black Hills Gold ring that had been hers. I didn't like it, but miraculously, it fit on only one of my fingers, the only finger that wasn't a knotted mess, my left ring finger. I asked my dad if I could have one of the posters from my grandma's big band days—"Dance to the Melody Kings!" The Band with All the Friends! Florence Avery on Piano and Accordion!—but my uncle was worried I'd damage it. My dad borrowed it and took it to Kinko's and had a T-shirt of it made for me.

Grandma Avery's laugh was a wheezy "hee hee hee," like air being squeezed from her accordion without any of the mysterious keys or buttons depressed. She fixed everything in her house with twist ties and Scotch tape. When we went to visit, my dad was always busy wiring the mailbox back onto the house or cleaning gutters, which left Grandma Avery free to sit next to me at the organ in her living room, where we'd play from her hymnal or the big book of jazz standards or her fake book, which didn't seem to have enough notes on the page to match what my grandma got out of the organ. I'd play the melody on the top register while Grandma Avery pounded out chords on the bottom keyboard. It seems now that we were always playing "Basin Street Blues." "Oh, honey," she'd say with a laugh, as I played the melody as straight as could be. "Jazz it up!"

I'd never been much good at "jazzing it up." I couldn't improvise the way she did. I trusted Mozart, Beethoven, Chopin, Bach, Scriabin, Szymanowski—and by then, Schubert most of all—ever so much more than I trusted myself.

At Grandma Avery's funeral, an old man sang "Danny Boy." No one suggested that I play the piano, though I kept waiting to be asked. Instead, I read a poem that I'd written. After the funeral, as the adults dealt with flowers—can we take these to the church?—we kids, my brothers and cousins and I, milled around the empty sanctuary. There were two pianos. Chris was at one and I was at the other. I don't remember how it started except that it was quiet at first, because we were afraid we'd get in trouble for playing. We started playing a twelve-bar blues, which Chris had taught me years before. I played the chunky chord changes, the closest I could come to improvising. Chris soloed, the true improviser. Soon we forgot we were, technically, still at a funeral. We were jamming the way Chris jammed with Andy, the way Grandma had jammed with me, or tried to. We played louder and louder and when we stopped we realized our dad was standing there, smiling. "Your grandma would approve," he said. I have won a few ribbons and trophies, taken center stage, and had my share of applause, but the happiest musical moments in my life are these: spontaneous Schubertian sing-alongs with my friends and family.

For years, I wore my grandma's pink-and-green Black Hills Gold ring, and for years my left ring finger was the only finger I had that *didn't* swell and lock up. I believed there was a connection, that if one of the medicines for rheumatoid arthritis was gold injections, maybe my grandma's gold ring had a protective quality, too. So maybe I got the benefit of gold therapy even though I refused those supposedly painful injections.

I was starting to learn that the line between medicine and magic is fuzzy, at best.

Chapter 8

Those two extensor tendons in my right hand gave out, too, less than a year after I stood on the rim of the Grand Canyon, less than a year after Grandma Avery died, just as I felt whole again. In February 1998, I was sitting in my music theory lecture class, stretching my hands before my piano lesson, when I felt the tiniest *ping!* inside my right hand. Suddenly my fourth finger and pinkie were hanging down, limp. I couldn't lift either one. I canceled my lesson, put an ice pack on my hand, and went to sleep completely certain I'd have my fingers back soon.

When I woke up the next day, I had a brief moment pregnant with peace before I recalled what had happened, the way you forget the events of a Friday night, a bender or a breakup, until you remember. Under my blankets, I tested my fingers: nothing. *This is the hour of lead.*

But I did nothing.

After several days, I scheduled an appointment at ASU's student health center—a clinic that specialized more in sexually transmitted diseases and strep throat than serious rheumatic diseases. But I went to Health Services to see a particular doctor, Dr. Bennett, whom my mother had ferreted out when I first came to ASU (probably a suggestion she'd learned at one of those conferences: find a knowledgeable rheumatologist in the town where your child goes to college. Make contact before there's a crisis). My mom, of course, had found the most knowledgeable rheumatologist possible: Dr. Bennett had had rheumatoid arthritis herself since she was a toddler. Her fingers were gnarled, she had the pendulum gait of someone who can't bend her knees, and her face had that trademark chipmunk look from years of prednisone treatment. But she had things I thought a person with arthritis wouldn't—or couldn't—have: a white lab coat and a stethoscope and pictures behind her desk of her beautiful toddler boy.

I sat in the chair in front of Dr. Bennett's desk and showed her my hand. She didn't even have to lift herself from her chair to get a better look at it. Immediately, she said, "Well, you've ruptured your extensor tendons! You need hand surgery."

She was not surprised. Only later did I learn that I was the only person who'd been surprised. Four years before, having brought the swelling on the backs of my hands to the attention of my doctors, my mom had written this in her notebook: *synovium covering tendon inflamed—can eat into tendon—get irritated by excess activity.* To most people, four hours a day at the piano with arthritic hands could be considered excess activity.

Dr. Bennett rocked herself back and forward to get out of her chair and then wobbled into motion, working her curled fingers over the pages of a directory like a hook, and I soon had an appointment with a hand surgeon in Scottsdale, fifteen miles north of campus. I didn't have a car, but Dr. Bennett was sure this was the doctor for me.

On Valentine's Day, I took a taxi up to Scottsdale to see Dr. Sheridan. A floor-to-ceiling fish tank filled the lobby. In the exam room, there were pictures of ASU athletes, all scribbled with messages of gratitude to him.

Dr. Sheridan sat across from me on his little swivel stool and delicately lifted my hand. "How long has it been like this?"

"Like a week," I said.

He explained that the tendons had definitely ruptured and by now the frizzled ends had probably wriggled up into my forearm or farther. He danced his fingertips up my forearm, briefly, lightly. He tore a scrap of paper off the exam table and sketched out what he wanted to do:

Plan A. The pointer finger has two extensor tendons wrapped around each other like a candy cane. Dr. Sheridan would make a tiny incision at the base of my pointer finger and fish one of those extensor tendons out. Then, working in a larger incision down the top of my hand, he'd swing that tendon over and graft it onto what was left of the fourth finger's extensor tendons, and then sew the pinkie tendons to it. The pinkie and fourth finger would extend together, but they'd be capable of flexing independently.

Plan B: If there wasn't enough good tendon to work with, he'd just sew the whole mess of my fourth and fifth fingers' tendons to the tendons of the third finger. He'd know when he got in there.

"I'll be back in just a minute," he said, and then he left the room.

This was worse than I'd expected. I looked at the smiling, sunny pitchers and catchers on the wall. I was out of place. I was a pianist. Wasn't I?

Midway through my sophomore year, around the time that Radu tore my rotator cuff, I'd officially declared my major as music theory and composition instead of piano performance, thinking that I could make myself want to write music instead of playing it, if it came to that.

There had always been a part of me that wanted to be a composer. All those silly little "sonatas" I'd written? In college I was learning that sonata form referred traditionally to the structure of one movement of a particular instrumental work. Sonata form, I learned—by parsing Beethoven's *Appassionata*, his *Moonlight*, his *Pathétique*—had specific rules for the introduction of thematic material, the modulation to related and distant keys, and the repetition of certain whole sections. I found the rules reassuring; I enjoyed music theory. My dad would have been surprised to learn that I loved the math of it, actually, and trying to solve riddles even after class was over, poring over the red-covered book of Schubert sonatas, pencil in hand, in my dorm room to figure out what the hell that low, ominous trill on G-flat was doing in my favorite sonata, Schubert's B-flat. But as I sat in the chair in Dr. Sheridan's exam room, I knew that I'd changed my major as a sacrificial offering. Take my plans to be a pianist, I'd told God by filing that declaration-of-major form, just let me keep playing.

I tried to think of this as a sports injury. I tried to hope that Dr. Sheridan could restore me to the field the way he had all these grateful, red-cheeked athletes who smiled from his walls.

When Dr. Sheridan returned I wiped my eyes with the still-unblemished back of my right hand. "Do you have any questions?" he asked.

Once again, the question I truly had was not the question a doctor could answer. What would poor Dr. Sheridan have answered if I'd asked, "What about Schubert?"

For years I'd been secretly working on and studying the Schubert sonata, and I had begun to think that I was getting close to being able to uncloak it, perhaps play it for my piano teacher at ASU. I dreamed of filling the blond-wood Katzin Concert Hall at school with the sonata. It would be like a wedding, a public declaration in front of God and everyone that I loved this piece and would honor it.

"No," I said aloud, unable to ask what needed to be asked. I needed my mother, but she was 2,300 miles away and had no idea that my extensor tendons had cut and run, that they were miles across state lines by now.

"OK," Dr. Sheridan said. I thought he would breeze out of the room to see his next patient, someone he could restore to athletic power, a sounder investment, a better bet. "Let's just sit here for a minute in case you think of anything." He tore a piece of paper off the exam table and sketched out a tic-tac-toe board for us.

I'll always be grateful to Dr. Sheridan for giving me those few minutes of access to him, for that quiet pause before the cutting began, because once the cutting started, it didn't stop. It hasn't stopped. When my tendon ruptured in my wrist, a crucial crevasse opened in my life.

Schubert's health began to fail in 1823, when he was twenty-six. Just as Dr. Dequeker and others have sought to "diagnose" cases of arthritis in paintings, many scholars have attempted to, from a distance of a century, determine for sure what caused Schubert's illness. It seems almost certain that he had syphilis. For the next five years, until his death in 1828, Schubert's health would follow a jagged, but downward sloping, line. He endured fevers, rashes, and aches. At the same time, he was showing signs of depression: bursts of activity and despondent lulls, melancholy, rages. He knew that this illness was profound and incontrovertible, that he would never be the same. Soon, he knew and acknowledged that it would likely kill him. But still he composed.

My surgery was scheduled for the end of the month. I called my mom and asked her to come. "But you don't need to come before the surgery," I said. "Just be there when I wake up." I wanted to give my boyfriend, Casey, the chance to take care of me. I sensed that letting Casey have this role was a gift I could give him, a way I could make him feel powerful and useful, but I hadn't yet realized how it made me small and helpless. I hadn't yet grown tired, so tired, of being taken care of.

Casey was a sad-faced drummer with a mop of brown curls, perpetually untied shoes, and big gray eyes. He would chew on his bottom lip during class and drum incessant paradiddles on his corduroy jeans. In the fall, when I'd met Casey, he was pining over a dazzling music-theater major named Joyce, a small, dimpled thing with a little girl's swayback posture and a dancer's turned-out gait. She wore tights and leotards to class. Casey wanted to make her something for Christmas, so I helped him pick out a glass jar and purple sand to make a candle for her. I helped him make a velvet bag to put it in. I didn't tell him that I'd eaten lunch with Joyce at Arby's and she'd bemoaned how very many boys she expected to receive gifts from that year, and how she didn't want to buy them all gifts.

On New Year's Eve, as my tendons frayed without my knowing it, Casey and I found ourselves at a party, together on a couch, snuggled beneath a blanket, about to kiss. The TV was the only light in the room. *South Park* was on and it had been 1998 for a couple of hours. My right hand, tendons still untorn, was clasped between both of his hands, which were sweating. He was shuddering. "Wait," he said. "What about Joyce?"

In a very rom-com piece of dialogue, I said, "I am not some extra in a stupid romance movie about you and Joyce," I said. "And anyway, where is she tonight?"

I was at least a little convincing; Casey became my boyfriend. When I brought him home to meet my parents, I urged him to show my physicist dad all the cool yo-yo tricks he could do. I left them alone in the kitchen, and when I came back my dad was rambling about how a yo-yo could be made into an impressive weapon, like a ninja star on a string. When Casey and I got into the car to go out to dinner, he said, "Your dad is intense. He started talking about narcolepsy and how some guy he knew fell asleep while debriefing Chiang Kai-shek." I was falling in love with Casey, but I swooned then for my dad, proud that he'd played exactly the part I'd wanted him to, the eccentric and mysterious spy-dad.

On the day of the surgery in February, Casey borrowed his roommate's car and drove me to the hospital. We took a wrong turn and found ourselves following the arrows to the maternity/delivery unit. "Could be worse," I said. "At least we're not here for that." I was twenty; Casey was nineteen and sweet and beautiful but naive and sheltered and wrong in so many ways. We were virgins; pregnancy was still the Worst Thing That Could Happen to us.

But we were virgins for different reasons, me and Casey. I was no longer afraid of contracting Schubert's nineteenth-century syphilitic death sentence, but I'd avoided even getting close to having sex with boys because there was always some moment when, in the arrangement of bodies, the boy would roll over or shift his weight onto my hand or my hip and I would shriek with pain and the boy would feel guilty and disgusted and afraid of breaking me, and I'd explain that it was my arthritis. Arthritis makes people think of their grandparents, which usually makes them uninterested in sex.

Because I knew that moment was going to happen, I'd cut things short, or cut them off, if the making-out threatened to proceed past the soft parts into the athletic demands of actually doing it, of this leg here and this hand here. And then it got so I didn't have to cut things off; panic would rise in my throat if things got to that point, panic that caused the ropy muscles on the insides of my thighs—the muscles I knew from physical therapy were called hip adductors—to pull closed, to shut the boy out. I didn't want to be in my body; I sure didn't want anyone else in there with me. My body was a messy apartment. Couldn't we go somewhere else? Like Schubert, couldn't we just occupy ourselves with friends and art?

For two years, Casey and I stayed together for the sex. The absence of it. We were one another's alibi. "People who've had sex, have sex," a friend once told me, to warn me: The only boys who would tolerate my inability to Do It would be the ones who couldn't, or wouldn't, Do It themselves, for whatever reason. We both knew that people had sex all around us, even in the practice rooms at the Music Building. Casey was a virgin because he was a Catholic. I was a virgin because I was an arthritic. Arthritis had become my religion.

When I woke up from surgery that February morning, my hand was hidden inside a giant padded shroud. A drain snaked out of the padding and across my body. They took me up to my private room. High on painkillers, I fell in love with the sconces on the wall. I fell in love with the word *sconce*. I insisted Casey bring me spaghetti, so he went out and drove around till he found a chain restaurant that sold spaghetti. He brought it back for me along with McDonald's for himself. Having not eaten since before midnight the night before,

I was famished. I ate my spaghetti and then sent him back out for McDonald's for me: two cheeseburgers and a chocolate shake.

Casey brought flowers. He'd asked the florist to put one of every kind of orange flower in a vase. She tried to caution him against it, he told me later, telling him it would be ugly, but he insisted, because he loved me and I loved orange. He brought our friends from music school—Beth and Sarah and Nate—to camp out in my room. Just like Schubert, who was so central to Viennese music parties that they named the parties after him, I was in the center of a ring of loving, talented musician-friends, albeit installed in a hospital bed instead of at a piano. Minor detail. The love was palpable.

Dr. Sheridan came to check on me. He pulled the drain out and spilled blood on Casey's ASU sweatshirt, which I'd spread across my lap like a blanket.

I was a rookie for that first hand surgery. I didn't withdraw from my classes. I didn't even plan to take time off from school. Surgery was on a Thursday; I told my professors I'd be back on Monday. "It's just my hand," I thought, and said.

It's a stupid thing for a pianist to say, but: I hadn't realized how much I used my right hand. I hadn't considered that my mother would have to shave my legs for me, that she'd have to wrap my arm in trash bags and tape it so I could take a shower, but that in the shower I wouldn't be able to squeeze the shampoo bottle or lather my hair.

I hadn't realized how painkillers would make me drowsy and muddled; unable to follow a lecture; and dangerously, deceptively happy.

I hadn't yet realized that surgery is traumatic, not just to the body part in question, but to your life. It's a cut in your skin but it opens up everything and you spill out, messy, and you lose your forward momentum and you can't go back to your life until you've managed to stuff everything back inside and close up the hole.

Sing it! *The wrist bone's connected to the . . . arm bone. The arm bone's connected to the . . . shoulder bone. The shoulder bone's connected to the . . . brain bone, oh let's call the whole thing off.*

I was on Percocet. I thought it would be fine, just fine, sooooooooooo fine, if my mom left on the fourth of March, my twenty-first birthday, as planned.

March forth. I'm fine. Onward. Go.

But that morning she had something to tell me.

"Your father and I are separating," she said. I knew it hadn't been a happy thirty-six years but wasn't there a statute of limitations on stuff like this? Wasn't this like returning a middle-aged kid to an orphanage? Wasn't . . . whatever.

"Oh, OK," said the Percocet. "Who gets the *White Album*?"

"The Beatles record?" my mom asked, puzzled.

"Yeah."

"Uh, I guess me? It's mine—"

"OK. What about the house?" *The* house, our very, very, very fine house, that eyesore yellow-and-green house, the only home I'd ever known, the house with the piano in it—

"We're selling it."

"OK."

And then she was gone.

In the next days, I took a series of city buses to go to physical therapy and my follow-ups with Dr. Sheridan. I had to drop a class to have the time to go to therapy. At therapy, they unwrapped my bandages and left me at a big table with my hand. My first glimpse of it shocked me, and I learned the next lesson of surgery: things must get worse before they can get better. The hand was pale, damp, and useless. "Lift your fingers from the table, one by one," the therapist said. Even the ones that hadn't been operated on couldn't do it.

The surgery had gone as well as could be expected. Dr. Sheridan had managed to salvage enough of my pinkie tendon to graft it to the fourth finger's extensor tendons, leaving the tendons of the third finger uninvolved. The result was that my fourth and fifth fingers could bend independently of each other, but when I went to extend them, they straightened together.

They fitted me for two molded splints that I would have to change every two to four hours. One kept my hand in a neutral resting position, like a palm flat on the surface of a basketball; the other kept my hand curled like I was gripping a soda bottle. I tried to taper the Percocet. I couldn't study; schoolwork was piling up. As soon as the Percocet fog lifted, a new fog rolled in:

My parents had been staying together "for the kids." I was the youngest, and now I was twenty-one. I was an adult. They were done, then? Could they really just leave me here like this? I wasn't ready. I was broken and needy and helpless.

Without the Percocet, I was weepy and exhausted. Beth would call—"Come and meet us for lunch at the Memorial Union," she'd say. How could my friends make such requests? I wondered: Didn't these friends know what they were asking of me? A shower, dressing, *wanting* to shower, to dress, to eat—

I couldn't go to class. I tried to do my music theory homework with my left hand, notating music with my nondominant hand.

My music composition teacher that semester, Dr. DeMars, was flaky and frazzled but handsome and kind. He wore jackets with patches on the elbows, just the way I'd always hoped my professors would, and his hair was a full-on salt-and-pepper Beethoven. My composition lessons were held in his cluttered office, his desk littered with manuscripts and oranges and stray pieces of machinery and instrument parts. Once, he'd held up a tiny spring in front of our form-and-analysis class and bounced it in the air. "Do you hear that?" he'd asked. "Isn't it beautiful?" On another morning, he'd greeted our twentieth-century-theory class by saying, "Good morning. Today will be in the key of D minor."

That spring, every time I showed up for a composition lesson with Dr. DeMars, I was like that joke about a country music song played backward: My tendon ruptured. My parents are divorcing. Our dog died.

I never got to spy on another composing student's composition lessons, but I have a hunch they didn't go quite like mine did. I'd come in to the room tearful and Dr. DeMars would look up at me with his lined, jowelly, friendly face. He'd almost smile, until he read my face, and then I'd sink into a chair and his eyebrows would fall and his voice would dip into a gravelly register and he'd say, "What is it?" When I told him, he'd lean forward in his chair and look at me over his always-broken glasses and say, "Oh, I could just cry with you. Shall I cry with you?"

And he told me stories about his own pain: Long ago, an old girlfriend, a budding poet, had committed suicide. "I've never forgiven Sylvia Plath for that," he said. Or how he'd been riding his bike home from school the week before and some mean children from the elementary school in his neighborhood threw oranges at him. He told me to use my pain to compose music. My lessons ran long; we played my songs and he hummed harmonies and we wrote them in with our matching pencils.

A music teacher is a special sort of beloved. Schubert's own elevated music teacher was none other than Salieri—yes, the same Salieri at the center of the (fictional) *Amadeus*. Gibbs describes their relationship as paternal and tender: In Gibbs's book, I learned that Salieri gave Schubert composition lessons and treated him to ice cream; in return, Schubert dedicated music to his dear master teacher.

I'd stopped taking the Percocet because I couldn't stand having both an addled body and an addled mind. Of course, pain itself will scramble your brain. But I hadn't accepted that. Nearly every night, I called my mom in tears. She worried that I was having Percocet withdrawal. She told me to call the doctor's answering service if it got bad. The doctor on call who got beeped when I called during an intractable, late-night crying jag called back and told me it wasn't Percocet withdrawal but probably a virus. I reported that to my mom, who dutifully recorded it in her notebook. And in the margin she wrote, *Bullshit!*

I was taking conducting that semester, part of a two-semester course that was required of music majors. In class, we took turns being the conductor, graded on our ability to conduct a crazy, hodgepodge band—our classmates on their respective instruments—through a set of short band pieces in a workbook. But after surgery, I couldn't play; I couldn't hold the baton—what place was there for me in this band? The professor said I could come into his office and conduct the audiotape that came with the workbook using my left hand. On each visit, he'd press play and sit back in his chair with his arms crossed as I flung my left hand around trying to keep up with the invisible musicians on the tape who had no idea I was there. I got a B.

I couldn't think. I couldn't eat. I didn't want to take Percocet. The tiny incision on my hand gaped and swallowed all of me.

My friends kept calling: "Come to the renaissance festival with us!" they said.

I called home: *Mommy, I want to come home I can't do this let me come home*—it was the call I never once made from nursery school or a sleepover or the first year of college—*Mommy, please.*

But I couldn't come home. I had school, and besides—they were packing up the house, they were getting ready to sell it, it wasn't really—

—*PLEASE isn't it my home anymore I need a home to come home to I'm not ready*—

Somehow they got me on the phone with dear Dr. White. "I'm fine," I squeaked falsely. "But I can't go anywhere. I can't do anything."

"Give it a shot," she said. "Go to the renaissance festival with your friends. See how you feel if you get out of your dorm room for a bit. Then see if you still feel like coming home. Oh, and take a half a Percocet. Right now."

I took the Percocet and promptly threw up.

I went to the renaissance festival and I don't remember anything except swapping out my splints under a tree while Casey hefted a giant, juicy turkey leg to his mouth with one hand and cupped his other hand under his mouth.

And then, finally, for spring break of 1998, when I was twenty-one, while everyone else seemed to go to Cabo, I went home, to paradise. But the house was hollow. My parents had cleared out their junk and ours. A Realtor had "staged" the house, which, as far as I could see, meant she replaced our handmade afghans with a basket of her own nappy store-bought afghans.

I wanted to be bundled up in the car, taken along on errands with my mom, nursed. The highlight of the visit was when Chris took me with him to the DMV. It rained and I was wearing Casey's ASU Windbreaker that was fleece on the inside. It was big enough I could pull it over my hand and my splint as my brother and I waited in the line at the DMV.

To justify my coming home, my mom scheduled an appointment for me with a performing arts hand therapist. "You keep wearing those splints," he said, "you'll never play piano again." It did not terrify me that he said this. It was a relief. Someone had finally said it out loud. He fitted me with a dynamic splint. It was molded plastic with Velcro straps, like the others, but out of the top sprung a traction system rigged of rubber bands and loops of Velcro. The last two fingers of my right hand hung suspended in little slings. All day long I was to curl them and let them spring back, working against the tension of the rubber bands, which could be adjusted.

The device reminded me of Robert Schumann's "finger tormentor," the device he is said to have invented to strengthen his fingers, thereby mangling his hands and ending his days as a pianist. Though Schumann referred to his finger-strengthening device, somewhat cryptically, as his "cigar mechanism," no one knows for sure what form this device took. Some say it was a benign finger-stretching device rolled under the fingers—like a cigar—on the table. Others, including the music history teacher who told me about it, insist it was an elaborate traction device with a sling around the fourth finger and a line attached to a pulley connected to the ceiling.

People love this story, and they retell it: that Schumann insisted on strengthening his perfectly healthy fingers and devised a crazy machine to separate his third and fourth tendons (just about the opposite of what my surgical intervention had done to my hand). People love this story, I think, because they like when illnesses and injuries have a cause. And because hubris, in that classical form of an already-great man daring to reach for more, more, more, is irresistible. But it might not be true. It's indisputable that in the 1830s Schumann was plagued with hand pain. But many people insist his hand wasn't injured by a device at all but because of syphilis (which, if true, would allow us to continue blaming horny Schumann himself). Still others suggest that the hand injury that Schumann wrote about could very well have been arthritis, but that theory hardly ever gets any ink. Finger tormentors, hubris, syphilis syphilis everywhere!—that's all very Romantic. There's nothing Romantic about arthritis.

The performing arts hand therapist found a place in Phoenix that could continue the therapy. They sent me and my finger tormentor back to the desert. Playing piano—not to mention the Schubert sonata—was unthinkable. Even listening to it was unbearable. My copy of *Horowitz the Poet* no longer held a fixed place in my CD changer; I listened instead to music with words that allowed me to feel sad but not dangerously devastated—mostly Jeff Buckley, Toad the Wet Sprocket, and the *White Album*, which got me the closest I could stand to devastation. The red-covered book of Schubert sonatas, which I'd carried back and forth in high school and which usually lay open on my dorm room desk, was shut and stuffed into the corner of a bookshelf.

Nearly five years after I watched Byron Janis play in that atrium in Denver, as I recovered badly from hand surgery in the desert while my mom worried about me long-distance, she wrote this in the margins of her notes, cryptically referring to the Broadway score for *Beauty and the Beast* the pianist-turned-composer had recently composed: *March 24, 1998: Byron Janis 70 birthday. Hunchback duet.*

Hunchback! Schubert's eldest brother, Ignaz, was a hunchback. But my mom's notation didn't feel like some mystical, embedded connection to my hero. In the context of the notebooks, this weird little note invites me to picture me and sallow old Byron Janis seated together at the piano, two key-smashing beasts, stabbing at the music with our useless, monolithic hands.

My parents bought me a used Chevy Cavalier so I could get to hand therapy and back without eating up half the day on unreliable buses or spending a semester's tuition on cab fare. I worried about sibling dynamics: my parents had never bought a car for any of my siblings. I felt spoiled. I was terrified my parents would sell my piano to pay for the car, but they didn't. No one even suggested it.

After my hand surgery, I finished out the semester relying on my "good" hand, playing left-hand-alone repertoire. In the music library, I sniffed out the substantial body of works written for the left hand alone, works by Bartók, Scriabin, Brahms. Composers write music for left hand alone for three principal reasons: as a feat of compositional prowess, to offer pianists opportunities to close the gap between what the left hand can do and what the right hand can do, and in response to injured pianists—most significantly, Paul Wittgenstein.

After Paul Wittgenstein was shot in the arm in World War I, the Austrian pianist was taken to the hospital, anesthetized, and taken into surgery. Unfortunately, while he was under, the hospital was commandeered by the Russians. When he woke up, he was a prisoner of war. A prisoner of war with one arm. A *pianist* prisoner of war with one arm.

Trapped in that Russian POW camp, Wittgenstein worked on his left-hand technique by tapping out all his piano repertoire on an upturned box and then, when he got home, set about using his substantial family wealth to commission left-handed music from famous composers like Ravel. Wittgenstein—a "key smasher," according to his piano teacher, an epithet that brought to mind that old evaluation of the piano judge who thought I'd barreled my way unfeelingly through Chopin's *marche funèbre*—had died the day before my birthday in 1961. Did *that* mean something?

I didn't want it to mean something. He wasn't one of the pianists or composers I'd wanted to grow up to be like. I never made a papier-mâché bust of Paul Wittgenstein or dressed up like Paul Wittgenstein for a Girl Scouts skit or read a biography of Paul Wittgenstein and imitated its prose in my diary. I didn't even know who he was until I was forced to make his acquaintance late that night in the music library, my own limp right hand in my lap. He looked like the Count from *Sesame Street*. I hated his ghoulish face, turned to face the camera over his right shoulder, his stub hidden inside the flaccid sleeve of his jacket, his left hand curled atop the keys of the piano, his expression a mix of defiance and fear, like someone you've surprised in the bathroom. "You lookin' at me?" he seems to be saying. "Please. God. Don't."

One of my peers, Akira, a star composing student from Japan, taking his cue from Ravel and Paul Wittgenstein, composed a piece for left hand alone just for me. But he didn't invite me to premiere it; he performed it himself in the student composers' concert with his healthy right hand in his lap, while I watched from the audience with my finger tormentor. He gave me the manuscript afterward, and there was my name in the dedication. I couldn't even be a key smasher.

That summer, I went home to Maryland, but this time I went to my mom's new town house, where my dad didn't live. Gypsy, our dog, had died just before my mom moved into her house, adding to the strange emptiness. Certain corners of the house—the kitchen, for example, with the white muslin curtains trimmed in red gros-grain ribbon, and the stained-glass fruit-bowl lamp with its hidden crystal heart—looked like our old house. I could trick myself into believing I was at home until I saw something that didn't fit—the foreign pattern in the kitchen linoleum, the ugly wallpaper in the downstairs bathroom. In the corner of my mom's new sunken, blue-carpeted living room, was my piano. But I could hardly play it. For the first time since I laid hands on the sonata all those years ago, I hadn't even bothered to bring Schubert home with me. The red-covered book, and my recording of Horowitz playing the sonata, remained in a box in storage in the desert.

I had my wisdom teeth removed. I sulked. I punished my mom. I viciously told her Gypsy probably died so she wouldn't have to live here. In the car one afternoon, being toted along on errands with my mom just as I'd wished for in the spring, I fiddled with the radio knobs using my good, left hand. Terry Jacks's "Seasons in the Sun" came on and my mom started singing along in the voice I remembered from church, ever so slightly sharp and more revealing of her Minnesota accent than her speaking voice, and I immediately, reflexively, changed the station. I wanted noise, thrash, cacophony, armor. "That's too bad," my mom said sadly. "I like that song."

I leaned my head against the window and felt my eyes stipple with tears. I wanted so badly to turn the station back to that song for my mom, but I couldn't, or wouldn't. I was spent, exhausted, and hurt. I'd yielded enough, given enough. I wanted to inflict on someone—anyone—what had been inflicted on me. I wanted to wallow and pout. I did, and the affliction was complete: everything hurt.

That summer, Casey cheated on me with a Joyce-shaped tuba player.

When school resumed, Dr. DeMars, my very own Salieri, told me again to make use of my (ever-doubling) pain in my music, and so I wrote tortured songs about Casey. Dr. DeMars defended my songs: "Sure, sure, it's all very *tonal*, but if these lyrics were in French, we'd be calling this art song," he said. We discussed the hundreds of songs Schubert had written, many of them settings of Romantic poetic texts. The Prince of Song had taken what was until then a secondary musical genre—the German *Lied*—and elevated it to serious consideration. Even Schumann, who would initially dismiss Schubert's sonatas for failing to live up to Beethoven's model, would call German lieder the only genre to get any better after Beethoven. And Schubert was the master and the innovator, the lieder leader.

We looked at "Erlkönig," which I'd learned about from Mr. Frezzo. That was the popular—very popular!—music of its day. "Sometimes you don't lead by standing on a chair and saying, 'I'm leading,'" Dr. DeMars said. "Sometimes you lead just by being your-self. And people follow." Some critics have taken Schubert to task for mixing high-brow and low-brow musical styles—and he is the uncontested Prince of Song! He seemed to be giving me permission to do the same, blend the classical music and the popular music I loved to create something original and worthwhile.

Mrs. Feltman came out to visit her son David, and she carved out a day just for me. She told me she'd had cancer. "But I'm better now," she said. "Knock on wood." We went to Milano Music and ogled the harps. We dug through boxes of sheet music together. She came to the music school with me and we went to yet another student composers' concert I should have participated in. When it had come time to select composers for this student composers' concert, I was the only composing student without a piece on the program. It turned out that my English-language art song sounded more like dismissible pop music to the other composing faculty. "You can turn pages," Dr. DeMars told me, unintentionally evoking Schubert, who had served as page-turner at the premiere of his own masterpiece "Erlkönig," but even that job was awkward and impossible. I couldn't get up from my chair next to the pianist quickly enough, pinch the wily pages between my wrecked fingers deftly enough, get out of the way smoothly enough to keep from ruining the music. So I sat in the audience, in the dark, with Mrs. Feltman. In the middle of the concert, in a much-too-loud whisper, she leaned over to me. "If I were your age, I'd put a feather in my cap for that boy right there," she said, and she pointed at exactly a boy I'd started to notice, a graduate student in music composition who wore loafers and carried a leather shoulder bag instead of a backpack. I thought about telling her then about my chaste and thrilling night in a dorm room twin bed with her younger son, but I decided to wait.

I had all the time in the world to tell Mrs. Feltman everything I needed to tell her.

Days after the concert, Dr. DeMars and the other composing teachers gathered and told me I should consider a change of major. I hadn't composed the amount of serious music I ought to have. Dr. DeMars was quiet; he didn't say anything about art song; he didn't stand on a chair and say, "Follow me!"

According to Gibbs, Schubert and Salieri eventually parted ways over a disagreement around Schubert's compositions (Salieri objected to Schubert's dedication to setting German texts instead of Italian). There is no evidence that Schubert's Salieri broke his heart, but mine did. A music teacher can, I think, break students' hearts in ways other teachers cannot. Dr. DeMars's betrayal stung, but it underscored the steadfastness of my other music teachers: Mrs. Feltman and Mr. Frezzo had not, and wouldn't ever, give up on me.

I defaulted to the most generic kind of music degree, my second change of major. From piano performance to music theory and composition to a BA in music, from artist to theorist to tourist: this is the ratcheting down of hope. I had accrued more music theory credits than I needed, but my break from the music school would be ragged and shameful: clearly a failure as both pianist and composer but foolishly insisting on collecting my generic degree in music, I still had to take a semester-long course in acoustics (taught by Dr. DeMars) and a few more semesters of studio lessons on a solo instrument. Even so, I had room in my course load. There was nothing left for me in the music building. I filled my schedule from the English department catalog: rhetoric, the short story, experimental fiction.

All throughout college, I'd been satisfying any requirement I could with English-department classes, mostly because I had no business in any other part of the university course catalog. The highest math class I'd taken in high school was Algebra II/Trig, and as I approached my final year of college I was still laboring under the misguided idea that I was "bad at math." I'd gotten away with satisfying my math requirement by taking college algebra and a course called Mac Literacy for Musicians. So when I found myself demoted from a bachelor of music to a bachelor of arts, I had many more music credits than I needed, but I suddenly needed some basic humanities classes and more French. The Language and Literature building, which housed the English department and the foreign-language department, was the only building on campus I knew almost as well as the music building, and I chose to serve out my sentence of exile from the music building there.

In retrospect, I know that I was simply modulating to a different language of composition—words instead of notes. Now, of course, I see that words are as much my birthright as music. That I grew up in a house lined with books, among people who love nothing more than a Sunday trip to a used bookstore. That even before I was penning insipid sonatas on lined paper, I was stapling notebook paper into books and labeling every other page with a chapter heading. That I have been a journal keeper for as long as I can remember. That at the times in my life when I could not play music—my day alone in the ski lodge, my hand surgery—I have consoled myself with books.

But I didn't, or wouldn't, acknowledge the tug toward writing as my chosen form of composition at the time. When Schubert was first able to quit his dreaded job as a schoolteacher and become the live-in music tutor for the Esterhazy children in Zseliz, he expressed relief and delight: "Thank God I live at last . . . otherwise I should have been nothing but a thwarted musician." Whereas Schubert's first separation from Vienna allowed him to "compose like a god" and avoid the thwarting fate, my expunging from the music school was involuntary. I was not ready to be a thwarted musician.

But thwarted I was, and foolishly I fixated on that instead of on the ways I was being enveloped and received by the English department. For my experimental fiction assignment, I tried to write a story in the form of a fugue. I typed it out on long sheets of paper taped together so the melodic lines would be recognizable as well as the way the harmonies stacked up vertically. I brought it to class rolled up in a film can. I recorded it on my four-track, four voices lapping one another and developing motives and themes according to what I'd learned in music theory class. "Brilliant," my experimental fiction teacher said. But when I showed it to one music teacher, he was outraged: "Where are the notes?" he demanded.

In acoustics class, we had to choose a topic for our final project. "I want it to be something related to your instrument," Dr. DeMars said. "I want it to be something that means something to you."

A week before, I'd been in the emergency room with that knee so inflamed with fluid that it had started to leak into my calf. In the emergency room, the doctor had done a Doppler ultrasound to locate the mass, a Baker's cyst behind my knee that was causing all the trouble. The doctor was impressed that I knew about Doppler, that I knew the tool he was using was called a transducer and that the gel, mostly vile sugar, formed a seal between the transducer and the skin so nothing could interrupt the ultrasound wave. So nothing could interrupt the message sent from body to box. "You premed?" he asked.

I didn't bother to explain that what looked like a decent premed education was actually the combination of what I'd learned about Doppler ultrasound in my acoustics class and many years of physical therapy, including such unforgettable lessons as my misguided taste of ultrasound gel years before.

"I'm a music major."

So when Dr. DeMars assigned the acoustics project, I told him I wanted to do mine on acoustics in medicine, specifically ultrasound.

"I'm not going to say no," he said, "but it's going to be hard for me to give you an A. I'd really prefer you do a topic with more relevance."

It was not a no.

I insisted on my topic because it was becoming clear to me then that acoustics in medicine was going to have more relevance to my life than the acoustics of a piano. My body was my instrument now, even if it was a warped lyre, out of tune, unplayable.

I really shouldn't have had to beg for approval of my topic: ultrasound is an acoustical phenomenon. When sound waves bounce off structures, they create echoes that indicate the size and shape of things—sunken ships, sea creatures, tumors, babies.

And more recently, ultrasound has been used not just for diagnosis but for treatment. Physical therapists use ultrasound to create deep heat and healing in damaged muscle tissues. Ultrasound can be used to break up fibroid cysts or kidney stones without surgery.

Musical acoustics, specifically, have medical applications, too. Though it wasn't yet on the market when I was writing my acoustics paper, another great topic would have been the Lung Flute. Invented by an acoustics engineer, the Lung Flute is a $40 treatment for a multibillion-dollar-a-year health problem, and it's purely acoustic.

When you blow into it, sound waves are produced that move at sixteen hertz (the same frequency at which the cilia in your lungs move). So a few toots on the Lung Flute can loosen mucus and get it out of your lungs—which is great news for the ten million people with chronic obstructive pulmonary disease whose cilia are bogged down in more mucus than they can cough up. In Japan, they use the Lung Flute to test for TB, and in Canada and Europe they have used it to test phlegm for evidence of cancer.

And that's to say nothing of the well-established benefits of music therapy: to help premature babies gain weight, patients with dementia access and share memories, autistic children deal with stimulation, stroke victims reclaim speech. There's no question that there's a complex, important relationship among bodies, illness, and sound: The stethoscope is probably the most readily recognizable icon of doctoring, which suggests that simply listening to bodies is still a crucial part of medicine. If I could write a new acoustics paper today, I'd choose this topic: many stutterers don't stutter when they're singing.

I got an A on my acoustics paper. But it was a pitiful parting gift: the school of music—the very art of music—had tolerated me as long as it could. I was being informally expelled.

Chapter 9

I had tried to prepare for this expulsion: in the spring of my freshman year of college, I got my first tattoo. Tattoos are like children in so many families: The first one's a big deal, so carefully planned. The rest just sort of happen.

For two weeks before I got the tattoo, I drew it on carefully with a ballpoint pen to make sure I liked it: a black, inch-high treble clef on the inside of my left ankle. It wasn't the most original tattoo; I was one of three freshmen in the music school to get a piece of musical notation tattooed on my body that semester.

But like everyone who has a tattoo, I believed mine was deeper, more meaningful: my tattoo was going to remind me that I was a musician, indelibly, even if a day came when I couldn't play piano anymore. Of course, as a freshman in college, still outpacing my arthritis at the piano (just barely), I hadn't actually believed there would come a day when I couldn't play anymore, but it sounded good. Secretly, I hoped the treble clef would work like blood on a doorpost: to persuade arthritis to pass me over.

After the treble clef tattoo, there was a string of bass clefs on the opposite ankle. The next tattoo came when I learned about the Latin phrase festina lente—"hurry slowly"—and learned that it was a popular emblem in the sixteenth century, frequently represented by a crab and a butterfly. "Butterfly and crab are both bizarre, both symmetrical in shape, and between them establish an unexpected kind of harmony," Italo Calvino wrote about this motto, and this symbol, in a speech he planned; he died before he delivered it.

Ten years into arthritis when I got the "crutterfly" tattoo on my right ankle, I had increasingly come to feel like a quick mind stuck in a slow body. I wanted to take every class, go to every reading, stay till the parties were over, meet everyone, and bike home at dawn. But my body wouldn't allow me to do all of that.

Even as Schubert's body failed him, even as he wrote in letters and his own original poems that he would "never be right again" and was "nearing final downfall," he composed. Music poured out of him, even when hospitalized. A friend described him as "superhumanly industrious."

Hurry slowly, I thought. Yes: I will hobble slowly to class but ask every question I can think of while I am there, during my recitative moments. I will solicit extra reading assignments, write the optional papers. I will limp everywhere I go, but once safe behind a desk or a piano or ensconced on a couch, on equal footing with everyone else, I will be a rocket ship of getting-stuff-done-ness, of making-people-laugh-osity, because I know the arias are coming. The sicker I got, the better my grades got.

Without knowing it, of course, I was submitting to a stereotype of disabled or chronically ill people, that of the "supercrip." As Nancy Mairs writes in Waist-High in the World: A Life Among the Nondisabled, "people with disabilities . . . know that they are scrutinized relentlessly for shortcomings and expected to fail. Work [or wit or gregariousness or intelligence or grades] of average quality won't gain them the necessary edge . . . they are required to show to earn a place among 'normals.'"

"Brother Body is poor," Rilke wrote. "That means we must be rich for him."

I didn't realize, as the crutterfly was emblazoned on my squishy ankle, that my empowering motto would push me for years and then I'd run out of gas, discovering that my attempts to hurry slowly, to be a riot of accomplishment and mental quickness, would become yet another way I apologized for my disease. I'd become so afraid that people were counting me out, so afraid that teachers and classmates and employers and coworkers were coddling me that I'd insist on being better, stronger, faster, busier, and more productive than anyone. I couldn't say no to any assignment, project, or task for fear that if I did they'd think I was "playing the arthritis card" or, worse, that they'd play it for me. "She's got all she can handle," I imagined them saying, shaking their heads in pity.

Tattoos are the logical extension of clothing as a deflection tactic. People comment on my tattoos, ask about them, admire them. They show me their own or confess that they've always wanted one—what is it like, does it hurt?—and I eat up the attention. My tattoos broadcast all the things my disease has rendered me but that strangers can't see: I am a veteran, an expert. Tattoos are an especially sweet method of redirection, because people admire that I endured pain to get them, even if they have no idea how much pain. Here are symbols people can understand the way they can't understand my bumps and flaws. Tattoos allow me to say, "Don't look at that, look at this!" And if people stare at me, tattoos create the possibility that they are envying my artwork, not judging my body or lurching gait.

Clothing for concealment, tattoos for deflection. My first, tentative foray into that third tactic—normalization—came with the next, and last, tattoo I got. It is on my back where I can't see it. No one can. I got it when I was fifteen years into arthritis, after my banishment from the music school. If I'd still been going to arthritis conferences at that point, I'd have been one of the vets. No one would ask me to slow down and wait up or open a soda can for them now. By then I had more scars—that snakebite on my shoulder, a raised squiggle on my left hand, hash marks on my belly—to boast about. And so it seemed necessary to make another, final mark on my body, a distinctly arthritis-y mark, to counterpoise the scars. To concede that I was, in fact, arthritic, but to insist that at least one instance of arthritis's graffiti on my body be something I chose. So I chose the Arthritis Foundation logo, but I gave it wings, and I put it somewhere only I can see it, and only if I use a mirror and make a point of looking. Such contradiction, such tentative acceptance.

Though I have never truly regretted my four tattoos, their permanence didn't sink in until well after the ink had dried and the ritual application of Lubriderm had ceased. There is no undoing them now, should I ever so wish, not without expensive and painful laser surgery. Needless to say, I have something of a policy against unnecessary elective surgeries.

When I look at the tattoos—just at *them*, at their shape and their color—I see that I like them. When I get out of the shower and put lotion on my legs, the tattoos around my ankles come alive, their colors deepening, the pliable skin softening. I find myself mesmerized by the shading in the butterfly's wings. I find that I can't really remember when the treble clef wasn't there any more than I can remember when I didn't have hand scars.

And most important, tattoos are permanent changes to my body, changes that invite stares and questions and comments, that *I* have made.

Evidence of arthritis is all over my body. There are bumps and bends and scars I didn't start out with. And then there are things I put there myself.

"Aren't you afraid you'll regret that?" people sometimes ask. "What if you wake up one day and wish you hadn't done that?" They point to my inked and aching ankles.

To which I always reply, albeit sometimes silently: What if you wake up and wish you weren't forty, or gray, or clumsy, or a type 2 diabetic, or not the dancer/athlete you used to be, or inscribed with scars and wrinkles? A lot of stuff is going to happen to our bodies, yours and mine, that we wish wouldn't happen. I thought I'd lose my virginity before I got gray hair, but it didn't work out that way. Our bodies become scribbled over with the evidence of what happens to and within us. Much of it is outside of our control.

Every day, every one of us—every one of us who wants to keep living, every one of us who insists on forging ahead, every one of us who has a spouse or children or officemates or friends who expect us to get OK with our bodies enough to show up to the bedroom or the soccer game or the big meeting or happy hour because they need our love and our brains and our wit and they'll forgive us for bringing along the old body—must reconcile who we think we are with that aging, crumbling, shape-shifting form we see in front of us. Isn't it OK for some of those permanent changes to be of our own doing? I'll be damned if I don't at least get to coauthor my history on my body.

Discussion boards are full of people querying the safety of getting a tattoo after major surgery—joint replacement, heart stents, brain tumor removals. Though Clinton Sanders, author of *Customizing the Body: The Art and Culture of Tattooing*, tells me that he doesn't think the intersection of body modification and disability has been seriously studied, the anecdotal (read: Internet) evidence suggests that it is very normal to respond to your body's modifications of you by modifying it. Tit for tat.

Without knowing it, when I branded my disobedient body with permanent art, I was joining the ranks of other damaged, disabled, deviant people who use tattoos (and piercing and other artful modifications) as a powerful way to reclaim their bodies. A Google image search for "mastectomy tattoo" yields more than a thousand images: a mosaic of fairies and Celtic knots and butterflies and stars and flowers—even the creatures from *Where the Wild Things Are*—all displayed on the flat, healed chests of women who lost their breasts to cancer. Tat for tit.

Just as I assume these women did, I used tattoos as a way of having some say in the changes that were written on my body ("Oh yeah, body? I see your scars and rheumatoid nodules and I raise you!"). My tattoos are comforting. My curled hands look nothing like the hands I had twenty, ten, or even five years ago. When I look at pictures of my body in its childhood, I can't even match up the parts I have now to their long-gone healthy counterparts. I doubt if I'd be able to pick a photo of my own bare feet—at, say, age fifteen—out of a lineup. But there's no mistaking my ankles for any others. When I look down and see ink, I am reoriented. I know where—and who—I am again.

Still, Sanders explains that even in this relatively tattoo-biquitous era, tattooing is still essentially fringe, "employed to proclaim publicly one's special attachment to deviant groups, certain activities, self-concepts, or primary associates." My tattoos are the stamps on that other, "bad" passport that Susan Sontag wrote about. They link me to that group of deviants, my primary associates, the pale ones who hobbled through cold hotel lobbies all those summers.

But my tattoos are also the good, old-fashioned tattoos of yesteryear, the sailor and soldier tattoos that John Irving waxes nostalgic about in *Until I Find You*: They are "keepsakes to mark my journey, the love of my life, a heartbreak, a port of call."

My right hand had healed fairly well from the hand surgery. Anyone who didn't demand virtuosity from her hands would probably have been pleased with the results: Nearly two years later, I could hold a pen, button a shirt, groom myself—the physical therapist's gold standard. But I held my hands to a higher standard. I needed to reach an octave, at least—better a ninth or tenth—in order to play most piano literature, even if I wasn't any longer a pianist, or even a composer. I needed more strength than I had to depress the keys of the grand pianos in the practice room and on the concert stage and at my lessons. I had to fulfill my lesson requirement every semester to stay on track to graduate as the most peripheral kind of music major—why didn't anyone ask me where I thought that would get me exactly?—and I could barely make it through a lesson, much less hours of practice. My piano teacher, the same one who'd been so proud when I'd won third place in a piano competition early in my college career, made the suggestion: "Why don't you take harpsichord this semester instead?"

The harpsichords, with their easier-to-push keys, were kept in a locked room at the end of the hallway on the fifth floor of the music building. You had to have permission to practice on them, and you had to be issued a big gold key that said "do not duplicate." The harpsichord teacher, Dr. Metz, was a lean, white-haired man with a tidy beard. He smiled when he spoke and pulled at his beard, his head cocked and his mouth open in an expectant smile, whenever you answered. He accepted me into the harpsichord studio, the small group of students who studied with him in private lessons and then met as a group once a week to play for one another. Another student in the class was also a chronically ill refugee from the piano studio, whose HIV medications made him unable to memorize piano music. "Memorization isn't really a convention of baroque music," Dr. Metz explained to me.

Dr. Metz set out to teach me how to read figured bass. If you looked at the harpsichord music quickly, you'd think it was piano music—there's the treble clef, there's the bass clef, there are the black notes that mean melody and accompaniment. But the left hand is responsible not just for reading notes but for deciphering a set of numerals. You're given a note to start from and then the numerals tell you the relationship between that pitch and the other pitches needed to make up the chord—but not the voicing. Should you put the C on the top or in the middle of the chord? It depends on what chord you are coming from and where you are headed. And then it is up to you to figure out how to slide most logically, most elegantly, from one chord to the next as your right hand plays the melody. It was a lot like playing from Grandma Avery's big fake book.

Figured bass troubled me the same way all improvisation did: I wasn't sure I had anything interesting, novel, to say musically. The music of my favorite eras—the late classical and early Romantic—were not without their calls for improvisation. Concertos frequently have cadenzas, in which the orchestra stops playing (caesura) and the soloist improvises a flashy demonstration of skill and musicality. Sometimes these cadenzas were written out, as in the case of Mozart's Concerto No. 27 in B-flat Major, K. 595, which he premiered himself in the last public performance he gave as a pianist. In general, though, I'd always preferred having my notes prescribed for me, even if I wasn't always compliant with the composer's orders.

I settled in for a semester of playing that music, music like that damned Chopin étude, that required my brain as much as—more than—my hands. My brain, impervious to arthritis. I see now I was being shown how to hedge my bets, I was being offered a trade.

On a harpsichord, you can't play louder or softer. No matter how hard you strike the keys, you're not going to get more sound out of the instrument. This isn't to say that how you touch the keyboard doesn't matter. The harpsichord is extremely sensitive to your attack. It might not be louder, but the quality of the sound can be hoarse and horrible if you are careless. And the harpsichord is less forgiving than the piano, too. It is more difficult to cheat, to fake it. There is no sustain or damper pedal to rely on when your hands can't quite hold on to a note, letting your feet do what your hands cannot. On a harpsichord, you have to hold the keys down for the whole duration, or the sound will stop. But the keys are closer together, and they are easier to press. On the harpsichord, I felt like I was handling a marionette. Trying to hold on to all the notes and decipher the figured bass, I felt tangled up in the music, brainy and puzzled. I felt tethered to the keys. I missed the bombast and ache of Chopin, of Szymanowski, of Liszt. I missed playing the piano. I missed Schubert, who still lived in a box.

But Dr. Metz was kind and patient with me, and he let me perform on the final studio recital and when I arrived early at his house for the end-of-semester party, before the sun had gone down and before the trays of food were put out, he put me to work. He handed me a roll of hot-pink garden ribbon and a pair of scissors and dispatched me to his backyard. "Tie one of these on each rosebush," he said. His backyard was a rare spot of moistness in the desert, a cool expanse of lawn ringed with county-fair-quality rosebushes, the fence around the perimeter festooned with twinkle lights that were on even before the sun went down. I set about to do my job. I didn't know why he was having me tie pink ribbons to all the blooms. I wondered if I was doing something important, I wondered if I was single-handedly responsible for protecting the prized flowers when the yard filled up with people. I still don't know why I was doing that job. I think now that he was giving me something to do to get me out of the house, out of his way. I could see him through the kitchen window, moving around his wife, Barbara, in a silent dance—he opening a cupboard, she ducking below his arm.

I looked down at a glorious yellow bloom in front of me, a flower the size of my face. I had a nearly irresistible urge to cut it off with the scissors I had in my hand.

Though I would continue taking harpsichord lessons even after I graduated, I never took piano lessons again.

As graduation approached, I reflected on my old childhood hero, Mozart, and the end of my own formal piano study. After falling for Schubert, I'd retired Mozart, stuffed him away like a plush toy I'd outgrown. But standing on the edge of adulthood, I longed for my old comforts. Huggy, childhood Mozart. That last public concert of Mozart's, in which he played the piano concerto in B-flat? It was on March 4, 1791. My birthday. To a girl born on Vivaldi's birthday, that's the kind of thing that feels like a sign. Then again, according to musicologist Alfred Einstein, Mozart's playing of the piano concerto in B-flat—why is all of my favorite music in B-flat?— signified the end. "It was not in the Requiem that he said his last word, however, but in this work."

I graduated with a degree in music. That summer, my remaining music friends and I fled to the beach in Los Angeles for the week. In the company of Beth and Deanna, these two extraordinarily beautiful and talented saxophone players, one jazz and one classical, I felt like an impostor.

I feared they saw me the way Wittgenstein's contemporaries saw the one-armed pianist or, for that matter, the way many people view disabled people: courageous, curious, freakish, feckless, virginal, vexing, pious, pesky. I knew my friends loved me and admired me for whatever limping music I was able to make against the odds. But I'm fairly certain they didn't see me as what I wanted to be: a pianist.

I was unable to find solace or inspiration in Wittgenstein—or, for that matter, in any of the other legendary musicians-persevering-despite-disability stories that I knew of. Beethoven? Sure, he was deaf, but that happened gradually and didn't start until he was in his late twenties, at least. He at least had a chance to get great before he started slipping.

And there was Leon Fleisher, who lost the use of his right hand to dystonia in the 1960s and simply plugged ahead, playing all the left-hand-alone repertoire and conducting, which I hadn't been able to manage, until Rolfing and Botox delivered his right hand back to him.

I should have been able to derive some inspiration from Byron Janis, himself a sufferer of arthritis. But Leon Fleisher, Beethoven, and Byron Janis had been granted something I envied: they had at least been given the chance to be great. Byron Janis's head start on arthritis was so much longer than my own. No one could dispute his greatness. He could always point to what he'd done and say, "Do you hear? That's me." All I have is a box of ribbons and trophies, a photo in a yearbook.

Listen. I know. Millions of kids take piano lessons, and very few of them become concert pianists. I understand rarity and odds better than most, I assure you. In all likelihood, I would not have been good enough anyway. But this cruel synchrony, to be gifted with music and arthritis nearly simultaneously, is what at times is almost unbearable. There is a peculiar pain in never having been given the opportunity to expand, honor, or exhaust whatever allowance of natural musical talent I had. If I failed, at least it would have been on my own terms. I know I am a better musician than my body will let me be. Unexpressed music is something, but it isn't music. Like pain, like language, music must be expressed. *Let it out*, people say. *Let it all out.*

This might be, more than anything, what connects me to Schubert. He did not have the meteoric rise that Mozart did. He grew—he began to grow—into his talent, but he died before he had the chance to do so. I did not die so young, but my playing did.

Could I have heard this in the sonata that first day in Providence? A "secret program," a coded narrative from Schubert to me? A lament for lost opportunity, lost music?

Schubert had been dead for a century before the music world discovered the spectral beauty of those last three sonatas. They did not appear in print until 1839, and the publisher decided to dedicate them to Robert Schumann. Schumann, in turn, dissed them publicly, writing that they "ripple along from page to page as if without end," sniffing that Schubert had renounced "shining novelty, where he usually sets himself such high standards." In 1928, Rachmaninov revealed that he didn't even know Schubert had written sonatas.

Until the twentieth century, Schubert's sonatas were penalized for not being, essentially, Beethoven sonatas. It is only in the past hundred years that we have come to appreciate them on their own merits, to see them not as Schubertian also-rans but as serious, compelling works that deserve their place on the shelf next to Beethoven (a spot on the shelf Schubert would have cherished, not resented). Schubert's sonatas are infectiously singable, because the Prince of Song brings his lyricism to bear on the melodies of these sonatas. My own anecdotal proof of that is the way the B-flat sonata wormed its way into my head more than twenty years ago and hasn't left.

And although the compositional structure of his sonatas is relatively traditional, he is something of an iconoclast, modulating to unexpected keys and tonalities. He rejects the supposed requirement that sonatas modulate from their home key to prescribed destinations, most of all the dominant key, choosing often to shift to related keys that Beethoven might treat as stopovers on the way to satisfying resolution. That everything must resolve in the expected fashion, Schubert seems to say with his sonatas, is nonsense: let me show you that there are satisfying resolutions that you (and Beethoven) never dreamed of.

But it is Beethoven's sonatas that have so come to define sonata form. According to Charles Rosen, "sonata form . . . is more or less those compositional procedures of Beethoven which were most useful to the nineteenth century, which could be imitated most comfortably and with the smallest risk of disaster." Schubert is often talked about like he is trying to imitate Beethoven's sonatas, like he is some kind of striving little brother who wrote a few pretty songs.

In his life, and in his music, Schubert lived under the shadow of Beethoven, but not altogether unhappily. His adoration of Beethoven is explicit in his compositions. In *The Life of Schubert*, Gibbs puts forth a theory that Schubert's Piano Trio in E-flat, Op. 100 (D. 929) includes a "secret program"—not just purposeful imitation of Beethoven but embedded references and musically encoded homage. Schubert "quotes" musically from a Swedish song of farewell, and from Beethoven's *Eroica* symphony, itself originally dedicated to a hero. Schubert premiered the Trio at a concert on the one-year anniversary of Beethoven's death, where it was performed by Beethoven's own musicians.

There's no question, Schubert loved Beethoven. As a schoolboy, the story goes, he is said to have sold his schoolbooks for a ticket to *Fidelio*. Schubert escorted Beethoven's body to the grave carrying a black-draped torch and then, it is said, went to a tavern with two friends and drank one glass of wine for Beethoven and another to whichever of the three of them who would be the next to go. Schubert was the next to go, one year later. On his own deathbed, he is said to have asked to hear Beethoven's Quartet in C-sharp Minor. Delirious, he is said to have murmured, "Take me away from here, from under the earth. Beethoven does not lie here," which his beloved brother Ferdinand—the same one who ripped off his compositions—interpreted as a request to be buried next to Beethoven. And he is.

If it weren't too risky for me to get any more tattoos—because of the surgeries that have happened with increasing frequency in the last years, and will continue to—it would be, in great black Gothic letters across my back, the epitaph that marks Schubert's gravestone: "The Art of Music here entombed a rich possession, but even fairer hopes."

CAESURA /
INTERRUPTION

I turn to stone, and my pain goes on.
> —Ludwig Wittgenstein,
> Philosophical Investigations

My apartment was small, a fourth of a shed, really, that had been cut up into apartments. It would be almost twenty years before I bothered to get my diploma framed. I left it in the fake-leather folder it came in. I put it in a low drawer with old birthday cards, and my CIA plaques. The Schubert book, with its faded red cover, was in a box somewhere. My diploma was an expired passport. I had visited music, but I was a resident of illness.

I hadn't really thought of Randy Cohen, my red-haired musical nemesis from high school, until one day, in the summer of 2000, when I saw him—impossibly!—walking down the street in Tempe, Arizona, just a block away from campus. I pulled over in the parking lot.

"Randy Cohen!" I shouted out the door of my car.

He plodded up to me in his Birkenstocks. "Hi, Andrea Avery," he said, genial, not as smug as I'd remembered him to be, and not surprised-seeming at all. Then again, he was out of place; I wasn't. Everyone knew I'd fled to the desert after high school.

"What the hell are you doing here?" I waved my crooked arm to encircle Tempe, my town, the sandwich shop where I worked, nestled right up against the back of the music building and Grady Gammage auditorium, where I'd collected my music degree, for whatever that was worth.

"I'm conducting *Titanic* at Gammage," he said. Of course. "You should come to the show," he offered. "Tonight."

I sat in the orchestra pit with Randy Cohen one last time, with empty hands and no instrument in front of me. From where I sat, I couldn't see much of the performance (which didn't matter; I'd seen it on Broadway with Casey), but I wasn't watching it anyway. I was watching Randy do what he'd set out to do, what everyone we went to school with expected he'd do, what he was made to do and wanted to do and supposed to do. I watched Randy tap his baton expertly; I watched the musicians follow him.

The first time I'd seen the show, I'd been sad, distracted by Casey's traitorous hand in my lap, thinking only of the sturdy tuba player he'd cheated on me with, thinking only of the red-chewed kiss a brass mouthpiece leaves on its player's mouth. We had foolishly tried for almost two years after his infidelity to stay together, feebly patching over the proliferating weaknesses in our sinking relationship after that first, fatal error. I suppose a musical about the *Titanic* wasn't really the best choice for a relationship-saving date.

This time, though, with nothing but the music and the tops of the actors' heads to go on, what I made of the story of the *Titanic* was this: If it had fulfilled its potential, if it had been the greatest ship that ever sailed, there would never have been a musical about it. A bigger, greater ship would have come along. *Titanic* is more spectacular in failure than it ever could have been if things had gone as planned. Was it a comedy or a tragedy?

After I'd been unofficially expelled from the music school and forced to take refuge in the English department, I was angry. That fugue story I'd turned in for experimental fiction was greeted with delight and interest by my English teacher and classmates, even though it was snubbed by professors at the music school. It was as if there were two volume knobs, like you find on a mixing console, and I had the "miserable failed musician" knob turned up to earsplitting volume and the "happy 'something else'" knob turned down to zero. I was going to be a spectacularly failed musician, then? I didn't want to be a success in this other way; I didn't want to be something else. I wanted only to be a musician. Deep down, I wanted it still.

We went to IHOP after the show, and I tried to tell Randy how proud I was of him, how proud I was to know him. But I couldn't bring myself to say that I was relieved to sit in the pit with him without being consumed with jealous fury, intent on proving that I was the pianist by leading mutinous revolts and undermining his authority, which I did in the high school pit. And I didn't apologize.

"What do you do now?" he asked.

"I'm starting grad school," I began, and before he could make me say it, I answered his next question. "In the English department."

Years before, I had mostly successfully convinced myself that it was a composer I wanted to be, not a pianist. But after my falling-out with Dr. DeMars I knew I had no prospects to continue my study of music composition. So I convinced myself that I could be a composer still, of stories. Schubert wrote once that "whenever I attempted to sing of love, it turned to pain. And again, when I tried to sing of pain, it turned to love. Thus were pain and love divided in me." My attempts to sing of love—to play music, or write it—had turned to pain. Perhaps I could sing of that pain—through writing—and turn it into love. I did not try to explain all of that to Randy. I just looked down at my blintzes.

Graciously (after all, he was a pupil of Mr. Frezzo's, too) he changed the subject and I didn't have to explain that I had fallen— no, been thrown—off course, that I was no longer that girl my classmates had named "most talented" in the yearbook (had I ever earned that title, anyway?), that I hadn't touched a piano in months, that I wasn't sure I would again. I kept my hands under the table, forfeited my fork to the unfinished blintzes.

Mercifully, Randy allowed the conversation to wend around music entirely. We didn't talk about Mr. Frezzo, or all those musicals we did together, or about Randy's own doubling successes as a pianist and conductor and orchestrator, all of which would soon have him appearing in those ubiquitous black-and-yellow New York Playbills, at the White House, and eventually onstage at the Grammy Awards.

Schubert's Symphony No. 8 in B Minor is known as the "Unfinished" Symphony. While one children's book, *Franz Schubert and His Merry Friends*, posits that Schubert skipped off to a picnic instead of finishing the symphony, some scholars argue that Schubert didn't finish it because it—he—hurt too much. He had contracted syphilis. "To a sensitive man like Schubert," reads the entry in *Grove*, "the association of the composition of his symphony with the events that led to his illness might have made a return to it repugnant."

That fall, as my music friends took off for New York or CalArts, I went no further than to the English department on the other side of campus for my new life. I rode my bike to school and made a point of taking a route that circumvented the southwest corner of campus. I avoided the music building. I'd knocked on wood, but less than a year before, I had learned that Mrs. Feltman's cancer was back.

I'd started to give up on one dream, but I hadn't yet been bullied out of the other: love, and making it. In some resilient way, I believed that I didn't have to choose between celibacy and syphilis. I could find what Schubert didn't: love and life.

Single, having left Casey back at the music building, I let my new friends from the Language and Literature building take me to Casey

Moore's Oyster House to cheer me up and we met some new boys and when we went home with them the one who was supposed to be mine took me to his bedroom and I discovered that he slept on a frameless futon on the floor and I wasn't going to be able to get down or up, much less do whatever was supposed to happen in between. So I stood at his CD rack and commended his taste in music and became his buddy. I did this a hundred times.

One night at Casey Moore's, I met Ryan. I was wearing a white vintage coat with a hole in the pocket. I was standing at the foot of the stairs on the patio and my friend Monica said, "Do you guys know each other? You should." Ryan was handsome, but thick and sort of ruddy, and more important he smiled constantly and he laughed a lot and he had a crown of golden curls that he styled compulsively by sweeping his meaty hand across his forehead in a move he called "the swirl." His hair was darker blond, sweaty, where it met his faintly freckled face. He'd just gotten back from Cologne. He was studying industrial design. He wanted to make furniture. He wore only black or charcoal gray, and he was proud of his European jeans with their unusual seam details. We were both drunk.

"Oh my God," I said. "Do you see that red-haired guy right there?" I said, pointing to a sporty guy in Tevas across the patio.

"Uh, yeah."

"I totally went on a date with that guy—one date—in my freshman year of college—"

Ryan looked, and laughed. "Yeah? Seriously? *That* guy?"

I thought Ryan was surprised because that guy, the guy wearing some kind of high-tech hiking gear shirt that was snug on his muscled torso, didn't look like my type. I was decked out in my vintage coat, my fishnets, my red shoes. Ryan's clothes looked European and snobby but his pink cheeks and thick build made him seem like a big Texan cowboy playing dress-up. We were both cracking up.

Laughing and grabbing Ryan's arm, I told him all about that one date from my freshman year: how the sorority girls on my floor dressed me and talked me into wearing mascara, and a boy in a white truck picked me up blasting Cat Stevens, how he took me to 7-Eleven and then we stopped at the guy's house—on the first date! To meet his mother and kid sister! Can you imagine! Ryan was laughing so hard there were tears in his eyes.

"*That* guy? *That* guy! That's my little brother!"

We were young and drunk and all too ready to believe that there were patterns, a design, to our lives. I already wanted to believe in magical patterns and secret programs, plumbing the depths of music history for signs and augurs, a piece of music premiered on my birthday, for example. Anything to believe that the project of growing up—becoming something, loving someone—was more than so much aimless fumbling. I wanted signs, and designs, and here was a handsome *designer* who had been foreshadowed by his brother years before.

Ryan asked to borrow the pen from my purse to write down his number and when he gave it back to me, I put it in my pocket and it fell through the hole to my feet. Ryan picked it up and gave it to me and I did the same thing. Again it fell. And again. "Man." He laughed. "That's a pretty coat but functionally it kind of sucks."

Ryan could draw. Our dates were almost always to the coffee shop, and Ryan would bring stacks of white drawing paper and some pens and we would draw together. "Draw a toaster," I'd say, and in a few strokes he would conjure one up. "Now a curling iron."

He drew pictures of me, flattering cartoony pictures. My eyes were always big and starry, my legs straight and my feet spread in a standing-my-ground stance. We did "exquisite corpse" drawings, folding a piece of paper into thirds and then taking turns drawing the feet or the torso or the head.

He educated me about midcentury modern furniture. Where anyone else saw neutered, emotionless space—the waiting area at the airport—Ryan saw a story. He knew how those chairs had been chosen to suit as many people as possible. He studied bodies and he knew how to make garden spades and laptops that people could use, things people would love without knowing why. He understood my gripes about low-slung chairs, which I couldn't get out of by myself, and he knew I didn't want to ask for help. When we went to a restaurant, he knew I'd want to sit at the high-top table because it was easier to hop down from a stool than to ask for help up out of a chair.

"I hate toothbrushes like that," I'd say in the aisle at Target, pointing at the bulbous, chubby, supposedly ergonomic tooth-brushes often suggested for people with arthritis, and Ryan would go off on a tirade about arcs and angles, distribution of weight and fulcrums and grip. "Yeah, I don't blame you," he'd say. He'd snort dismissively at the toothbrush, another embodiment of faulty design. A designer's misguided idea of what's good for people, not based in actual user experiences. I thought my dad would like Ryan.

We dreamed up a line of silly De Stijl–themed T-shirts, laughing all the while, sure that we could market them to pretentious art students: "De Stijl crazy after all these years. . . . In de Stijl of the night."

Every Sunday afternoon we drove up to his mom's house in his black Volkswagen, holding hands in the center console. After dinner we watched TV with her, the *Crossing Over* show, or the awards show with Bjork in her swan dress. Sometimes after his mom had fallen asleep on the couch, I would change into my bathing suit in her bedroom and Ryan and I would go swimming, float-dancing in the water, where I am weightless, and we'd kiss. I was falling in love with him and with belonging to this family.

Late, still with damp hair but our skin chlorine-dry, euphoric, we'd get back into his car and descend from Scottsdale into Tempe and we'd go back to his house and go to bed and within minutes there'd be trouble: What were we going to do about this sex thing?

From his humid bedroom with its whirring fan and his computer casting blue light on our bodies, I felt nostalgic for our afternoon. I wanted to be fully clothed with Ryan, armored. I longed to be in a coffee shop with him. I wanted us to be laughing brains together, forever. I loved Ryan. I wanted him, and he wanted to have sex.

We'd try, we'd start, but then the familiar sensation would return, the panic came from my groin to my stomach to my throat and my hip adductors would clench and I'd say, *No, no, no, I can't.*

He'd get up from the bed and pull his weird, European jeans on and say, "Maybe I should take you home."

In the driveway of my apartment, he'd leave the car running and smoke a cigarette.

"Can't you wait?" I'd ask.

"For what? It's like we have all 999 of the pieces of a 1,000-piece puzzle," he'd say. "It's just this one little piece that's missing."

"But we have the other 999," I'd say. "Isn't that enough?"

I couldn't believe that that one little piece was enough reason to toss the rest. I couldn't believe that this thing that was wrong with me—what exactly *was* wrong with me?—this thing that had already taken so much, was going to take this, too.

We'd break up on Sunday nights, over and over again, but by the following Saturday afternoon one or the other of us would call and say, "Want to get coffee? I'm De Stijl into you. Bring paper and pens."

Until finally we found ourselves in my driveway again, and Ryan said, "You know what? I don't think you're ever going to have sex. Sometimes your arthritis wears on me." And that was the last time. There was no coming back from that. After that, there was no way we could be disembodied together the way I wanted us to be, in brain communion, or the way he wanted us to be, in sex.

I wished I could swap out my whole midsection like one of our exquisite corpse drawings, just get rid of the whole chunk of me that included my heart and my aching hip joints and my organs. Ryan loved my face and my brain and my taste in shoes, but everything else got in the way.

Oh, I know, love is not about sex. Love is not about bodies. Sure. But if I take an inventory of all the times I've felt most acutely loved, they are these:

My father is on the beach at Chincoteague on his hands and knees, pale and freckled in the sun and out of his coat and tie, the station-wagon keys glistening on a chain around his neck, building a giant tortoise out of sand for me.

My mother is on the family room floor with me, cutting a sewing pattern out of the delicate tissue, telling me, "You can't skip any of the steps on the pattern. They are all important."

Erica is braiding my hair, her thin fingers trawling my scalp, her knees against my back.

Matthew has his arms around me, cupping my hands in his, as we show off a toad we collected at the campsite.

Chris and I are heaping all the blankets, cushions, and pillows in the house in a pile on the family room floor so we can play a forbidden game we invented called Mounds, where we leap from the arms of the tweed couch into the nest we've created.

Sharing the piano bench with someone I love, singing.

A body is an inescapable necessity. My body has made me hard to love and, I feared, incapable of loving. Add it to the list: like pain and language and music, love must be expressed.

There are no moments without bodies, and maybe there is no love. What if I can't get down on the floor or in the sand with my own children? What if I can't braid my own daughter's hair? Let it out; let it all out.

So I can't really begrudge Ryan the sex he wanted. How are you supposed to know someone loves you if they can't show you? *I love you this much.* See? It doesn't really work without the arms.

I tried to meet someone else. Back at Casey Moore's—Nabokov in my head, *Here will Jack always stumble, here will Jane's heart always break*—I sat at a high-top table with my friend Caroline. Two boys in jean jackets approached us. The one with the pompadour and the tiny, angry rock-and-roll pins on his lapel seemed to like me. I got up to go to the bathroom, unfolding my rigid, bent legs from under the table. "Wait. Why are you walking like a gimp? Are you a gimp?" he said. What a pickup line. Ryan had been my last best shot.

Six weeks later, I was in my dark apartment getting ready to go to a Halloween party without Ryan. I was going to be Velma from

Scooby-Doo because I could wear both my glasses and a shin-length skirt that would cover my bent knees. Chris called.

"Andy died," he told me.

Andy Swindells had been sick for so long. I thought he'd always be sick, but alive. My brother had been trying to get ahold of him and wasn't getting a call back. Worried, he'd gone to Andy's apartment. Andy's wallet and keys were there. There were towels on the floor and there was shit and blood and that's it. He'd contracted meningitis.

By the time my brother found Andy at the hospital, he was dead.

I went to the Halloween party and no one knew who I was.

My mother told me that Chris sang "The Wind Cries Mary" at the funeral.

Dr. Metz had issued me a new harpsichord key after I graduated in 2000, but I couldn't bring myself to go to the harpsichord practice room because I'd have to walk through a crying, curving hallway of piano practice rooms to get there.

I barely practiced, but the harpsichord studio is where I went on the morning of 9/11 after I couldn't stand being in my apartment anymore. I sat at the harpsichord and looked out the half-circle windows at the impossibly blue sky and I cried, and that felt something like music, like purging.

At Christmastime, I went home to Maryland, to my freshly fractured family. We'd have two Christmases: first at my mom's town house and then at my dad's apartment. My brothers and my sister were there. It was the lull between eating and board games, the bullshitting hour. The table was still cluttered with dishes. I was seated on the side of the table against the wall. From where I sat, I could see my piano, which sat untouched, except for when my sister played it. I was bracing myself for the day someone suggested that Erica get the piano instead of me. My mom was in the kitchen getting a plate of cookies ready for all of us, and Chris, our prodigal clown, returned to us after years of stoned, stony absence, was holding court, telling us about something he'd seen on TV. His honking laugh kept interrupting the narrative, but we were all getting it: "midget" tossing.

Family legend has it that Chris was the first person to ever make me laugh, working at it as I hung in my electric swing in the foyer.

Now, my face got hot, my eyes started to sting. I wanted to leave the room, but the only refuge was up the stairs to the guest bedroom. I was pinned between table and wall, my gimpy legs tucked under the table, out of sight. I couldn't stand it.

I thought of the blinking hand that signaled that your time to cross the street was almost up, how I'd gotten to the point where I couldn't cross a street in the time allowed, how boys in cars would yell, "Out of the way, freak!" as I hobbled to the curb. I thought of the boy who called me a gimp in the bar, or the supposed friend who, when she learned that I was getting somewhere with a dance major who worked at our coffee shop (he'd held my hand) said, "Hmm. Dancers with cripples. I don't get it." I thought about the other friend who thought it necessary to pass that information along to me.

"Stop it!" I screamed at Chris, stunning him, freezing his beloved face in an expression of shock.

"What?"

I pulled myself from the table and hauled myself up the stairs slowly and sideways, using the railing, unable to wipe the hot tears from my eyes because I needed both hands to make my escape. There are no easy exits when you are the gimp.

I was crying on the bed when Chris came in. "I didn't mean anything, Irms," he said, using my nickname.

Chris and I have always had a near-twin-like ability to reconcile our spats with code words or gestures. A jutted-out bottom lip means *I'm sorry, I was an asshole.* "Baaaaaathroom tissue," uttered in the snootiest British accent, was plucked long ago from a TV commercial. "Hello, Mr. Star" (in same accent—Benny Hill and *The Goodies* had taught us that everything's funnier in a snooty British accent) came from an afternoon spent drawing at the kitchen table, when I tried to draw a person and the features were scrunched too close to the center of a moon face. I said it then, one of the first times I discovered that to laugh at myself meant I could elicit a

precious laugh from him, which was and still is the best feeling I
know, my favorite song. There are many of these code phrases in
our private language and they all mean, *I love you. Remember when
we were young together? Do you remember everything that came before?
Remember how we'd fix heaping, sloshing bowls of cereal and carry them
down the stairs so we could eat in front of the TV, against the rules, while
Mom and Dad were out playing tennis together? Remember when Mom
and Dad played tennis together?*

"Don't you know that people laugh at me?" I screamed. "Don't
you know that I'm a gimp? That I'm a cripple?" I had never said it
aloud before.

"I don't think of you that way," Chris said, his eyes red around
the edges. "Come on. You know I don't think of you that way."

"You can't talk about people that way," I said. "I'm one of them."

Chris climbed up on the bed with me and I wanted to cuddle
with him the way we had when we were younger, before drugs and
divorce and so much pain, for both of us. He was crying.

"Don't paint me like I'm some kind of asshole," he said. "I'm not.
Andy—" he said, and stopped.

Andy, who'd been gimpy longer than I had, whom Chris had
cared for and walked slowly with and helped and loved and sang to,
finally. Andy who'd been dead for only a few months. How could I
begrudge Chris the chance to retell whatever story made him laugh?
How could I have forgotten how much, and how clearly, he loved
the most broken people—Andy, and me? We were quiet for a long
time, both crying.

"Andy, and September Eleventh, I just don't see the point,"
Chris said. "I don't want to kill myself, but sometimes I think if
the Metro went off the rails or something, maybe that wouldn't
be so bad."

It was code, and I knew exactly what he meant. I felt it, too.

The next day, my mother and sister and I went to Holy Cross
Hospital—the same hospital where I'd gone for all those mornings
of physical therapy—to see Mrs. Feltman.

She was sitting up in bed and her hair was mussed but not that much more than usual and there on the bed stand was her tube of red lipstick. "You look beautiful," she said to me.

"You, too," I said.

Her husband stood by the window with his back to us, worrying the window blind cord with his hand.

"I still think of that drawing you made of me," she said. "What a hoot."

That was the last time I saw her. We spoke on the phone over the next couple of years, always with the idea that we would get together one of these days. The last time I spoke to Mrs. Feltman after that day at the hospital was on Mother's Day, 2004. "I'm coming to visit in September," I said. *Try to hold on until then*, I didn't say. *Thank you*, I didn't say.

"I love you," I did say.

I didn't see her again before she died on July 30, 2004, the birthday of Nannerl Mozart, Wolfgang's eclipsed older sister. Nannerl had the undivided attention of Papa Mozart for the first four years of her life, and she took lessons that no doubt filled the house with the music that Wolfie consumed, that his brain steeped in, reforming itself plastically in the original "Mozart effect." But eventually she came to describe herself as just "her brother's pupil."

The winter after that final public concert Mozart gave, on my birthday in 1791, he swelled up, vomited, and died. No one knows for sure what he died of; among the theories are poisoning, scarlet fever, meningitis, tuberculosis, parasites, chronic heart or kidney disease, even—from at least one theorist—systemic juvenile idiopathic arthritis, and rheumatic fever. Despite its similar name, rheumatic fever is not the same thing as rheumatoid arthritis. Rheumatic fever is most definitely caused by a bacterial infection, specifically a strep infection, whereas the role of infection in RA is still unclear. It follows, then, that rheumatic fever can be resolved through antibiotics, whereas RA cannot. But the illnesses share a name because the symptoms of acute rheumatic fever—fever; pain;

joint tenderness, swelling, and pain; fatigue—are very similar to those of RA, especially mid-flare. Rheumatic fever can be serious and deadly; in fact, in *Little Women*, after Beth appears to recover from scarlet fever, she gets progressively more ill with a resultant rheumatic fever and heart disease, and dies.

So neither Beth nor Mozart had rheumatoid arthritis, but I feel nonetheless knitted to both of them through our shared agony of burning through your bedsheets with fever, so inflamed that the touch of a blanket is torture. And probably, on that last November day, Schubert knew, too.

A week after Mrs. Feltman died, I received a copy of the funeral program from my mother, which included a five-by-seven portrait of Mrs. Feltman from the 1950s—black-and-white, diffuse, before I knew her. In the picture, she was handsome, elegant, the beauty queen she always loved to remind me she'd been growing up in Pennsylvania. She was a class act: I never, until the last time, saw her in anything other than a dress or a skirt and blouse. Even a hospital gown is a *gown*. But the picture didn't capture her charming dishevelment; the bodices of her tops and shirtdresses were frequently catawampus and misbuttoned, like she'd been in a hurry. She wore pearls, brooches, scarves. She wore red lipstick always and it was usually on her teeth. Her hair was tinted Lucille Ball–red, too, and she had a little cowlick, even if the front parts were well-behaved. She sang along with the melody of my playing at the top of her lungs, filling up her antique-stuffed living room with her great big sweeping dances and rollicking laugh. She was sturdy, healthy, permanent.

When I was growing up, the wall of my parents' bedroom above their bed was covered with a mosaic of family pictures, in all sizes and mismatched frames. In a tidy row right above the headboard, stretching from my mom's side to my dad's, were pictures of each of us: five-by-seven Sears portraits lined up in order of age. Because the pictures were all taken on the same day, I am fixed at a year old; Chris is forever a chubby toddler; Matthew is a clever, golden-haired kindergartner; and Erica is a bookish, shy-smiling third grader.

In this same row were pictures of my fresh-faced parents, black-and-white college class portraits. My dad looked like Buddy Holly, and my mom was easily beautiful, full-lipped, twenty, in a black turtleneck and short, early-sixties curls. Above that nice, neat row parallel to the headboard, the pictures morphed into a cloud that grew up and out. There was an imaginary line of division down the middle of the wall, to the space between my parents' pillows—my mother's relatives on this side, my father's on that side—but the line was approximate and not fussily maintained. Pictures were never taken down but new pictures were added until they stretched nearly to the ceiling and to each wall. They seemed to emanate like dreams or angels from the bed itself.

In their quantity and familiarity, they offered benediction, confirmation, approval: *This is a family*, the pictures told me as I stood on tiptoe on my parents' bed, *and this, here, is your spot in it.*

Mrs. Feltman was not *family*, not technically, but the picture from her funeral program brought to mind the gallery over my parents' bed. I decided then: I would make a gallery of my own. I e-mailed my parents to ask them for black-and-white pictures of my grandmothers, portrait shots. And I asked my mom for the picture of her, the one that hung in their bedroom, the one in the black turtleneck.

My mom e-mailed the pictures without asking any questions. But my dad could not resist. "What are you doing?" he asked.

"I'm just, I don't know, I'm making something."

"Well, if you tell me what it is, I can send you the best picture for the job," he said. Perfectly reasonable. I hesitated—would he take over, tell me how to do it, advise me to "measure twice, cut once," like so many school projects? I told him:

"I want to hang up pictures of all the women who inspired me to play piano," I said.

"Oh," he said. "That's a nice idea. I'll see what I can find."

Soon I had the pictures—my mom's picture just the way I remember it; Grandma Avery in round wire-rimmed glasses, spit curls, a bow-tied blouse, and a jaunty jacket with its collar popped up in the back; Grandma Torvik in a bob with bangs, a gauzy filet crochet dress and a string of pearls—and I laid them out across my desk along with Mrs. Feltman. But the women wouldn't cooperate. They looked off in different directions: two up and to the left, the others up and to the right. One was sepia tone, where the others were fuzzy blue-gray. So I scanned them and photoshopped them so they were all the same hue, and all facing the same way. My dad would approve of my fastidiousness.

These are the women who bequeathed to me, through blood or habit or instruction, or eventually in the form of a grand piano itself, music. In the pictures, the women are all about the same age, though they were never the same age at once, though they had never before all been in a room together.

The e-mail came just days after my dad sent me the photograph of my Grandma Avery for my wall of musical muses. The subject line was "A suggestion":

> *I had an idea last night and I strongly suggest you give it some serious consideration. I think you really ought to add a photo of Erica to your pantheon of musical muses . . . I think that she did have an influence on you in your interest in music and piano; she provided a role model for you in your earliest years, as a person you could identify with, mimic, and yes—compete with. Please think about it. Love, Dad.*

Great pianists can come from healthy competition. According to Byron Janis in his book *Chopin and Beyond: My Extraordinary Life in Music and the Paranormal*, the legendary pianist Vladimir Horowitz—"the poet," whose recording of the Schubert sonata I'd played to frayed ruin, whose first student was Byron Janis, incidentally—confessed, "I should never have become a pianist. I wanted to become a composer. My sister was a very, very good pianist and I got competing with her, and to make money I decided to become a pianist."

Maybe Nannerl played some part in cultivating Mozart's early genius.

But what I took from my father's suggestion was that piano wasn't securely in my column after all. Even this was something I borrowed from my sister. We'd performed together just once—Schubert's "Marche Militaire" for four hands, of all things—and up until I received my dad's e-mail, I had thought of it as Erica accompanying me. I thought I was the Mozart and she was the Nannerl. The truth was, I hadn't viewed my sister as real musical competition after the first year or two I took lessons, if I ever did. I was secure. I'd always been certain that the neighbors who heard piano streaming out of our screen porch knew that it was the youngest Avery who did all that playing. Besides, I had *things* my sister didn't: boxes of piano certificates and trophies, and that antique glass ornament that Mrs. Feltman—who had been Erica's teacher, too—let me pick off her Christmas tree to keep. I had the degree in music and technically the piano itself (even if it was sitting in my mom's house in Maryland).

Still, all of that seemed small and inconsequential next to the realization that in my father's eyes, my music was incidental to my sister's. All that painful cleaving and clinging I'd done to claim the piano as my own was for naught. To him, even music was more rightfully hers, yet another hand-me-down.

I was furious at him, and at myself for being so infantile, so territorial and shaken. I put the pictures in a drawer.

Maybe the memory of Ludwig's judgment seeping in under the door inspired captive Paul to upturn that box and make something of his new one-armed reality. Maybe. But I still think I know the private, if fleeting, deflation Paul must have felt when he managed to get a message out of the POW camp and, by way of his mother, to his friend, the blind composer Josef Labor. He asked his dear friend Labor to write him a one-handed concerto. A brilliant idea, something that had never been done!

Labor replied that he'd already begun just that thing! Paul's genius brother Ludwig had made the suggestion.

CADENZA /
IMPROVISATION

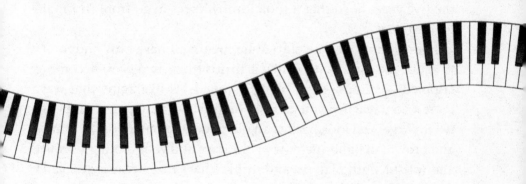

Are these books my books? Is this foot my foot? Is this body
my body? Is this sensation my sensation?
                                    —*Ludwig Wittgenstein,*
                                    Philosophical Investigations

I was at Target when I decided to get my knees replaced. I
was looking through the greeting cards while a little boy,
kindergarten-age, tugged at his distracted mom's purse. "Mom.
Mommy. Mom! MOM!" he screamed. "Mommy. Why does she look
like that? Why, Mom? Mom!" His mom was either well practiced
at ignoring him or truly absorbed by the push-button "sounds-of-
ocean-solitude" display in front of her. "Mommy! Why. Do. Her.
Legs. Look. Like. That?" he persisted, brow furrowed, eyes glued to

my legs, which were stuck in a bent position, lacking about thirty degrees of extension so that I looked—always—as though I were about to hop. A billion times over this had happened, and I'd always tried to be game about it. So I looked at him, intending to smile beatifically in his direction, expecting him to hide apologetically behind his mother's legs, expecting her to mouth "I'm so sorry" silently and steer him by his little shoulders to another aisle.

You can't blame the kid, really. He was only stating what I really should have been screaming at my own image in the mirror during the five years or so that it took for my knees to go from "normal" to, well, *that*.

I don't know when it started happening. I have only endpoints to gauge the speed with which arthritis froze my knees. Becoming crippled—as opposed to being maimed—is like aging that way: there's no day when you go from being six to being seven to being twenty-five. You look back at an old photo of yourself at six, sturdy and brown, in hand-me-down corduroys and your brother's T-shirt and waist-length pigtails, and think, That's me? Because you can't reconcile it with the angular, pale person you've become.

When I graduated from high school in 1995—I know for sure— my knees were fine (oh, that favorite word of mine) because I have pictures of my legs, sheathed in opaque white tights, sticking out straight and long from under the hem of that unfortunate baby-doll dress I thought made me look Grunge in a Good Way.

I have a picture of me in jeans and a flannel shirt of my dad's, comically wielding an ax in Flagstaff, Arizona, circa 1997 or 1998, and in it my legs are almost straight—but it's hard to tell if the slight bend in them is just the stance I chose as I hefted the ax over my shoulder or if it's a stance my body imposed on me.

There are pictures of me from the Best Summer Ever, the fabled summer of 2000, that beautiful, ideal summer when Beth and Deanna and I hit the road for sunny California a week or so after collecting our bachelor's degrees in music. On a gray day, we rented cruiser bicycles at Venice Beach and there is a picture of me, in capri-length jeans and a lightweight black sweater, straddling the gigantic-looking yellow cruiser, at a full stop, tipped slightly off-balance with one foot on the ground, leg bent. What I know about this picture is that the bike was actually the right size for me, the *real* me anyway, the me who was a few inches taller, but that the leg length I'd started losing made it hard to reach the pedals, hard to plant my feet when stopped. My locked-up knees made it painful to pedal the bike, and I remember wishing the activity—oh, the day, the trip!—would be over soon. But I smiled hugely for the camera, because I knew that this was a *fun* thing we were doing and if I said anything it would make my two dear friends feel bad.

The sky was gray the whole time we were in California. We went to the beach anyway. I love the ocean, but I couldn't get down onto a beach towel on the sand like my friends could because I wouldn't be able to get up. These two beautiful girls—in their bikinis—set to work industriously and unself-consciously digging a hole in the sand two feet deep. When they were done, I could lie on my towel with them and then, putting my legs into the cool, damp hole, I would find myself sitting on a sandy ledge. From there, they stood on the edges of my hole and pulled me up and out by my hands.

We headed into the water—water, where I am spaghetti, where I am finally on equal footing, where my disability is nearly invisible. I am a good swimmer and the ocean is handicap-accessible, with its sloping ramp. Easy in, easy out. We rode the waves together, three heads bobbing happily on the surface. But then a huge wave came and we were all tumbled onto the sandy floor. I was upside down and then flat on the shore, unable to get up without my sand shelf. And there was another wave coming. "Help me," I yelled. They had righted themselves and they came to me. The wave was looming. We three struggled awkwardly, my two friends trying to help me up by my hands because they knew that was the graceful way I preferred. Finally the wave was too close. "Permission to lift you up gimp-style?" Beth hollered. "YES!" And so they lifted me from under my arms, in the way that always made me feel the most like cargo, like an invalid.

Later in the week I went swimming alone in the gray Pacific and I swam into a riptide and a freckled, unattractive lifeguard—not at all the way I'd pictured it—dragged me back to shore without saying anything.

And then there is a whole series of pictures from 2003 in which, despite the long, wine-colored crepe dress I'm wearing to mask it, I look like I'm about to fall into an invisible bench, the bend of my knees is so pronounced. In all of these pictures I am several inches shorter than both my mother and my sister—which isn't strange except that when I'd left home after high school, I was about five eight, my mother about five seven, and my sister about five six.

I'd always been tall. Not freakishly so, just a bit taller than average. Tall enough to be in the back row of class photographs and to be asked to reach things on high shelves for teachers and other kids. But looking back on my college and graduate school years, between 1995 and 2003, I realize that no one commented on my height, no one asked me to reach anything, I was placed in the middle or—horror!—front rows of group photos.

The bend in my knees had gradually stolen about four inches of my height from me—such that after the divorce, my mom's new boyfriend called me a "delightful little person" after meeting me, a description that sounded wrong to my mom (and later, to me). Delightful, sure, but *little*?

Because my knees had gone and gotten stuck in this position, unable to straighten and with only the slightest amount of flexion, I adopted a weird gait.

Try it: Sit in a chair with your feet flat on the ground in front of you and your knees bent to a handsome 90 degrees. Now slide your feet away from you until the bend in your knees is slightly more obtuse, about 110 degrees if you can eyeball it or if you happen to have a goniometer or protractor on hand. You must keep your knees bent at this angle, no matter what. You may want to duct-tape a medium-size red rubber playground ball to the back of each knee.

Now. Stand up. No arms on your chair? Sucks to be you. Rock back and forth until you've gained enough momentum to propel yourself forward and out of the chair and hope you don't overshoot and fall forward, because getting up from the floor is even harder.

Once you're up, take a few steps, but you mustn't bend or straighten your legs. Your feet must stay flat on the ground. You'll kind of shuffle to where you're going. A boy you become friends with later will say, "When I first saw you walk it looked like both of your legs were asleep." In comparison to the other things you've heard, this comment will seem gentle, artful even, and you'll think for a moment, does he *like* me like me?

If there are stairs between you and where you're headed, you'll have to walk down them sideways, step by plodding step.

People ask me now if my knees were painful when they were like that. I don't know. I guess so. Pain is like noise. When it's persistent, your glorious, efficient body tunes it out. No sense paying attention to a constant car alarm.

What was painful during those years was going to parties. Trying to score the seat on the couch next to the arm so I'd have something to use to pull myself out of its depths. Going to the bathroom to find a low toilet seat and the sink countertop too far away to lean on to get up. Learning to pee standing up and hoping no one found out.

What hurt badly was meeting a sweet-faced boy at a dinner party with a fucked-up hand that looked like a flipper, short and weak from some childhood illness, and thinking we made a perfect pair. Going on a walk in the hot August night with him, having him say, "Hold on. Wait. You really walk like that? I thought you were goofing."

What hurt, perhaps more than anything, was climbing the stairs to my brother's town house for that first Christmas celebration as a broken family and having my suddenly single father open the door and—before the "hello there, Punkin'" and the beard-scratchy kiss on the cheek I was desperate for—scan my lower body and say, "Ugh. Is that all your knees bend these days?" I'll remember that forever, but I don't recall if I got the kiss or the "Punkin'."

So you can't blame the little boy in Target for his question. Why *did* my legs look like that? The more I thought about it, the more my internal monologue took on the cranky timbre of a preschooler. *Why?* Why had I told myself, over and over, that everyone had something to deal with, some cross to bear? Why had Ryan and I filled pages of a sketchbook with dresses we imagined would be perfect for someone like me, stiff, armor-like Schiaparelli-inspired dresses that belled dramatically between waist and shin to cover up the sins of my legs? Why hadn't I called an orthopedic surgeon and looked into knee replacement?

Because I was twenty-six. At twenty-six, Schubert became ill with whatever killed him. But I was not Schubert, and I was not dying. I had life ahead. At twenty-six, the idea of trading in my original parts, no matter how faulty they were, felt something like defeat. Joint replacements have come a long way in the last twenty years. But still, under ideal circumstances the new joint should outlive its bearer. Go ahead and give seventy-five-year-old Grandma a new hip. Grandma, go to town. You'll die before the pit-resistant titanium wears out, before the joint starts loosening.

But if I started this process now, this swapping out of eroded, misshapen joints for smooth titanium ones, how many times would I have to repeat it? My dreamboat knee-and-hip guy, Dr. Armstrong, gives my new knees a generous twenty-year life expectancy, and since I plan on living at least long enough to see all my friends get arthritis—ha!—I can expect to replace them two or three more times before I die, each "revision" (how delicious that those operations are called that!) more difficult than the last, each time the wafer-like patella getting thinner and thinner.

In order to want to get rid of a body part, you have to have some measure of hate—disavowal, at least—for that part. And it's not hard to find someone who claims to hate part of her body; it's not even hard to find someone who has gone so far as to swap it out, a snub nose for a generically straight one, small breasts for large.

But if you hate your body part—your nose, say—because of its shape, because of its fixed wrongness, because you just don't feel it represents you, your hatred is contained. If you hate your body part because it was decimated by a disease that is still in you and always will be, and that is voracious in its appetite for organs and systems—then you are opening the floodgates for a self-hatred with no end.

If I were to hate my legs, what would stop me from hating my hands, my feet, my elbows, myself? I refuse.

At times, I admire my body. My rotator cuff tear did exactly what the therapist said it might: it healed itself. Years later, when I looked into shoulder replacement, sure that the doctor would once again tell me my bone was so soft and unhealthy as to be unfixable, the MRI showed no evidence of Radu's work. "Are you sure you tore your rotator cuff?" this surgeon asked. I am sure. I have my memory and, better yet, I have my mother's notes with the arthroscopic surgeon's report.

My body has been as kind as it can be. It has timed its destruction cleverly and elegantly. I didn't tear the extensor tendon in both hands at once. Much in the same way my hands were planning their coup while I lavished attention on my shoulder, my knees were silently rebelling while I coddled my hand. But they were polite about it. They have good timing.

My knees were not always my biggest problem. For years they'd clicked when I bent them; they flexed and extended not fluidly but like a ratchet or the door of a car, falling into notches of open- or closed-ness. My body has been graceful in this way, if no other: It has never given me more than one arthritis crisis at a time. If there is one rule my body has taught me and then followed, it is this: There is only room for so much pain at once.

My knees cooperated when I needed to attend to the clutch of pain in my abdomen when I lost my appendix. My knees hauled my body to all those hand therapy appointments, and my knees would wait to fail me until I had hands that could minister to them, that could deftly rub vitamin E into my knee scars to keep them pliable.

My body has a good timing. It is teaching me how to live in it as gently as it can. So it's hard to want to take a knife to it.

I've had this disease since I was twelve, an age when I was still awed by the world, OK with confusion, game for anything, elastic.

Awesome, whatever. Here's the part when they introduce letters to math class. No point resisting, I'll get the hang of it. Here's the part where I get a "chronic" illness called "early-onset polyarticular rheumatoid arthritis." Sure. Cool. I just hope I get a boyfriend. Continue doodling Batman logo on canvas Keds.

And although the words *joint replacement* had been invoked long ago, way back at the beginning of my relationship with arthritis, hospitals, blood draws, and physical therapy, soberly invoked by a Dr. White as an "inevitability," more to my mom than to me, I hadn't ever considered it.

Instead, I'd devoted an awful lot of energy to accepting my deformity. To developing a kind of grace. To masking it. To learning how to pose in pictures so that I didn't look too weird. To developing responses to questions from strangers. Ballsy questions like, "Why are *you* taking the elevator to the second floor?"

To the boy who asked if I was a gimp, I replied: "Why are you acting like an asshole? *Are* you an asshole?"

That kind of response was rare. Mostly, I insisted on viewing these occasions as chances to educate! To inform! To reach out! The irritated hotshot professor who asked me why I was riding the elevator to the second floor when she had to get to the sixth and was late already found herself with a sassy TA, a chipper elevator companion to the sixth floor who spewed a measured, minute-long speech that went something like this: "I have rheumatoid arthritis, a chronic autoimmune disease that causes all the joints in my body to become inflamed, painful, and deformed. It also causes intermittent, low-grade fevers and fatigue. I may look healthy to you, but I have difficulty climbing stairs and that is why I chose to take the elevator today."

Dumb, well-behaved girl. What I'd gone and done, early on, was develop a Great Attitude about my arthritis. Doctors, teachers, guidance counselors would comment on it, musing about how I never seemed to wonder "Why me?" And so I learned, early on, that this was prized above all. I was told—though never overtly, of course: Don't complain; don't be angry. Don't be one of those bitter disabled people who victimize themselves and blame the world (this is one option from the same limited menu that includes the supercrip). Thing is, a good dose of Why me?—or, rather, What the hell? Why *anyone?*—is a good thing. A Great Attitude can be taken too far; dealing with what life hands you, rolling with the punches, being a trouper can mean not calling the doctor when you should.

And my Great Attitude has meant smiling when insult is added to injury.

I was tired of being a curiosity and a cause.

And up to the day when that little boy in Target accosted his mother with his insistent questioning, I'd reserved my bitchy responses for adults who ought to know better than to call a girl a gimp when she's minding her own business. Up until then, I'd been gentle with children, trying to smile at them when they stared. But not this day. I looked at the little boy and he didn't look away. He stared. He said, again, fiercely, "Why do her legs look like that? MOM." I didn't smile benevolently. I hissed at him, "Because I was rude and I stared at strangers when I was little."

And that shut him up. His mother glared at me and then she piloted him to another aisle. And I was instantly transformed into the villain: in this case, the scary lady, myopic, always with a dowager's hump, frequently wielding a cane, usually wearing a moth-eaten cardigan, living in the creepy Victorian house on the corner that kids dare one another to approach. This is me, played by Cloris Leachman in a character role.

I was freakish, objectionable, disfigured, broken, and I'd refused to be a saint: Bad Disabled Person. I gave disabled people a bad name. I was mean and scary. Shit. I had two cats and a hundred cardigans. I was one boarded-up-Victorian-house-on-the-corner from being *that* lady.

I didn't want to be that—I didn't want to be any of these things anymore. I wanted another choice: I wanted to be invisible, anonymous, unremarkable. More truthfully, I wanted to be the one to decide what was visible about me. I wanted to decide when to be anonymous, when to be weird. I wanted to be remarkable for my always bold, frequently dubious fashion choices. I wanted to have control. I wanted people to ask me where I got my shoes. I wanted people to stop me and say, "Excuse me, sorry, I hate to bother you, but who cuts your hair?" I wanted people to stare at me because I was rocking Material Girl fingerless lace gloves with an Ethel Mertz shirtdress, not because my body was strange.

I wanted, more than anything, to be happy. I didn't want to live a plan B, always comparing myself to some seven-year-old piano whiz.

I'd realized that piano was not going to be the thing that was most extraordinary about me. But in Target, I decided: neither would it be arthritis. I'd be *something else.*

Movement IV

TEMPO COMODO / AT A COMFORTABLE TEMPO

If someone has a pain in his hand, then the hand does not say so (unless it writes it) and one does not comfort the hand, but the sufferer: One looks into his eyes.

—Ludwig Wittgenstein,
Philosophical Investigations

Chapter 10

That day in Target, I was on my way home to Fred.

I'd met Fred at Starbucks. One day, from my regular perch on the purple velvet couch, drinking the coffee the baristas hadn't let me pay for, I saw a new employee with ears that stuck out like jug handles. He strode over to the counter with the half-and-half, wiped it down with his towel, sighed heavily, and snapped the towel over his shoulder.

The story is, I knew then that I would marry him. The story is, I was attracted to his vulnerable ears, which suggested that he'd been picked on in elementary school and therefore likely had depth of soul, and his no-nonsense work ethic, which presented a challenge.

By that time, I'd learned from my mother that if you're going to feel lonely, it's better to be alone. To be lonely with someone else is unbearable. I believed it had been decided for me that I'd be—permanently, fundamentally—lonely, and so I'd decided to be alone. What I'd learned from Ryan was that the things my defiant body wouldn't, or couldn't, do were more compelling than anything I could do.

But there must have been some quiet, mutinous, mutated part of me—some part as tiny as a gene or as invisible as my immune system itself—that had refused to learn that lesson. Some stubborn, stupid part that believed my body was a contender, that it could endure another bout. Thank God for that stubborn, stupid part that made it impossible to resist the challenge presented by this new barista.

He was the new assistant manager, sent there to cut down on the shrinkage, the corporate loss (my free coffee). "He's not that friendly," another barista said. "Good luck with that." Fred was a challenge I had been preparing for since I was little: weaseling reluctant smiles out of men with work on their minds.

I went there every day. If Fred was one of two people manning the cash register, I would let other people go in line until I was sure I'd end up in his line. I'd babble nervously: "So I was thinking I'd get my regular iced grande nonfat mocha but I'm thinking maybe I want to try something else I like the flavor of coffee I'm not one of those people who hate coffee and I don't like the froufrou Frappuccino thing and I also don't like umbrella drinks or anything like that I'm more of a beer girl do you have any coffee drinks that taste like Guinness? But anyway I do like caramel so I was thinking of the macchiato but I don't want to get something that's so sweet it doesn't taste like coffee anymore know what I mean and is macchiato even a real word?"

Barely smiling, Fred would organize the Sharpies in a neat row on the counter until I was done. "Name, please?"

One day, though, I noticed that he'd written my name on the cup before I told him. Progress.

And then he was taking his ten-minute cigarette breaks with me. "What do you like to do when you're not at work?" I asked.

"Play video games."

"That doesn't sound like something we can do together."

"It's not."

But he kept taking his ten-minute breaks with me, his Starbucks-issue white digital timer on the table in front of us, ticking down the seconds.

Another time, as if picking up the earlier conversation:

"I like to play pool," he said.

"Me, too."

"Let's go play pool sometime."

Beeeep!

I pursued him in ten-minute segments. "It's 'Decker,' right, Fred?" I said, my address book open in front of me on the table.

"Yeah."

"Well, I've got some room here in the D's."

"What?" He exhaled a breath of smoke, his lips turning up in a faint smile. There it was.

"I said, I've got vacancies in the D's."

"Are you asking me for my phone number?"

"I am, and you're not making it easy."

"Well, why don't I get yours, too, and when I get back from my trip to Idaho, we can go play pool," he said, pulling out his flip phone and entering my number.

Beeeeep!

We went to play pool on a Thursday and I wore the strangest outfit I could come up with. "You were wearing a skirt *and* pants," Fred says now. "That was weird."

"And a ruffle-front Western shirt," I say, making sure we both know the story by heart.

"I know. I looked down your shirt when we were playing pool," Fred reminds me.

I'd worn a strange outfit to give Fred every chance to reject me immediately. Better that he decide I was too strange right off the bat, before he got a chance to see my body. My linen pants and silk wrap skirt and Western shirt and cat-eye glasses were my armor.

His truck was immaculate, but I spotted a stray french fry between the seat and the console and I knew that he was not perfect and that he'd cleaned the car just for me.

As we circled the pool table, chalking our cues, we hardly looked at each other. We looked instead at the green felt field, the tally of balls. We gave each other every reason to put an end to this before it got started. "I'm a Republican," Fred said.

"I'm going to adopt my children," I said. He stood up and looked at me for a long time, chewing his lip, and after a few more dates I would understand why.

"Don't ever ask me to quit smoking."

"Don't ever ask me to get rid of my cat."

"Why would I do that?"

"You haven't met my cat."

"Do you have many friends?" Fred asked.

"I sabotage friendships," I said.

The next day, I worried when Fred hadn't called. I got out my colored pencils and drew a comic strip: In the first panel I drew me, blathering proudly about sabotaging friendships. In the second panel, a Tinker Bell–size version of me floats down and tells me to shut up. "What she means to say, Fred, is that she hopes to see you again and get to know you better." I put the comic strip on his windshield at work. He called.

Later, I learned that the sadness I detected in Fred had less to do with his ears—though they'd been an issue, too—and more to do with a hard-edged, hard-living, absent father and a baby that Fred and his high school girlfriend had given up for adoption. I sewed a pocket onto the front of his barista aprons for all of his Sharpies. When I folded his freshly washed green aprons, I stacked them in his bureau drawer next to the comic strip.

When I slept at Fred's house, in his super-cold, air-conditioned room, on his blue sheets, we would try to have sex like I'd tried so many times before. But when the rising panic came and the hips said no, Fred would lie beside me and say, "It's OK. Don't worry. I don't care if we never do it."

I know it sounds like some kind of Princess and the Pea riddle, but that's all the more it took. It would be a year before I would have the first of my joint replacements, which would restore my height and mobility and make this project of living in my body ever so much more bearable. When I met Fred, I was arguably at my lowest physical point: slow, lurching, shrunken. But my body was incidental to him, a perk that came along with my brain and my heart, not the whole point, and so I was finally able to be a body with him. It was a paradox, and like all paradoxes, really that simple. He assured me he didn't care if we never had sex, and so we had sex.

One Saturday afternoon, before he went to work, it happened. It hurt, but not any more than I'd heard it hurt for anyone else and, best of all, not in an arthritic way.

Afterward, I called my sister to tell her. And then I went to the Scottsdale Museum of Contemporary Art and walked the echoing halls, sure that the other people would be—should be—able to see that something was different about me. Could they tell I'd had sex? If people stared at my lurching limp, I didn't know it. I believed they were staring at me because I was in love; I glowed like a lamp. In the gift shop, I bought a blue stained-glass pendant on a silver chain and in the car in the parking garage I pulled it out of its box and clasped it around my neck. It hung there between my cared-for breasts, the silver chain snaking over my clavicle, rattling with crepitus as I managed the clasp. And I loved the way it looked on me.

We joke about that day because Fred is now a locksmith and he is in the business of getting into things other people cannot get into.

Fred took me home to meet his mom, his sister, and his two little nieces, Emily and Stephanie. I wore a simple sleeveless black-and-white dress, no armor. I put my hair up in short little knots I hoped would impress his hairdresser mother. In the car in the driveway, he took off his baseball cap and rubbed his head. "Look," he said. "I don't know what they're going to say to you. I apologize ahead of time if they say something lame."

They never did.

His mom told me later that when he first told them about me, he gushed about the strange way I dressed. "Every day I see her," he said, "she looks different. And it's like getting to unwrap a Christmas present."

When I introduced Fred to my dad, the first thing my dad did was mock-interrogate Fred about one of Fred's photographs that I'd shown him, an otherworldly close-up of a VORTAC site near the airport. "How many fences did you jump to get onto federal property to take that one?" he growled, smiling. It was a good sign that he was teasing Fred this way, and that Fred could take it. Double-swoon.

When I got home from Target that afternoon in 2004, to the house that Fred and I had started renting together the summer before, just six months after the pool hall and five months after I bought the blue "lamp" necklace, I made an announcement. "I want to get my knees replaced," I said.

"Thank God," Fred said. "It's about time."

Early on the morning of April 8, 2004—what would have been my Grandma Torvik's ninety-eighth birthday and also, in 1810, the date that a thirteen-year-old Schubert began his piano Fantasie for four hands, perhaps his earliest work—I took a shower and used the special iodine sponge the hospital had given me. I scrubbed my bent knees. In the kitchen, I stood against the wall and Fred marked with pencil how tall I wasn't. He wrote the date next to it. Then he and my mom and I packed into the car in the still dark and drove the deserted freeways to the hospital. In the waiting room, my mom said, "Let me take a 'before' picture."

"They're *all* 'before' pictures," I said.

Then I was taken back to the waiting room and wrapped in toasted blankets while I waited for the anesthesiologist, a doctor who explained to me that his name was difficult to pronounce and best remembered as "Dr. Chocolate Bar." Fred and my mom came back and they each held one of my hands.

They sent Fred and my mom back out to the waiting room. They took my glasses and put them in the "patient belongings" bag under my gurney. The nurse buzzed out of my screened-off partition in the pre-op holding area and didn't pull the curtain all the way closed behind her and I could see, across the aisle in the other bay, the blurry figure of an old man waiting for his own surgery. And he was blurry because my glasses were in a bag beneath me and because there were tears swelling in the corners of my eyes. No matter what, when I woke up I would never be the same, because once you take out someone's knees and put hardware in there, you can never go back. Fred and my mom had gone as far as they could. The rest was something I had to do alone.

I was a child then: aware but unashamed that the old man across the way was seeing me cry, waiting for the doctor to come and fix me. And I was, suddenly, adult. I thought, "This is what dying will feel like." Other people can tend to you, minister to you, care for you, but at some point they have to turn around and go back to the magazines and the coffee and the ticking clock. Healthy, living bodies, with their hugs and their sex and their handshakes, are so good at creating the illusion that you can commune, collude, or combine with someone else. But a sick, injured, or dying body reveals the truth: we are totally alone in these shuttles. Everyone else is back there, on the ground. If we're lucky, we come back in one piece. But we're never the same after where we've been. Illness is, indeed, a place.

Dr. Armstrong, raiser of llamas, wearer of blue lab coat and fetching ties, Clint Eastwood lookalike, made a match set of parallel incisions on my legs. Each was about six inches long, one down the front of my left knee and one on the right. One leg after the other, he moved the patella aside. He removed the crunchy, nasty surface of the end of each femur and fit a metal covering over it. Then he did the same thing to the top of each tibia, sanding it down to a nice, flat unarthritic surface and then boring a hole into the center of the bone, planting a metal stem in there. He built two little sandwiches then, one in each knee, following this recipe: a slab of metal on the tibia, then a plastic shock-absorbing disk, then the top part of the joint. Then he put new backs on the patellae and returned them to the front of each knee and then he sewed me up.

I woke up in post-op with two long, straight legs, heavily bandaged and cloaked in stark white support hose designed to prevent blood clots. I spent six days in the hospital, up several times each day for physical therapy—a few steps at first, just from the bed to the chair on Day One, but then down the hall, then doing laps around the nurses' station, pushing my walker ahead of me. My lower back was a riot of muscle pain because my bent-knee position had caused me to have a swayback posture in order to look anyone in the eye, and so for years I hadn't really stood up straight.

April 10: up to walk A.M.—*down hall and back. Up to walk* P.M.— *2x around circuit. 500 feet. & able to stand up so as tall as me.*

Whenever I wasn't walking, and at night, exhausted, I was lulled to sleep by the rocking motion of the continuous passive motion machines, brilliant trough-like devices, padded with sheepskin. My legs were strapped into the machines that would gently coax my knees through a totally respectable range of motion, from perfectly straight (oh, zero degrees where have you been all my life) to 45, then to 90, then 100. "What a trouper," the nurses said as I begged them to crank it up—can't we go to 110?

The nurses told me that some people hate those machines, but I loved them—I loved the gentle, repetitive motion. I loved the hushing white noise, the metronome for my dreams. I loved looking down to catch a glimpse of my legs moving painlessly (to be fair, I was still plugged into a powerful epidural) doing what they were supposed to do. I liked the look of TED hose because I think opaque tights are a very smart, mod, put-together look that ought to make a comeback.

One morning, about halfway through my hospital stay, a new therapist was sent to work with me. Virginia was old and fat and gray-skinned, with the puckered lip wrinkles of an ex-smoker. I was already seated in the blue plastic hospital recliner when she got to my room, ready to practice bending and straightening and then standing and walking. We started through the exercises but— perhaps because I'd overdone it the day before—I was struggling. "This is hard," I said. I did not say "I can't," though I was doubtful that I'd make it through the twelve reps. I tried. My leg was shuddering. I didn't think I could do it again. Fred was there, and my mother, too. Witnesses. I did not say—ever—"I can't."

"You're a wreck," Virginia said.

Violins in my ears.

I'd walked several times that morning, with my mother or Fred as my escort, before Virginia had even shown up. I'd been showing off to Fred how I could do precisely this exercise. I was no wreck.

This was Ms. Babuska all over again. But this time, I did not—I could not—get up and leave the room. This time, I felt a voice— mine?—bubble up from my belly.

"I know I'm not a wreck," I said softly. "I've done every exercise I've been assigned twice as well and three times as often as requested. So I don't care what you called me. But what really scares me"—*the crescendo begins, a far-off rumbling of the timpani*—"is that some of the people you work with—frustrated people, people in pain, old people"—*trumpets!*—"might actually believe you. You're out of line, you're full of shit, you're not allowed in my room anymore"—*Cymbals! Cymbals! Cymbals!*—"You have no idea; you should be disbarred or excommunicated or whatever they do with people like you; they ought to take away your goniometer and your TheraBands; you're an insult to your profession."

And then I finished with my best line, which I delivered through clenched teeth like the Terminator as I stuck my foot into her lap, my leg perfectly straight: "Measure. My. Flexion."

They didn't send Virginia to me anymore. Well trained by my mother, I recorded the details of the incident. I filed a letter of complaint with the hospital, and the administrator came to personally apologize. I received a letter of apology on hospital letterhead and I filed it in the notebook alongside all the letters and notes my mom had kept.

But they wouldn't let me leave the hospital till I'd had a bowel movement. And it wasn't happening. The night nurse, a woman, kept threatening a suppository and I was looking for any way— preferably a mouth-and-digestive-tract way—to avoid it. "If it hasn't happened when I'm back on tomorrow night," she said, "we're going there."

My day nurse was a hot male nurse named Rod, which felt to me like a really hot-male-nurse-y name. And up until the bowel movement ultimatum, visits from Hot Rod had been a real treat. But the pressure was on now. "I don't want a suppository," I told him.

"How about some hot prune juice?" he asked.

"OK."

He brought me a Styrofoam cup with a straw. "Just sip it," he said, leaving.

Another boy, a nurse's aid, came in to empty my Foley catheter. I felt like I should make conversation with him, if he was dealing with my urine.

"Do you like your job?" I asked him.

"Yeah, it's better than construction, which is what I used to do," he said, busy with the bag of my piss.

"I think I'm going to throw up," I said.

He gave me a bedpan and I threw up half a cup of warm prune juice and that morning's pain pill.

He left with all my fluids.

I rang the call button. "I have to go to the bathroom," I said. Rod showed up.

He helped me out of bed and into the bathroom. He positioned me on the toilet and closed the door and told me he'd be right outside.

The prune juice, that which I hadn't puked up, worked. It worked too well. "Rod?" I called through the door. "I need help in here."

He came in and wiped me clean and I tried to float out of my body so I wouldn't be part of this scene where a muscular, sporty, adventure-type guy, a guy I suspected would never approach my kind in a bar, was wiping my ass.

"That'll do it," he said. "You get to go home now. Congratulations."

Until I was discharged, I tried to scan Rod's broad face for some indication that he now thought of me not as a girl but as an invalid on a toilet, but it wasn't there. "Hair looks cute," he said when I braided it to go home. When I went back to the hospital months later to thank him (and to show off my perfectly straight legs, hoping I'd also run into Virginia), I learned he'd taken a job as a helicopter nurse in Alaska.

I'd arranged for six weeks of help for the knee surgery. Though I was sure Fred could take care of me, I didn't want to exhaust him. I was hoping he'd marry me, and I worried that if he got too much thin before thick, too much bad before good, he wouldn't want to. My mother was there for the operation and for four weeks after, my sister came for a week, and my dad came for a week after that. But I recovered more quickly than I'd expected. I was driving after two weeks, and so by the time my sister showed up, I was stir-crazy and bored.

Here she was. A Brooklynite in the sun-drenched, car-crazy red state she wasn't fond of, to take care of me. I had her all to myself. We hit the thrift stores, one of the things we both liked to do. She looked for natural fibers, neutrals, skirts for contra dancing. I looked for flashy vintage. We separated as soon as we were inside the door. We'd occasionally cross paths in the store, but we reunited only when it was time to leave.

One morning, I buzzed around the house straightening up. I did the laundry, washing a whole load of Fred's green Starbucks aprons. I cleaned out the cereal bowl he'd left in the sink before going to work. I thought she'd be amazed at how super a crip I was being, that she'd praise me. She watched me and when we got in the car to go to another thrift store, she said softly, "I don't get it. What are you getting out of this relationship?"

I shrugged off the conversation. "He does housework, too," I said.

How could I explain to my fiercely independent, feminist sister (whose disapproval, even minute, sends me wobbling like a Weeble) that perhaps because I've been tended to and done-for more than

I ought to have been, I want almost nothing more than to care for a home and the people inside of it? I want to be upright, speedy, wheeling, capable, a contributor. That those times when I sat in a chair with a magazine and my feet up while Fred vacuumed felt too much like all those other long days in chairs, stiff or sore or bandaged or drugged and unable to help. In these intervals when I can pull my weight, I must. And I want to. Because I will be sidelined again and again. Recitative, recitative, aria. I must have enough caregiving credits in the bank to get me through those times when I must be cared for. It's not Fred or any other man who says this is so—it's me.

I'd progressed through everything they'd asked of me at physical therapy. I did the bike and the treadmill and the leg lifts. I'd even learned how to get down onto the blue gym mats on the floor and then up again, something I hadn't done in years and something I wanted to be able to do to play with Fred's two nieces—or, dare I dream, my own children.

"Erica," I said. "There's something I need to do. Stairs." Our house didn't have stairs. Most buildings in Arizona don't have stairs. Buildings are low and, as my mom commented when she first brought me out for a college visit, "the sky is such a part of the landscape here!" So instead of trolling yet another Goodwill, we drove to every shopping center and office complex we could find that had stairs. My sister didn't say anything about how much gas we were using or our carbon footprint. As we climbed a brick staircase, she helped me with my form. "That looks good," she said. "Good job."

When I got to the top and I turned around, dizzy with exhaustion and sudden fear—where was the railing? Could I stop my feet if they got started? Would I fall? How do I get down?—I was overwhelmed with gratitude to see my sister there with me. She had always been with me, even if it seemed like we had nothing in common, even if our phone calls had become terse and infrequent. Here she was, having taken time off work to care for me. To babysit me, without payment of any kind. She was not my competitor, as much as my dad had tried to create that tension between us.

My family had always been there, all of them wishing they *could* go ahead of me, pioneer this path for me, help me with this, do it for me, make it easier. There simply hadn't ever been anything they could do. I was alone in this and I always would be. But I was not—I will never be—lonely in this. Not with the family I have. Not with Fred.

In fact, when I retell my memory of the *Challenger's* exploding that Tuesday morning thirty years earlier when, as I remember it, I was home alone, my dad balks. "You weren't alone!" he says. "I was there, and I can prove it." He produces his journal from January 28, 1986. In detail, he has recorded the notes he prepared for his bureau chief for his absence, the meetings at work that he shuffled to be there with me. In all of this—that ordinary sick day and the many extraordinary sick days that came after—I was never as alone as I thought I was.

The first part of your life, the first half, maybe, is supposed to be ascension. You're supposed to get steadily bigger, stronger, smarter, better at stuff before you start going down. That's the promise, anyway. The myth. My heartbreak is that I started downhill before I'd had a chance to get all the way up. My challenge has been a life of going in contrary motion: trying to go up while my body goes down.

Going down, there is gravity to contend with. Going down is so much harder than going up. Going down, it is crucial to have someone there ahead of you.

"Good form," my sister said as I panted over the railing. "Keep it up." And we started down together.

Chapter 11

The Monday after Christmas 2004, my knee scars faded to white and my legs working like new, I came home from work eager to try out the bread machine we'd received.

"I think we should take down the Christmas tree first," Fred said.

"No." I pulled off my shoes with the toe of the opposite foot, kicked them toward the wall where my new height of five eight was marked in pencil.

"I really do. I think we need to take down the Christmas tree." He took my bag from my shoulder and put it down.

"You're crazy. Trees stay up till New Year's. That's how it works. It's fake anyway; it's not like it's going to die." I was always having to teach him how to play house.

"Well then you need to look at it." All the lights were on.

"Why?"

"Look at the tree," he said. Our cats, Fitzgerald and Target, mewled at our feet, sniffing my shoes.

There was a little velvet box pushed into the branches of our fake tree, not far from the ornament Mrs. Feltman had given me.

"Oh," I said. "Is this *that* moment?"

"It is."

I took off Grandma Avery's Black Hills Gold ring and slid on the one Fred gave me. It went on easily. When Fred looks at me, I know he sees the version of me that I see. He is the only person in the world who does.

We went to Petco and bought cat food, and then we went to Starbucks to celebrate and it was perfect. Romance: someone to do all the long-day Monday evening errands with. A lifetime of extraordinary ordinary.

Aria: That spring, my stomach started hurting. I knew it couldn't be my long-gone appendix. It hurt just below my rib cage like a bruise. I was compelled to reach inside my button-down shirt and press on it, like Napoleon.

"Gallstones," the doctor said.

The Internet told me about the four F's of gallstones: They tended to affect people who were forty, fair, fat, and flatulent. I was twenty-eight and fair. I didn't think I was fat, but I've never been able to tell. I didn't think I was any more flatulent than anyone else.

Nonetheless, I was not surprised that I had gallstones. I'd long thought that if there was something weird a body could do, mine would do it. I've never had any good reason to be comforted by statistics. What are the chances, indeed.

My gallbladder was removed and I was brought home and installed on the couch before 10:00 A.M. I spent a few days on the couch, with Fred bringing me Tang and pain medicine. My cranky black cat, Fitzgerald, slept on my feet and nipped at Fred's hand when he came to pet me. One day, as I lay there tucked in tightly, the Steri-Strips still holding my incisions shut, I stretched my hands in a lazy Percocet yawn and my fourth finger and pinkie on my left hand dropped. It didn't hurt. I got up and got myself an ice pack, displacing Fitzgerald. I knew I'd be seeing Dr. Sheridan again, but I didn't want to overwhelm Fred. I hid the ice pack under the Mexican blanket. He found it when he came to check on me.

"What's this?" he asked.

Busted. "Oh, my hand hurts."

"Like, something big or small?"

I couldn't lie to him. "Big," I said.

I want to protect Fred. I know what it's like to be in my body. When something snaps or aches, I may not know what's going on, but I know exactly where the ache falls on the pain scale. I know—I am starting to know—an ache from a sting from a rupture versus a flare. My body and I have a private language. Sorry, Ludwig. If I say I'm fine and I'm not, I at least know I'm lying. I don't truly have control, but I have more than Fred does. All he knows is that one day something works and the next it doesn't. He doesn't know if I'm lying when I say, "I'm fine, I'm fine." It's no wonder my mother kept all those notebooks, tracking every bit of data and detail. It was the only way for her to feel like she knew what was going on.

When I asked my dad if he remembers that time he painted the house Technicolor yellow while I was sick inside it, watching black-and-white movies, he e-mailed me an elaborate schematic he'd dug out of a box somewhere and scanned. It shows a hand-drawn blueprint of the house's paintable surfaces, each one numbered and circled. A key in the corner tells me that the numbers were circled only when that surface was done. Below the schema is a list of all the sessions in which he painted, how long he worked, and what ancillary tasks he performed ("removed gutters to paint"). There are asterisks, and the key tells me these indicate rain days. He has indicated where he ran out of gallons of paint.

When I cross-reference my dad's painting chart with my mom's notebook, I learn that on October 24, 1989, as my dad caulked, scraped, and painted the north- and west-facing gables of our yellow house in two sessions, from twelve to three and again from four to five, my mother had me at Children's with stomach pain, joint pain, and diminished appetite. In the margins of this page I find one of the drawings that pepper my mom's notes. This sketch is an arrangement of circles and ovals—pills, each marked with milligram dosages, dancing up and down the right side of the page.

My mom refers to 1989 as "the bad year," and it occurs to me that by this time, they may not have spoken to each other about the minutiae of their respective October twenty-fourths, but they both turned to paper and pen to record data.

And I am finally able to imagine—if not understand—what drew them together in 1960, what they talked about for the seven years of their marriage before Erica came along, and it is this: the worship of information. The power of data, of numbers and weights and distances and dosages or notes, to make shape out of shapeless, erosive time. To create order, beauty, and hope where there is only messy living. To control the uncontrollable, or to feel like you can.

The second hand surgery, in July of that year, didn't go as well as the first. I try not to get mystical about it; I try not to wonder if it didn't go perfectly because my mother wasn't there. She wanted to be. I told her, "No, let's let Fred take this one."

Dr. Sheridan agreed that a dynamic splint—the finger tormentor that had worked so well the first time around, that the music performance physical therapist had given me—was the way to go. I was worried: With the first surgery, I'd been in that splint for months. I didn't think of myself as some foot-stomping, self-serious bridezilla type, but—the wedding was planned for October 9, John Lennon's sixty-fifth birthday. I didn't want to wear the claw with my gown. How would we do the rings if I was still wearing it?

I spent the whole summer before our wedding doing hand therapy. Again. After a few weeks of moving pegs from a peg board to a pile and back again, I knew that my hand wasn't going to heal unless I asked more of it. I hadn't played piano in years, a drought that had seemed unfathomable to me back in the days when I couldn't walk past the piano without playing it. As I looked down at my warped, gimpy left hand feebly attempting to stack blocks or pinch a marble, though, I knew that I hadn't given up on piano, or my hands, entirely.

I believe that you must use your body the way you need it to work. If I was going to ever ask my hands to play the piano again, I would have to ask them to do it now. To show them what I needed from them.

"Can I play the piano?" I asked the therapist.

"I don't know, can you?" she joked. She looked up from the electrical stimulation electrodes on my forearm, little devices that would strengthen my hand muscles in small ways, despite themselves. Seeing that I wasn't joking, she cocked her head, worried-looking. "I don't know that I recommend it," she said.

That wasn't a no.

So Fred and I rented a piano, a walnut-finish upright that looked and sounded like that old Wurlitzer, even if it lacked the cozy smell of ammonia. It was delivered and set up in our living room on a day when Fred was at work, right in the spot where the Christmas tree had been. I still had a box of my old piano music from college. It lived in the garage with my platform walker. After the piano movers left, I went out to the garage to get the box. I couldn't lift the whole thing, so I opened the lid and looked inside. Nearly immediately, I spotted the worn red spine of my book of Schubert's sonatas. I did not reach for it. I knew I wouldn't be able to get through even the first measure and I was not looking to have my heart broken. I would start with my brain. I started with Bartók, and when that went OK, I went back out to the garage to get Haydn. I wasn't taking any risks on anything I actually loved. No Chopin, no Mozart, no Beethoven, no Szymanowski, no Piazzolla. No Schubert.

I began my self-prescribed course of hand therapy. When I was ready, I moved on to Bach for the exquisite dexterity required to move between runs of adjacent notes. I bought a book of ragtime favorites for the flight required—the long-lost ability to leave a bass note resonating and then hop, untethered, up to the middle register and end on the right chords. *Oom-pah, oom-pah.* I cautiously retrieved books and pieces one-by-one, gradually increasing the size of the stack that lived in the walnut bench or on top of the console.

The music I wasn't yet ready to play—including the Schubert—stayed in the garage. I played for half an hour a day, then an hour, then two. Fred never complained that he couldn't hear the TV in our tiny house. "Sounds good, baby," he'd say, even though it didn't.

We were married at the zoo. My dress was a 1950s-style ball gown with a popped collar and three-quarter sleeves that showed my matching hand scars, no finger tormentor. Under my gown, I wore crazy hand-painted heels that tied with lime green grosgrain ribbon. The shoes had an arthritis-friendly rubber sole.

The wedding was perfect: Moments before the ceremony, as I stood on the top of a hill with just my dad, waiting for the first strains of "Love Me Tender" to cue our entrance, he said, "Well, shall we head on down to the execution?" I laughed because I knew that he meant "execution" as in the execution of a long-held, elaborate plan. At our wedding, Chris played the guitar and sang the Beatles song "I Will," as much because I wanted to dedicate it to Fred as because Chris had taught it to me, playing it for me on his Walkman in the backseat of our station wagon on one of our long trips. Matthew read a poem I asked him to read. In her toast, Erica recalled how I'd gushed to her when I first started dating Fred that we were like old people together. "Here's to the day you actually will be old people together," she said. It is a different kind of toast you give a young couple that has already had more sickness than health.

My knuckle has swollen around my beautiful set of rings and I can't get them off to get them cleaned. As far as I'm concerned, this is a fine problem to have, and I'll deal with it when I really have to, like for my next MRI.

Soon after our wedding, I noticed a lump on my right elbow. It was sore, large, the size of a gumball, squishy, positioned precisely where the bony, jabbing part of my elbow had been just the day before. It was not then—though it would soon become—hot, red, painful to the touch, even the touch of a sleeve.

I didn't have that worried, self-searching, sure-of-imminent-doom moment I've seen on Lifetime. My lump didn't mean cancer, because this is not that story.

What I did think is this: There goes another one. This isn't to say that my elbows had, till that point, been unaffected by this disease, this unruly houseguest I've been hostessing (graciously, I think). In fact, they were and are stuck in a permanent bent position, fixed in a jaunty, rigid, just-about-to-jump kink. But until that day, they were benignly affected. Stuck and a little misshapen, but generally painless and the only nuisance they presented to me was that jacket sleeves often hung too long on my bent, shortened arms. That was a problem I gleefully got around by hemming my jacket sleeves or, better yet, buying jackets in the petites department. Who me, petite? OK!

My elbows were not unaffected, but we—my elbows and me—had reached a kind of peace. *OK, Elbows. You don't straighten, but you also don't hurt. I can live with that.* So this lump didn't mean cancer, but it meant a violation of the tacit contract my body and I had been hammering out through several iterations and years of bitchy negotiations.

There goes another one, I thought. *Right Elbow, you have joined the ranks of Left Shoulder, Right and Left Wrists, and Right Middle Finger. And Knees and Left Hip, too—but you remember what we did to them, don't you? You were there, of course, Right Elbow, you turncoat, you bitch. Knees and Left Hip acted up and we traded them in for metal ones. So watch the fuck out, Right Elbow, because I've googled this moment and I know you can be traded in, too. Anything you can do, titanium can do better.*

We are in a pretty good place, my body and me. Détente. But there are violations of this contract, still. I don't know what each day is going to be like. Just when I think I've got a handle on this disease, something new turns up. I trot to the eye doctor saying, "I dunno, Doc, it's the weirdest thing. All day today half my field of vision has been dark and blurry, so anyone I look in the face looks like the Phantom of the Opera and I think driving might be dangerous. What do you think it is?"

"Well, there is this thing that can happen in some patients with rheumatoid arthritis. It's not common, but . . ."

Episcleritis, he says. Inflammation of the episclera. He prescribes steroid eye drops, which, I'm amazed to find, I can taste in the back of my throat, quinine-sour like the Plaquenil tablets I chose instead of gold injections all those years ago. Everything's connected inside, I guess.

Even that colitis I was sure I picked up in the hospital in 1994 might have been my own doing. My mom's notes say this: *colitis could be r/t RA . . . would be a consistent picture . . . often shows up after RA starts.*

All of my mucous membranes are dry, which the doctor attributes to Sjögren's syndrome secondary to RA. My thyroid gland has conked out entirely. Hypothyroidism and Sjögren's syndrome are both autoimmune diseases, and I learn that with autoimmune disease as with tattoos, having one increases the likelihood that you'll have others. I'm an autoimmunity *wunderkind.*

Another day I go to a neurologist because I've been having spells—not dizzy, exactly, but more like a spine-tingling instant when my hearing and vision seem to dilate and then contract, and I feel a small jolt like at the end of a fast, downward elevator ride. The Whooshing Electrical Bounce, I call it. The neurologist does all kinds of tests, asks all kinds of questions—have I ever been treated for mental illness?—and then says, "Well, there is this thing that can happen in some patients with rheumatoid arthritis. It's not common, but . . ."

It's called *atlantoaxial subluxation*, and it means that the first vertebra, atlas, is sliding down on and squishing the second axis. Just as I was with the knee "revision" surgery, I am in love with the poetry of these names, but I am afraid of what they might mean. The doctor does some imaging tests, says he'll call in a few days to let me know what he sees. "Don't do anything very *jostly,*" he says. In the meantime, I read about it on PubMed. One of the side effects of atlantoaxial subluxation is sudden death. I don't tell Fred that until much later.

I don't die suddenly before the doctor calls. He says I don't have it. But my relief is short-lived. I'm not quite thirty years into this disease, and my twelve-year head start on it is shrinking. My chances of having atlantoaxial subluxation, or any number of the other serious complications of RA that can threaten my heart, my eyes, my mortality, will increase the longer I'm sick.

I don't trust this body as far as I can throw it.

And there are new questions, now that my arthritis doesn't always enter a room before I do, now that it can sometimes be my secret again. How much do I pull toward arthritis, how much do I push it away? Practically speaking, if my elbow flares up, how long do I let it hurt before I go to the doctor?

And more troublingly: Do I claim the title of "disabled" for myself, or do I reject it? If I claim it, is it permanent? Can I give it back? Is it a once-a-member-always-a-member thing, like the International Thespian Society? Do I have to explain myself to more legitimately disabled people? When I involve myself with the Arthritis Foundation as a volunteer and fund-raiser, thereby doing some real (albeit self-interested) good, am I inviting people to strengthen the association between me and my disease?

My relationship to the label of disabled is complicated because my disease is so unpredictable. I don't live my life at a fixed distance from the word *disabled*. I have always refused to get a hangtag for my car, even when I was recovering from joint replacement. I struggled with owning that word when I looked gimpy to the outside world. But when I awoke from my knee-replacement surgery, suddenly restored to my full height of five eight, and a few weeks later when I could once again conquer stairs and chairs of many heights and pants with vertical stripes didn't look weird on my right-angle knees, the outside world rescinded that word—never mind if I'd started to identify with it. I cannot get my footing.

Dr. Armstrong was able to fix my knees and my hip. My new metal parts made my body normal-looking, acceptable to me and to most strangers, but the changes to my identity by that time were permanent. I'd spent the first ten years of this disease being sick in a body that looked relatively healthy to others. Then I was a sick body that never let anyone get past, to the humor and the music inside. Finally, post-surgery, my body and my self were once again out of step: suddenly, rendered close to normal by the miracle of surgical science, I was accused of "passing" by a quadriplegic with whom I sat on a panel about women and disability.

I'm bi-abled, I guess, and so I feel a kinship with bisexuals who don't quite fit with the gays or the straights: I'm too disabled among my able-bodied friends, too able-bodied to fit in with the truly disabled ones. My disease isn't curable, and it's progressive and possessive; it's a bigger deal than most people think it is. Bolstered by steroids and titanium, I can pass for able-bodied. Thanks to modern medicine, I can get through a day without stares and comments. But my hold on this acceptable outer form—the bumps and scars noticeable if you look closely—is tenuous and can be rescinded at any time.

However, I'm not sure it matters at all whether I'm disabled or not when there's a day to get through (papers to grade, dinner to make, fifty pounds of cat to get to the vet in four carriers, carefully balanced on my back) and there's a call-it-whatever-you-want body that needs to be plied with some combination of pills and ice and heat and rest to get through it. My body—and my diagnosis, and the labels you or I might hang on it—is a means to an end. It is not the end. I am the things I make. I am not the shape I take.

With one hand, Paul Wittgenstein pulled the notes out of the piano that other people needed two hands to wrangle, and yet his sister wrote condescendingly, I think, of her brother that he was "trying to do what really cannot be done." A forty-page scholarly article in the *Journal of Musicology* sympathetically details Wittgenstein's notebooks, heavily notated manuscripts, letters, and diaries to expose his elaborate efforts to "pass" as a four-handed pianist.

When you have been broken, it seems, you must never forget it. You must never reach, lustily and with whatever working parts you have, for the things you wanted before you were broken, because then you are "passing."

I want to rise to Wittgenstein's defense the same way I want to speak up for Simonetta Vespucci, the "Venus" who may or may not have had arthritis. I refuse to reduce Vespucci to mere specimen, and I refuse to reduce Wittgenstein to a sad-sack almost-pianist whose central passion was the hand he didn't have. I would imagine that, given the choice, Wittgenstein would opt to retain his stolen hand, and probably Vespucci would choose not to have her swollen wrist and sausage finger, whatever their cause—but who knows? Maybe not. Not everyone with a disability goes around wishing it away, I can tell you that for sure.

Schubert composed my sonata just weeks before he died, likely having long before accepted that he was dying. His illness changed him, as illness does, and it changed what he created. Perhaps something as immortally beautiful as the B-flat sonata could be created only by someone who has accepted his own mortality. It's a romantic notion, for sure.

Or, less romantically: If Schubert or Wittgenstein or Vespucci served as creators or transmitters of art, of beauty, perhaps they did so not *because* of their bodily imperfections, nor even *despite* them, but just *with* their ill or broken selves. To argue that the mere supposition that a beautiful Florentine muse has an illness is to eclipse all other features of her identity, or to insist that a disabled pianist going about his work and chasing his passions is doing so to convince the rest of us he's as good as an able-bodied pianist, is to define these people not by any number of other features of their identity but by this one attribute only.

Or consider Byron Janis, who did cloak his illness in secrecy, but not out of some concern for his ability to "pass" in the judgment of other people. Byron Janis kept his arthritis a secret for decades, and in his book he describes the burden of this secret and how he allowed himself to keep playing as long as he didn't play more than a few subpar concerts in a row. "I could deceive myself," he writes, "but I would never betray the music."

Great music is better, whole-er, holier than any single player. Playing music, even with a perfect body, is an act of hubris. All musicians are trying to pass—as angels, or superhumans. To read the notes a composer laid out for you, to assign them to fingers that you then marshal through passage after passage, and then to hope that what you produce with bones and muscles and keys and strings and hammers and felt comes close to matching what was born in another person's heart, is to confront the very problem of bodies.

Music, played correctly, transcends even intact bodies. If, sitting in a concert hall awash in the Waldstein Sonata, you're thinking about the musculoskeletal health of the pianist's fingers, either you're doing it wrong or the pianist is. And if you are listening to a broken pianist play and listening only for evidence of her brokenness, the same is true. Even complete bodies are impediments, they are feeble musical tools, but they are the only tools we have if we insist on having music. And we do. I do.

And though it's taken twenty-some years of prematurely, unnaturally ill health for me to learn that, I recognize that it's not an extraordinary or unique discovery. It's the same discovery any owner of a chronically mutinying body—whether it's cancer or obesity or multiple sclerosis or diabetes or merely aging—might make.

In 2006, in the space of a few months, my left hip went from painless to excruciating, and I had it replaced. I was so grateful that I had good, strong, titanium knees to get me through the hip replacement. One crisis at a time, indeed. In 2007, my left knee replacement fell apart for no good reason, reminding me that being three years out from surgery didn't mean being out of the woods. That I am never out of these woods. They call it late failure. "This is kind of from the 'shit happens' medical file," Dr. Armstrong said. He went in and fixed it, putting a longer metal stem into my tibia and slathering extra cement over the whole mess. A few years later, the very same thing happened with the right knee, and Dr. Armstrong and I moved through our choreography for the fourth time. For both of my knee revisions, I'd asked him ahead of time if I could have the components he took out. He brought them to me in recovery. I keep them on a bookshelf near my piano.

For three years running, my dad makes a special springtime trip to Arizona just to help me cocaptain a fund-raising team for the Arthritis Foundation's Arthritis Walk. For three years in a row, we are the top fund-raising team. A hundred friends show up to the zoo, the same place where Fred and I were married, at 6:00 A.M. to walk with us. I've named our team "Chip and Old Block," playing up the joke about how different I am from my pocket-protector father. But I hope that he decodes my secret meaning: that I am of him, and like him, and that I am proud of those things. The first year, he surprised me with pendants he had fashioned for each of us to wear during the walk: his is a hunk of wood with "Old Block" carefully Sharpied on in Gothic script. Mine is tinier, and it reads "Chip" in an updated deco font. He drilled holes in each and strung them on the silver hardware-store chain he likes so much. We wear them every year, and I love the feeling of mine banging against my sternum. In his increasingly wordy and effusive e-mails—my dad is softening—he addresses me as "Chip" and he signs off, "Old Block."

The cutting happens quickly, and I nearly miss it.

I'd asked to keep my knees, these totems of my surgery, because I want some assurance that it is my body that is sick, not me. I wish I had my appendix and my gallbladder and even my ovarian cyst. I have worked so hard to dissociate from my diseased body, to stand apart in coolly intellectual observation.

And so I head into surgery again, but for once I am not the patient. I have persuaded Dr. Armstrong to let me watch him operate on someone else. It's a hip replacement.

I'd told myself to be ready for it, the moment when scalpel touched flesh, to watch for the doughy give of the skin beneath the sharp point, the quick, clean line and the bright, fresh blood. But my TV-fed imaginings will have to substitute for any actual impression of that moment, because Dr. Armstrong starts cutting nearly immediately and I miss the moment when it starts, the moment when the skin is broken.

The patient, T.H.,—now a hulking mass turned on his side, draped in blue paper—had told me, "Yeah, you can watch. I don't care. Just don't go poking your fingers in any holes." I laughed, and agreed, because while I knew I wanted to watch, I couldn't imagine wanting to touch anything. I wanted to observe, to stand apart. To see.

See. That is exactly it. I have to see. Rheumatoid arthritis has been at work in my body for almost thirty years, and evidence of it is all over me: fingers, knotted and fused; elbows, stuck in awkward flexion contractures.

The *damage* shows in the joints, in the knobby, tell-all nodes where limbs meet. But it is a disease of the connective tissue; it lurks in the blood and the soft tissues and the spaces between the joints just as, according to Claude Debussy, music lives in the spaces between the notes. I have only the nodes on the time line to tell the story of my body—the flares and the ruptures and the surgeries and the scars, the arias and the recitatives.

I am always anesthetized for the arias.

And so I am here, in light-blue scrubs, positioned at T.H.'s head, just behind the drape, watching. Dr. Armstrong breezes in, hands upturned in front of his face. He is always dashing, but today he looks even more like a knight to me, with a mask over his face and a scrub cap that covers his whole head and flares out above his shoulders. He steps into a gown someone holds up for him. Another nurse helps him with his gloves, and then he begins and I nearly miss it.

After Dr. Armstrong draws his hand across the skin, I see the flesh part and then I see pink-orange strata: skin and blood and fat. From where I am standing, just behind the patient's head, next to an anesthesiologist who is not Dr. Chocolate Bar as I'd hoped it would be (because, Dr. Armstrong explained, Dr. Chocolate Bar has leukemia), I can't see all the way into the canyon. After a while, there is cutting—a bone saw that doesn't faze me—and then Dr. Armstrong's hand disappears into the hole, up to the elbow it seems. There is a pluck and a pop and he pulls out a shiny dark apple: the hip.

I hadn't expected to want so badly to reach into the hole, into the man's body, to find out if it's hot in there or to know what blood and fat feel like slipping between gloved fingertips, but I do. I have been where this man is now. I have lain in the adjacent pre-op stall, swaddled in toasted blankets, waiting. I'm willing to bet that for weeks this man has lain awake at night, kneading at the place where leg meets groin, trying to massage away the deep, untouchable hip pain.

"You OK?" the humorless scrub nurse—the real boss of this room—asks me, wanting to make sure that I am not going to pass out and steal attention, become the problem. "I am smiling," I announce, because she cannot see me behind my mask.

And there it is. As T.H.'s hip is placed on a towel-lined tray and someone else grabs it to measure it, I wonder where my hip joint—the real, original, organic one—is now. Wherever it is, does it have arthritis? Did it stop having arthritis the moment it was excised from my body, free of me? I have been blaming my joints, but maybe they are not the problem. I entertain a brief, impractical fantasy: If I had every affected joint in my body replaced with cobalt chrome, would I still have arthritis? Who has this disease, anyway? Me or my body?

And suddenly, epiphanic, I know: There may have been a time—a year after diagnosis, maybe five—when arthritis could have gone away and I could have returned to the life I was living, unchanged. But not now. Now disease is the underpinning, the premise, the constant. I am bound to it and it to me. This is not to say that I wouldn't get rid of it if I could. It is to say that even if I could expunge my disease, I could never go back to being the person I was before I got sick. I'm not sure I'd want to.

Disease has changed me for good. It has formed my appetites and curiosities. I don't need to stalk my disease in operating rooms to see the full story, to understand it. It is always present. I cannot stand apart from my body. I am one thing, homogenous, harmonious. It is me and I am it.

I am not my body, but neither is my disease. Arthritis shows up in my joints but it is written into me at the most basic level; it's in my DNA. It is as much a part of the very fiber of me—and as separate from the physical parts of me—as my soul is. I am not afflicted; I am imbued. God is in the space between the molecules, and so is disease.

And so is music.

If music is in the spaces between the notes, then what happens if there are no notes at all? Can there be music? John Cage would say so. The absence of notes forces you to hear the music that is happening around you, despite you.

Eventually, I brought Schubert in from the garage. But instead of playing the first movement, which had had a hold on my heart since I heard it in Providence almost thirty years ago, I turned to the second movement. This *andante sostenuto* movement, in C-sharp minor, begins slowly, mournfully. I had time between key depressions to really hear the sounds, to plan where my hands would fall next. It is not flashy, but the sixteenth notes in the middle section, in A major, stopped me short. I could not simply sight-read it, not with these uncooperative, out-of-practice hands. But there was a flutter in my chest: this was not out of reach. If I could practice—truly practice, in the way I never much wanted to as a child—I could play this. I could not believe I had overlooked this achingly beautiful andante movement in my lust for the first movement.

As a young pianist, before arthritis, I was seduced by finger-flashy pieces. As I matured, teachers nudged me toward more cerebral music, like the étude from the piano exam disaster, or the harpsichord repertoire that Dr. Metz fed me. But what I had missed swinging between those two poles—the physical and the cerebral— was the middle ground. Pieces like this second movement of the Schubert, which was neither flashy nor as densely cerebral. This movement required some dexterity and of course a great deal of concentration, but it also had these big, wide-open spaces between notes, all connective tissue, gaping rests that needed to be filled with resonance and feeling, not action and planning. This movement was full of heart, that perfect fulcrum between thinking and acting. Heart, the physical motor that permits all action. Heart, the abstract locus of intangible feeling.

My struggle with arthritis had long felt like a battle between brain and body—which of the two defined me? Would my brain ever be enough to make up for my problematic body? But my attempts to become disembodied were futile and misguided. As the second movement of the sonata was beginning to make clear, to be any of the things I want to be, I need both brain and body. Rather, I need their perfect merger: heart.

I have relied on my brain to understand and articulate and endure my relationship with my body, but my experience in this body has also made my brain richer and more layered and more empathetic. Even Schubert is reported to have written that "pain sharpens the understanding and strengthens the mind." That has been my experience, so I can refuse neither my mind nor my pain. Schubert relied on both to produce his work, including my sonata, and I would rely on both to play Schubert. I am learning to live in that connective space between brain and body, with heart, and I would learn to play piano there, too.

Chapter 12

F red and I are at the first meeting with the adoption agency. One of the things I want to find out is if we qualify. This agency has said that they require that couples they work with have a "demonstrated history of infertility." We do not have that. I have been on birth control pills since I was a teenager—partly because the medicines I take are so toxic and partly to shrink the ovarian cysts I've continued to get. On the form that says "demonstrated history of infertility," there is an asterisk. At the bottom of the form, I see that the asterisk allows for other possibilities: "Or other health concern."

It's not that I can't get pregnant, not for sure. For the first half of my thirties, at least, my doctor said, "If that's something you'd like to try, we can do that." But getting pregnant would have meant taking me off the methotrexate. Methotrexate has long been the real gold-standard of RA treatment; I was prescribed it on its own in the early days of my disease and now I took it alongside a TNF inhibitor to increase its effectiveness. The TNF inhibitor could likely be continued during pregnancy, but methotrexate is a "Category X" drug, meaning it mustn't be used during pregnancy. Stopping methotrexate would have meant being less aggressive than we ought to be. It would have meant, maybe, losing ground. Ground I could not afford to lose if there would be a lifetime ahead of me as a mother.

Some women with rheumatoid arthritis go into remission when they are pregnant. About 75 percent. I have no reason to think I won't be in the other 25 percent—for whom the disease usually gets worse during pregnancy. I have always been "something else."

So we have come here to see if I am sick enough to enlist the help of an agency who will show our folder to a pregnant woman who will believe I am not so sick I cannot raise her child. This is precarious.

"It's not that we have a demonstrated history of *infidelity*," I say, rambling, "though I mean I can't know for sure that *infidelity* won't be a problem for us—" I look at Fred to get a nod of encouragement, agreement. His eyebrows are up and his mouth is open. Fred knows better than anyone that I chatter when I'm nervous. I look to the adoption lady across the desk. She looks shocked, too.

"Every single time she said 'infidelity,'" Fred begins softly, "she meant 'infertility.'"

"I figured," says the nice adoption lady, no doubt accustomed to nervous couples.

I tell her all about my arthritis. I tell her that I believe my job isn't to grow a child but to be strong and healthy to raise one. I make a point of mentioning that I work two jobs and belong to the Y and play the piano and run the vacuum cleaner from time to time. At the end of the meeting, sensing that I am fishing for some label or pronouncement I haven't gotten, the adoption lady says, "Yes. Yes. This is a good enough reason. You're fine."

Two weeks later, we are at our first of two required adoption education classes. The classes are held in a conference room at the agency and the couples huddle in two-person islands around the table. There is a lot of bending over backward to demonstrate to these adoption people—the people with the babies!—how kind and generous we are. We are handed pieces of cardstock to write our names on, so we can all get comfortable and get to know one another. A lot is going to be shared today, they tell us. One guy doesn't have a pen. "Oh, please here take mine," everyone says, and the guy is pelted in a hailstorm of pens.

There are eyes everywhere. The adoption people tell us there are snacks in the back of the room. Everyone avoids the soda except for one pudgy, dull-eyed woman, who cracks open a Coke. "Hmm. High-fructose corn syrup," I hear everyone think.

Halfway through the day, after lunch, they break us up: women over here, men over here. We are supposed to share what brought us to this point. All the other women have "demonstrated history of infertility." They talk a lot about the fertility drugs they've taken, about mourning the fact that they will not get pregnant. Some have already lost babies, through miscarriage or stillbirth, though I doubt if any have lost nine, as Schubert's mother did.

I am silent, because if I ever mourned that loss, I mourned it long ago. However, there must have been a time when I thought it was possible for me, because I can remember putting my potbelly teddy bear, Huggy, inside my nightgown so his taut, rounded bottom would look like a belly, and admiring myself in the full-length mirror hanging on the back of my bedroom door. But that was so long ago. That was *before*. It's been a long time since I considered trusting my body—this crafty, mutinous, misbehaved body—with such an important task. "Why are you here?" one of the women says to me.

"I want to be a mother because of the one I have," I say. I want to let my daughter wear whatever she wants, as long as it is clean and weather-appropriate, the way my mother did me. I want to teach someone to sew and knit and play the piano. I want to keep notebooks, and battle insurance companies, and take temperatures, for someone else, even if it means being terrifyingly locked out of the feverish, hurting body.

In the men's group, I learn later, they talked about how much babies cost.

The next weekend, we are back for the second installment. This time they are going to bring Actual Birth Mothers and Successful Adoptive Families in to talk to us. There is talk where there will be Real Babies!

A couple comes in with their nine-month-old and I suppose they tell us something about how these cheeks and curls became their daughter, but I am not listening. No one is listening. The baby is crawling on the floor beneath the table. Soon she is at my feet and she has pulled my keys out of my purse. Automatically, I reach down and take the keys. I give her my cardstock name tag to play with instead. "You can pick her up," the mother says.

I reach down and pick up the baby, feel this happiest of hefts in my hands. I pat her diapered bottom and lift her to my chest. Instead of delighting in her powder-sweet smell or tulip-lipped smile, I am thinking, Are you people getting this? Are you seeing how I can lift twenty pounds no problem? I am not too sick to do this.

The baby fits snugly in a hammock I make of my arms. But the welcome weight of her is countered by another weight in my belly, this one slimy and unwelcome: I am OK enough right this second to mother, but what about tomorrow? A year from now? RA is a disease of vicissitudes, and I am horrified to think of having a baby like this and being unable to lift her from her crib, both of us crying. I look over the top of her fuzzy head at Fred. It is perhaps fortunate that the process of adoption will likely take years. We will proceed cautiously. We will feel out the slope of the line my arthritis is on. We will be grateful that, while pregnancies sometimes happen by accident, adoptions usually do not.

And anyway, I already have sixty-five teenagers. I am a high school teacher, which means my heart is an ever-expanding locker bursting with delight and grief and amusement and frustration and love. So much love. I may never have the chance to earn the mother I have by becoming a mother. But I can chip away at the debt I owe so very many teachers, and I try every day to do so.

Years after my last harpsichord lesson with Dr. Metz, I received an e-mail from him out of the blue. The subject line was "Oh, Wow." He and his wife, Barbara, had come across an essay of mine in a magazine. "Life is so good, so sweet, so embraceable," his message began. We kept in touch for a short while after that, and he sent me a Taylor Mali poem called "Undivided Attention," which he called his "guiding light." In it, the speaker, a math teacher, has to compete for his students' attention with the sight of a piano being hoisted into an eighth-floor window and with the magic of first snow. "Let me teach like a Steinway," the poem ends, "spinning slowly in April air, so almost-falling, so hinderingly dangling from the neck of the movers' crane. So on the edge of losing everything. Let me teach like the first snow, falling."

Dr. Metz is gone now, too—but I have adopted his guiding light as my own. I fashion myself as a kind of Mr. Frezzo / Mrs. Feltman / Dr. Metz / Catherine Hammond with more than a little Grandma Torvik thrown in for good measure. In my classroom, I have my framed picture of Joe Theismann. "Redskins fan?" people ask. I nod rather than explain that I am a fan of Joe Theismann because of the sense he seems to have made from his "career-ending" injury. He broke both bones in that leg that night, but his body let him be painless. And so Joe Theismann knows what I know, which is that the body is a magnificent, benevolent machine. And I like Joe Theismann because he also said, of breaking both bones at once, "If I'm going to do it, I'm doing it all the way." This of course reminds me of my overachieving stay in the hospital with appendicitis, an ovarian cyst, and colitis.

Through a mutual friend, I end up on the phone with Joe Theismann, and we compare notes about the extraordinary pains a body can bear, about the body's ability to be chivalrous and protect its inhabitant from pain. He tells me that his own leg looked to him like a flounder as they loaded it onto the stretcher on the football field. He tells me, "You're the quarterback of your life."

Schubert, Wittgenstein, Theismann: I apparently have a thing for Austrian guys.

At Back-to-School Night, after my ten-minute song and dance, a parent comes up to ask me if I am a dancer, and I laugh. "You seem so comfortable in your body," he says. I don't exactly agree. I will never be at home in this body. But—finally—my body is at home in my life. When one of my sophomores, Lindsay, shouts across the quad that she found a way to use *pillory*—a vocab word—in dinner conversation with her parents, or when the boys soccer team joins my "crochet for charity club" and they spend hours wrapping their clumsy fists around crochet hooks to make hats for kids with cancer, the dissonance between the life I don't have—might have had, should have had, could have had—is finally silent. It is irrelevant.

Bizarrely, nowhere am I less self-conscious about my body than in front of a room full of sixteen-year-olds. From time to time I worry that I have broccoli in my teeth or that my fly is down, but I never worry that they are laughing at my skinny, crooked arms or my swayback, bent-forward posture.

Maybe they overlook my flaws because they are in the grips of body mutiny themselves. They know what I know, which is that it can all change in a day: they could wake up tomorrow to a voice that squeaks or hair in new places or breasts that draw attention, good or bad, or a face stuccoed with zits. They know it, and they know that I know it.

They know that I am not judging their bodies, their hair, or their faces the way it must feel the whole world is. I think they know that I am concerned with their hearts and minds and their ideas. But they can't possibly know how grateful I am that they extend the same generosity to me. If they love me, it is not for my body. And that is precisely what allows me to demonstrate the meaning of *maelstrom* during Vocabulary Charades by extending my bare, crooked arms and whirling around in the middle of the classroom, the way I never would have done when I was their age, only three years into arthritis and physically healthier than I am now. Their forgiveness of my body's shortcomings is what makes it possible for me to enjoy being in my body. They give me this, every day.

They vie unselfconsciously for the little gold stickers I dole out as rewards.

Leah shows up on "Dress Like Your Teacher Day" in trousers, a vintage cardigan, cat-eye glasses, and cowboy boots. "Look!" she squeals, bounding happily across the quad at 7:30 A.M., her hair still wet, dragging her backpack by its straps. "I'm you!"

That she has chosen my skin to be in makes me laugh and makes my heart swell with gratitude. That she has chosen to be me on this day makes me happier to be me, too.

I am discussing fate with my tenth graders. I ask them if they believe their lives are predetermined. I ask if they think they are fated, ill- or otherwise. It's no, no, no across the board. They do not remember Choose Your Own Adventure books, but like me they cut their teeth playing in a toy world where a car can become a robot and then switch back again, where we girls can do anything—right, Barbie? They are fifteen. They are half adult, half child. They are learning to express their dearest truths—"you're not the boss of me!"—in new terms: They believe in free will, they say, and rugged individualism. Fate/God/Destiny is not the boss of me! YOLO.

But there is one exception: Hulking, sweet-faced Dakota says, "I think it's all planned out for me. I mean, I think it's not God, exactly, but something, or someone, knows exactly what I'm going to be and do, and me, I just have to figure out how to be happy with it. I have to make peace with it, even if it's not what I thought I would be or do or whatever."

Though I worry Dakota may be relying on this faith a little too much, chalking up a 33 percent on the last test to "what was meant to be," I recognize his point. I ask him if he thinks this is a hopeful stance—is it testament to the elasticity of the human spirit that we can decide to be happy with our lot, no matter what it is?—or is this a resigned stance and depressing as all hell? After all, Dakota can still be anything. He is probably thinking he'll make himself perfectly happy being a gajillionaire real estate mogul when the NBA plan falls through. I decide I would really like to have this conversation with him when he's twenty-five, when he's gotten close enough to touch the net and then been felled by injury. I want to know if he is happy when he sits at his gajillionaire desk, still able to smell the cloying stink of the locker room, when he is haunted by the squeak of shoes on the hardwood.

I am at a swim meet at school. I try to spot the students who are mine when they turn their heads up to breathe. They pull themselves out of the pool, they hug themselves and they are so lean that their fingertips meet at their spines. They shiver and run on tiptoes back to the other side of the pool, waving covertly and mouthing, "You came!" A senior boy is sitting next to me on the risers, under a tent that flaps in the breeze. A stripe of sunlight paints our laps.

"Oh man," he says.

I look at him.

He is looking at my left hand, at my scar. It has not healed as well as the right. The last two fingers still hang down; the scar is bumpy. "What happened?"

I do not have a script prepared for this. I have only ever responded with saltiness to teenage boys who comment on my body.

"I have arthritis," I say. And that's it.

Quinlan is quiet. He looks at the pool and then back at me. He puts his warm, sweaty hand on top of my hand, briefly, pats it gently and awkwardly, so quickly I'm not sure it has happened. "That sucks," he says in a hoarse whisper. "I'm sorry."

If this seventeen-year-old boy is so kind, is it possible that others were, too? Were there kindnesses I missed?

In cataloging hardness, have I forgotten softness? People forget: the full name of the piano is the *pianoforte*. It is named for its full dynamic range.

Just like Schubert, I am descended from teachers. And like Schubert, I tried to avoid becoming a teacher by default. Unlike Schubert, however, I loved teaching from the moment I stepped foot into the classroom. On the first day of graduate school, after finishing teaching my first section of English 101, I called my mother. "Mom!" I sang. "I loved it. It was so much fun! I think I want to be a teacher!"

"I could have told you that." She laughed, no doubt thinking of her own mother.

For the three years I was a graduate student in the English department, I taught freshman composition and creative writing. One semester, I taught in the very same classroom where I sat as a freshman student of Catherine Hammond, the first teacher who explicitly challenged me to "find the form" for the music I had in me. It could be writing, she suggested. I was starting to agree, and also to see that it could be teaching. Teaching writing. Composition, after all.

But at the end of those three years, I followed bumper-sticker advice and decided that I would set free this thing I seemed to love, teaching, and see if it came back to me. I also had to consider practical matters that my mother had made sure I understood: health insurance with no gap in coverage, sick leave, retirement savings. So I took a job in marketing and after five sad years in a cubicle, I found my way back to the classroom, a tenth-grade English classroom in a private school. I felt leaving the marketing job the way Schubert must have felt in 1818 when he quit teaching to dedicate his life to his art: "Thank God I live at last."

For Schubert, being a teacher meant becoming a thwarted musician. But not for me. It is in teaching that I have found the perfectly balanced expression of all the things I have ever wanted to be—writer. Performer. Mother. And yes, musician. When I interviewed for my job, the principal looked at my résumé and said, "Piano, huh? Can you play?" I said yes and so—sweet symmetry!—for several years, I am the rehearsal pianist for the musical. We rehearse every day between January and March. I get to the auditorium before the kids do and I put my pencil and my metronome and my score on the top of the piano. The kids come clomping in and dump their backpacks. They huddle around me at the piano for their vocal warm-ups, and sometimes we break into sing-alongs, our own backstage Schubertiade. If I am practicing a passage from the instrumental score, they stand politely and watch. "You're so good," they say. I do not tell them that I am not good. That I used to be good. "Thank you," I say. "Are you ready for rehearsal?" I help them with passages in their solos that have them stumped. I sing the melody as I play. I tell them, "Meter is tricky. This one's a doozy. Put a little oomph in it. Jazz it up." I tell them, "Sometimes you have to rob Peter to pay Paul."

From this high school stage, I think of Mr. Frezzo, teaching at my old high school but planning to retire at the end of 2017, and Randy Cohen, off in New York City. Facebook allows me to see that Randy is part of the musical crew that received a Grammy for *Hamilton*. Facebook also allows Mr. Frezzo to scold me when I use *fuck* in a post. I am chagrined but charmed.

The school musical is *The Wiz*, the funktastic 1970s version of *The Wizard of Oz*. Quinlan is the Wiz. Maren has been cast as Dorothy, the part that Diana Ross played in the movie. Maren reminds me of Lauren, my dear friend from high school theater and CIA summer performances. She is stunningly, easily beautiful, with powder-fresh skin and bright eyes and long brown hair that curls at the ends, all on its own. Maren's voice is lusty and strong, bell-like in its high register but soulful and gritty in its low register. Maren is one of the only students who gets funk. Her hips move involuntarily when she sings.

Maren was in a car accident when she was nine and her left leg is mangled, rippled, bowed, shorter than the other one. She walks in a rolling gait, flat-footed with her right foot and on the tiptoes of her left. Her head bobs up and down when she walks. She is always smiling.

I am in the director's classroom one evening after rehearsal as he discusses costumes with the moms who are helping with dressing our cast. "Let's put Maren in a longer skirt," someone says. "You know, to cover it."

This is not my conversation; this is not my job. I say nothing. I go home. I cannot sleep.

The next day, another meeting in the director's office. "We can't put Maren in a long skirt," I say. "We just can't do that."

"I don't want people to be distracted by her leg," someone says. I know that this person means well, and wants to protect her also, but from a different thing.

They will be not distracted by that, I think. They will be distracted by our white, funk-free cast.

"But Maren doesn't cover her leg," I say.

She wears the cutest, flirtiest skirts. Sometimes she's right there with the rest of them, this close to violating dress code. She's on the cheerleading squad. She's the *captain* of the cheerleading squad. Maren's leg may be one of the first, most immediately noticeable things about her, but it doesn't take long for her to redirect your attention. "Not down there, up here," her voice and her smile say. And then you cannot take your eyes off her.

"We can't do this," I say. We cannot send this message to her. We cannot even take the risk of letting this beautiful girl—whose body-love is so hard-won—think that her leg is something she should be ashamed of. So the audience might be distracted. That will pass. And even if it doesn't, who's to say they shouldn't be? That is the less expensive outcome of the two.

"Do we need to write it into the script? So it makes sense?" they ask.

Why do we assume that the characters in our books aren't gimps? Why do we assume that people are perfectly healthy unless a big deal is made of it, unless it becomes the point of the story? How do we know that Dorothy doesn't have multiple sclerosis or a port-wine stain on her face or a mangled leg? Because if she did, she'd ask the Wizard for a miracle cure before she'd ask to go home? Look, we seem to say to the characters we are starting to love, if there's something wrong with you, you'd better tell me now, before I'm two hundred pages in.

The last big number of the play, "Home," is a go-big solo for Maren. We've been working on it together. The blocking has her standing at the corner of the stage. I am in the orchestra pit, below her. We need to time this carefully. I need to be able to see and hear her to know when she says the cue line, so I can start. She needs to see and hear me so I can cue her in the slow parts, the parts out of time. The geometry of this moment is such that I can see her face but not her legs, or her short skirt, over the top of my piano. She can see my face but not my hands. She nails it. She is going like a house on fire.

Sick leave: These words presume that sickness ends, that the fever subsides, that the aches dissipate, that the leaden blanket of fatigue lifts, that you'll return.

Sick day: That sick is the exception, the anomaly. That there's another kind of day. That twenty-four hours ought to be time enough to recover.

When I must, I take sick days. But when I call in, I am calling in sick(er). I am taking a sick(er) day. After all, I am chronically ill. I am always sick. I don't mean I am *sickly*, I am not the bubble boy, I do not overdo it with the hand sanitizer, I am not rolling my eyes and sighing, "Oh, you know me—if there is a bug going around, I will get it!" I mean that my baseline measurement of wellness is skewed. I mean that out of every five-day workweek, there is at least one day that I go to work with a fever or a limp or unable to make a fist or rotate my neck. I mean that if these were injuries, if these symptoms had an identifiable cause and I could reasonably expect them to be resolved, I'd be entirely justified in calling in sick. But because they are chronic, recurring, unabating and my "normal," I cannot. There is no sick leave policy that could—that should—cover that. So I go.

I have good days: I can squeeze the shampoo bottle with one hand, stand up while I brush my teeth without alternating which arm holds the toothbrush, button my pants and tie my shoes and zip my jacket and style my hair.

On these days I sing in the car, I squeeze in a few rows of knitting at coffee before I get to work. I make my tenth graders stand up and act out the parts of *Oedipus Rex*. For my part, I play a suppliant, splaying myself on the floor in a posture of distress in front of my benevolent, fifteen-year-old king Oedipus. I spring from the floor at the bell—See you tomorrow! Don't forget the vocab quiz!—dust off the knees of my trousers, circulate in the breezeway before the next class. High fives for everyone.

But there are bad days, and I do not know when they are coming.

On these days, I wake to find I can't open my hand, that I've kicked off my covers and my skin is covered with a patina of sweat. Standing, I find that my arms are curled to my torso and won't loosen. The shower I take is long and hot. I squeeze the shampoo bottle by propping it against the wall of the shower and pressing it with my forehead, my hand below. I cannot raise my arms voluntarily; during the night they have turned to stone. I touch the fingertips of my most compliant-seeming arm to the wall of the shower. I walk my fingertips up slowly, like the itsy-bitsy spider climbing up the waterspout. This is that old trick I learned in physical therapy after shoulder surgery. With my fingertips touching the wall above eye level, I rely on gravity to get my hand to the top of my head. I lather as best I can with one hand, but it is not very soapy. I need friction. For friction I need motion. I have no motion today.

I squeeze the toothpaste tube by laying it flat on the counter and pressing on it with my elbow. I hope that the gel will follow a suitable trajectory so that a pea-size amount ends up on my brush. I sit while I brush my teeth. When one arm gets tired of holding the million-pound toothbrush, I switch. After the teeth, I rest for a moment.

I go to the closet. On these mornings, I pay special attention to what I wear. On these mornings, I ask my husband to help zip me up or button me and he does so, sweetly and gently. On these days, I do not succumb to drab, elastic-waist clothes that are easy to get on. If I am dressed to the nines, it is likely because my body—my body which has been through so much—deserves, on this day more than any other, something nice to wear.

I wear Doc Martens on these days, with an orthotic insert stuffed inside.

On these days I add ibuprofen to my breakfast. My car, a Mustang, is a 305-horsepower cocoon. If I must move slowly, my car must move fast. Hurry slowly. Stuffed into the driver's seat, I am strapped in, bolstered. I can keep my hands on the wheel and be absolved of the responsibility to hold them up, working against impossible gravity, or let them dangle. I can move fast. I can turn the wheel by sticking my hands in the holes in the steering wheel. My commute takes thirty minutes. That is usually enough time for the medication to take the edge off. By the time I get to work, I am softening and already forgetting.

If I think I can afford it—in expenditure of energy, that is—I stop for coffee. My body makes my coffee decisions, and I let it. The barista at Hava Java knows my name and my drink. What he cannot divine is whether I want it hot or cold. My order doesn't seem to correspond with the seasons. I will order a hot latte on a 120-degree day and an iced latte on a 50-degree morning. A hot cup, denuded of its protective coffee sleeve, can be gripped tightly in a rigid hand that has clenched up during the night. The muscles and tendons in the hand can be warmed, coaxed to open. A cold drink can be held to the top of an inflamed wrist to take the swelling down, and I will not have to entertain the questions an ice pack would invite: "What's wrong with your hand? Did you hurt your hand?"

On bad days, I try desperately to give my students the teacher they had yesterday, even if I do it from my very comfortable desk chair, which furniture-designer Ryan, still my friend, taught me is the famous Herman Miller Aeron chair.

Sometimes I have to improvise.

The morning is long. Halfway through, between classes, coffee gone, I go to the bathroom to run my hands under hot or cold water, to sit for a moment, to press my cheek, which is hot, against the wall, which is cold.

By lunchtime, the ibuprofen is in full force and I can rejoin the world. I eat with the other teachers in the cafeteria but I am too quiet. "Something on your mind?" they ask. Yes. My body is on my mind.

When I get home, Fred receives me. He takes my book bag from my shoulder. He leads me to the blue recliner, the Todd Oldham for La-Z-Boy he bought me when I was in the hospital, a chair that Ryan would probably tease me for owning but that is my life raft on days like this. The one that is easy to get in and out of. He settles me in, gently removing my shoes and my socks, packing all the ice packs we have around my perimeter like I am a fresh-caught fish. He layers as many blankets and afghans on top of me as he can find. He tucks in the edges, wrapping me up, calling me a burrito. He brings me water. He leaves me alone. This is what I need from him. He gives me the remote and lets me put it on MTV, something delicious and trashy and shrill. He doesn't change the channel even as I sleep, feverish, in front of the TV. At eleven he helps me into bed, pulling a nightshirt over my head for me. We say nothing, but we both hope tomorrow is different. And sometimes it is.

I will demand a lot of my body, still. And my friendship with my body will be demanding. I know that arthritis will spread unpredictably; it will affect organs and systems I had assumed were impervious. I will never get the news that it's gone for good. I'll never be an Arthritis Survivor. I'll have it and have it and then die with it.

So it's not cancer. It's not a lot of things—it's not rosacea, it's not asthma, it's not diabetes, it's not multiple sclerosis, it's not typhoid or syphilis (!) or tuberculosis. It's not any number of chronic ill-nesses that range from pain in the ass to serious life-fucker.

I don't tempt fate by wishing to trade my disease for another, not when the drugs I take to treat my arthritis come in boxes warning me of lymphoma, and that seems like a reasonable risk to take if it will keep arthritis at bay. "Eh," says my (former) doctor. "With RA, you have an increased risk of cancer anyway, so whatever." I don't wish for cancer, but I do wish my mangled fingers and rigid elbows were met with the kind of awed respect a beautiful bald head is. I wish there were a Lifetime movie about it, filmed somewhere misty in Vancouver, starring Zooey Deschanel or Emma Stone as me. They both have voices that sound hypothyroidy. Lucky for me once again: goiter chic!

I wish people knew that arthritis is more than a pesky ache that keeps a "Silver Fox" business baron from golfing with his pals, more than an easily overcome pang that is answered with a couple of Advil and before you know it, you're back to tossing a ball with your grandkid or lunch with the Red Hat Society or gardening or power walking or stenciling.

My sickness is an epic opera without end. Sometimes it feels like the Ring of the Nibelung on repeat. Sometimes I wish my sickness had the beginning, middle, and end—for better or worse—of some kinds of cancer. I wish I could give you a heroic, linear story: Disease picks a fight, person nobly fights disease, jury decides whether the person lives or dies—or the disease does. Whatever. It's not. It's lather, rinse, repeat. It's *da capo al fine*: go back to the head and play through to the end.

Repeat.

In 2014, I had my left shoulder replaced in a seamless, textbook surgery. "The best result I've ever seen," the surgeon said. The next year, I tried for a repeat on the right shoulder. But things didn't go as smoothly; a different surgeon performed the operation and when I woke up, I had no sensation in my right hand or arm. A nerve had been seriously damaged in the operation. For days—and then weeks—my right arm hung flaccid and powerless. I couldn't wiggle my fingers or squeeze even the softest Nerf ball. The neurologist stuck a series of thick needles in my hand, grimaced, and proclaimed that I might never get my right hand back. A specialist at the Mayo Clinic also threw up his hands. Nothing to do but watch and wait, they said.

My mom stayed with me for almost a month, and then she left and my dad came. Every day of that long, miserable summer, one or the other of my parents took me to physical therapy or to Starbucks, where I practiced left-handed penmanship from a workbook I'd ordered on Amazon. I barked into my laptop and my cell phone to send text messages and to write, using a version of the adaptive technology I'd learned about in my first assignment at the CIA all those years ago. It was easily the darkest stretch of my life so far, and yet now that I'm through it, I'm sweetly nostalgic for those days in the car with my parents, for my mom sincerely oohing and aahing over my impressive left-handed cursive, for my dad gleefully insisting on buying me a pair of Nike LeBron Zoom Soldier 8s, cleverly designed to be easily worn by disabled athletes, on the very day they "dropped." I could pull them on and cinch them with my one working hand. "It's a medical expense," my dad said. "Sweet shoes," the teenage boys at school say.

It's partly the long repeats in Schubert's sonatas that give some, and maybe gave Schumann, the sense of their rambling length. But perhaps the blame is misplaced: Maybe Schubert's not to blame. Maybe the pianist is to blame.

Robert Levin, in "Performance Prerogatives in Schubert," argues that Schubert leaves a great deal of musical opportunity—and responsibility for originality—up to the performer, especially when repeat signs are used. Repeats of whole sections *are* boring—in the hands of a pianist who doesn't embellish or inflect her playing the second time around. Levin argues that "nothing is more destructive or dramatic immediacy than the reiteration of a singular passage . . . for at the moment of literal repetition the sense of singularity is destroyed."

As for repeats in Schubert's sonatas, Alfred Brendel advises that while a performing pianist should keep in mind the pacing of her entire program, "the player at home may happily indulge in repeating the exposition of a Schubert sonata a dozen times for his private pleasure."

I guess I must have made it. I must be a responsible, settled adult. Because my house in the dry, hot desert is as cold as I want it. And I have my piano. After several years of renting the little upright, I hired a piano mover to bring me the piano my grandmother and parents bought for me, the Kawai. My mom took pictures of it on her end as they unscrewed its legs and turned it on its side and swaddled it in blankets and belts. She put boxes of my piano music in the mail and the music showed up before the piano did. I retrieved my other boxes of music, the ones from my college years, from the garage. I dug through the boxes looking for a particular, beat-up red book. I knew what I would play first.

For two long weeks the piano was nowhere, on a truck in the middle of the country, and then it appeared. The piano movers had a big German shepherd that had traveled with them across the country. The dog took a nap on one of the blue quilted blankets. I took pictures as the piano was unshrouded, as its legs were screwed back on, as it was set upright. After the movers left, before I let the cats out of the bedroom, I lifted the lid and turned to Chopin, to the funeral march I hadn't known enough sadness to play.

I picked it out, reading slowly at first and then realizing that my hands, my hands that had been through so much, still knew this. My fingers knew where to look for the notes, even if they couldn't reach them. My tendons, which had been severed and sewn, did their job. It was true. I'd had no business at all playing this music at fourteen. But now. Now I knew it had been played at Chopin's own funeral, and at John F. Kennedy's. Better, I thought, to have awkward hands but a heart and brain that worked. Now I thrill at playing the music that disappointed me before, the Chopin étude I botched on the piano exam. I open my old harpsichord music and play it on the piano, grateful for music that fits in my hands but challenges my brain. Without music like this—if there were only Liszt—I'd be shut out; I'd have nothing to play.

As soon as my fingers reacquaint themselves with my piano, they clamor for Schubert. The sonata, the piece of music I love more than any other. There may be a reason this sonata spoke to me. And still continues to speak to me.

In *Extraordinary Measures: Disability in Music,* Joseph Straus, among the first to really examine the intersection of music and disability studies, evaluates Schubert and his music specifically through the lens of illness, and it is in his words that I finally solve the mystery of why that sonata captured me the way it did: "For Schubert," he writes, "disability is not something that can be unequivocally overcome. Rather, it is something that must be lived with, accommodated. Its traces can never be expunged, but leave a permanent mark on the musical body, just as syphilis marks the physical body. . . . In Schubert's music, there is the sense that wisdom is something otherworldly, to be won only through suffering."

Next, Straus offers an entire harmonic analysis of my sonata through the lens of illness and disability. I understand the analysis because of my years of music theory training and because of my years of arthritis training. That G-flat trill that posed a harmonic problem for me as I pored over the score Straus explains this way: "If the G-flat can be understood metaphorically as a wound of some kind . . . then the wound remains open, unhealed at the end of the movement. The musical body remains in a nonnormative, stigmatized state—it is still disabled. But the disability, instead of being cured in triumph or mourned as a personal tragedy, is accepted and accommodated."

Oh, my Schubert.

If I was going to have a life with arthritis in it, I am so glad I have had the piano as my companion. Byron Janis was, I think, referring to muscles and tendons when he wrote that "piano is good for arthritis." I would argue that muscularly, piano has probably been very hard on my arthritis. Excessive practice probably caused my tendons to rupture sooner rather than later, but I believe that those tendons would have ruptured eventually. But I do think that piano has kept my arthritic hands stronger and more mobile than they would otherwise have been. And piano has been good for arthritis in a more meaningful way: piano has given me something to reach for with my arthritic hands, some reason not to give up on my fingers. Without my five-year head start, without my muscle memory of playing piano, I doubt I would have pushed my hands to recover from their surgeries. I probably would have capitulated to the physical therapist's only expectations of diseased hands like mine: hold a pen, button a shirt.

One of Schubert's most beautiful songs is "An die Musik," the text a poem by his dear friend Franz von Schober:

> Oh lovely Art, in how many grey hours,
> When life's fierce orbit ensnared me,

Have you kindled my heart to warm love,
Carried me away into a better world!

This is one of Schubert's most famous songs, and it features a theme that was deeply true to Schubert himself: that music diminished misery. How fitting that I encountered the sonata for the first time at an art-therapy session. Music has made my arthritic life better. And perhaps I am a better musician than I was or would have been—not despite my arthritis, but because of it. Maybe it takes scars to play Schubert and Chopin correctly. Maybe that judge so long ago, the one who said I wasn't old enough to play the funeral march, was right.

It is hot in Arizona. Though not as quick as they used to be, my hands are warm and they move freely, limbered, over the keys. I play as late as I want, as loud as I want.

On a high shelf above the piano, next to the Bastet cat statuette Fred bought for me at the Smithsonian, are the four black-and-white portraits, These women, my pantheon, forever young and beautiful and all of them dead but my mother.

When I conceived of the idea, I thought these were the women who gave me music, but now that they are arrayed together on the wall, I see that they gave me so much more than that. In this wall of pictures, there are four mothers, four wives, two teachers, a professional musician, and a nurse. These are things I hope to be, the things I am meant to be, the things I will need to be, even if not by profession.

Below the shelf, next to my collection of metronomes, is my Grandma Torvik's pitch pipe. My mother gave it to me ten years after Grandma died. "I love to think of her in that little schoolhouse," she says, turning the pitch pipe over and over in her palm. "She taught everything: music and math and PE. Everything." My mom is silent for a moment, then she hands me the pitch pipe and its little red box. "She would be so proud of you," she says.

It is petty, perhaps, but important to me that she gave the pitch pipe to me and not to one of my siblings, all of whom Grandma would be so proud of, all of whom are musical, all of whom are healthy and happy and sober and whole. But in the pitch pipe I hear my mother telling me that my grandmother would be so proud that I am a teacher. That I have not strayed from where I belong. I am recognizable. I am something I was meant to be. I have not squandered my inheritance of talents after all.

I did not follow my dad's suggestion to include my sister on the wall of pictures. But below the shelf, in a matching silver frame, is my secret concession, my cryptic message to my CIA father, my encoded homage to my philosopher sister. It is a fuzzy, low-resolution picture of Paul and Ludwig Wittgenstein as little boys. Ludwig is nestled into the protective embrace of his big brother. Paul's right arm, the one he would lose, hangs at his side. No one is a genius or a gimp yet. They are little boys. They are siblings. That is all, and everything.

Once a month, Fred and I do it in the bathroom. Fred washes his hands while I pull my pajama pants down. I swab one of my thighs with an alcohol pad while he pulls the gray plastic cap off the needle. We don't have to say anything; we know what the other will do. This is our dance. I squeeze the flesh on the top of my thigh and he gives me my medication injection. After, he kisses me. He always kisses me after.

Sometimes he watches me getting dressed, layering garments and baubles and bangles and beads and artfully mismatching colors. "You're fearless, aren't you?" he says.

No, but: Finally, I truly don't care if strangers notice my bumps and jagged parts. I refuse to cover my scars. It's taken me thirty years to realize that someone's staring at my faulty body doesn't hurt any more than someone staring at my bizarre outfit. I've finally transferred my boldness in fashion—my willingness to play, my eagerness to stand out and be unusual, forged over years of pairing fingerless lace gloves with my Brownie jumper, an eagerness that predated this illness by at least a decade—to my body.

It is handy that my mom taught me to sew, all those years ago. I can move a zipper from the back to a more accessible side seam.

Better yet, I can make my own clothes from scratch—fantastic, unusual clothes that no one else has. This body deserves that. I think of my mom every single time I deftly, painlessly knot a length of thread, rolling it between my fingers and then pulling on it.

I have found that sitting at a sewing machine, with my foot on a pedal and my fingers in the fabric, feels a bit like sitting at the piano. I get lost; I create. If I sew this sleeve perfectly on the first try, then I get to do the other one, I tell myself, playing.

And it is like this at the computer, too. At the keyboard.

My first semester at college, for English 101, still raw and anguished, I wrote my personal narrative essay about my failed piano exam. It was that essay that promoted the poet Catherine Hammond to write at the bottom, "If you have this kind of music in you, your task will be to find the form. It may be writing."

It is writers who will save Schubert's sonatas from deadly comparison to Beethoven's. Charles Rosen invokes Stephen Jay Gould's writing about chimpanzees: "There are no essences, there is no such thing as 'the chimpanzee.' You can't bring a few into a laboratory, make some measurements, calculate an average and find out, thereby, what chimpness is." Rosen says, "Sonatas are like chimpanzees."

But we do this; we group things to make them easier to manage: chimpanzees, sonatas, disabled people.

Sonatas can have one or two or three or four or five movements, maybe more. Sonatas can have cadenzas—Mozart wrote out a cadenza for his piano sonata in B-flat, K. 333. I suppose a sonata could have a prelude.

Schubert's sonatas may always be penalized for not living up to Beethoven's, but Schubert was not trying to *be* Beethoven. As Alfred Brendel writes, Schubert admired Beethoven too much to challenge him on his own terms. Harmonically and melodically, Schubert "relates to Beethoven, he reacts to him, but he follows him hardly at all."

I am a wounded storyteller, the kind Arthur W. Frank writes of: "The mystery of illness stories is their expression of the body: in the silences between words, tissues speak."

I have not left music behind, but I acknowledge that there will be periods in my life when I cannot play the piano. It is the periods of silence—their duration, their frequency, their weight—that give meaning to sounds.

I may not be the pianist I wanted to be, but I have found my voice. I suppose I am a composer after all.

DA CAPO AL FINE /
START AGAIN

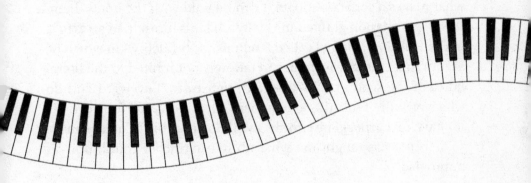

*A touch, which hurt yesterday, no longer does so today.
Today I feel the pain only when I think of it. . . . My grief
is no longer the same; a memory which was still unbearable
to me a year ago is no longer so.*

— Ludwig Wittgenstein,
Philosophical Investigations

I am playing the Schubert sonata with Mrs. Feltman—the
now-impossible first movement. We are in her living room on
Blossom Drive. She looks the way I choose to remember her,
tall and sturdy, her red hair glowing in the sun, the way she looked
on the day we shopped for music in Arizona. But me, I am older.
My hands have scars she wouldn't recognize and a wedding ring

she never saw. It is both a past and a future that never was and I want the dream to last forever.

I have played through the first two pages, and I am approaching the repeat sign that comes at the end of the exposition. This is the musical notation tattoo I should have gotten. It tells me: *Go back and do it all again. Go through all of it again—the modulation from major to minor, from well to ill, the victories and the losses, the rending and the mending, the climb and the fall.*

And so I do. If there is so much room for interpretation even in what makes a sonata a sonata, I can be bold with the notes themselves, permission granted me by Byron Janis himself, in an article in the *Wall Street Journal* called "In Praise of Infidelity," in which he argues that true musical interpretation is not limited to the literal notes of the score. He invokes St. Augustine: "Love God and do what you will." I substitute "Schubert" for "God" and I drop octaves if I have to. I arpeggiate chords. I will do anything to make music.

Arthritis has taught me what no music teacher could: how to improvise.

And so I start again, at measure 1. Who knows how many times I will start again? As many times as I want to, as many times as I need to. The notes are prescribed for me, but I'm not making music unless I make the notes mean something, unless I play it differently this next time through, heavy with knowledge of all that's come before.

"Let's put some oomph in it!" Mrs. Feltman calls out to me. "Make it different this time!"

I will.

Acknowledgments

I want to thank everyone at Pegasus Books, especially my editor, Jessica Case, for her intuitive, insightful, expert, and generous work on this book. My work would not have found its way to Jessica were it not for my agent, Rob Kirkpatrick of the Stuart Agency, who brought his own musical and literary brilliance to helping me tell the story I wanted to tell and got it into exactly the right hands. I would like to thank Erica Ferguson for her keen, perceptive, and artful copyediting and Maria Fernandez for her stunning book design.

In seventh grade, my English teacher mentioned she couldn't wait to read the book I wrote someday, a comment that has sustained me for many years. I am happy to finally be turning this in to you, Kay Katz! I am the beneficiary of many other teachers who have shaped my tastes, improved my reading diet, and generously and patiently responded to many thousands of my words. Thank you to Nancy Sullivan, Catherine Hammond, Larry Ellis, and Jacqueline Wheeler. I owe a huge debt of gratitude to the creative writing faculty at Arizona State, many of whom went beyond the role of teacher to become lifelong friends and mentors: Ron Carlson, T.M. McNally, Sally Ball, Jay Boyer, and Alberto Ríos. To the music teachers who also nurtured me—Ron Frezzo, James DeMars, Randall Shinn, Rodney Rogers—I hope you hear music in this work and know that your efforts were not wasted.

I want to thank Rose Weitz for her steadfast friendship and encouragement, which have buoyed me, and whose invitations to speak at her Women's Studies classes at ASU have allowed me to refine this book as well as my understanding of myself and my body. Thanks, too, to Rosemarie Garland-Thomson and Mary Felstiner for their wisdom and their writing. These women taught me how to pay attention to my experiences in my body and make something beautiful from them. Miriam Savitri Axelrod was a remarkably sensitive and generous reader, and to her I am ever thankful.

Many writers and artists have inspired and encouraged me, taking away from their own precious desk time to read and respond to my work. Thanks to Elizabeth Gilbert, Stacey Richter, Gregory Spatz, Caridwen Irvine-Spatz, Tayari Jones, and Natalie Serber. I am eternally thankful to Squaw Valley Community of Writers for the opportunity to improve my work in a magical setting with gracious and talented writers. Joe Theismann, thank you for a much-needed pep talk and for coaching me to be the quarterback of my life.

I would like to thank my cousin, Peter Torvik, who lent his expertise to the music theory elements of this book, as well as the brilliant and magnanimous music theorist Dr. Joseph Straus specifically for helping me with the music theory and history and more generally for his remarkable work in the intersection of music and disability.

When you are a chronically ill writer, your medical team is part of your writing community. I wish to thank Dr. Donald Sheridan, Dr. Dennis Armstrong, Dr. Dana Seltzer, and Chris Reynolds and

Diana Rivera at Desert Hand Therapy. For her crucial early care of me as well as her ongoing support (and for reviewing my writing on rheumatoid arthritis), I owe huge thanks to Dr. Patience White. Thanks, too, to Dr. Gary Hoffman for his expert review and helpful input on my writing about the arthritis disease process, diagnosis, prevalence, and treatment.

The love, support, and patience of my friends, even through my long silences, mean more than they know. Lauren, Davey, Beth, Sarah, Kat, Jen, RB, Betsy, Sharon, Keith, Gabi, Barb, Patrick, Andy, Lisa, Rich, thank you. Marc, thank you (I hope you like the book, and I really hope you like the font). Thank you to my students at Phoenix Country Day School, whose creativity and authenticity inspire me—I've been your student all along.

For seeming to intuit when I want to be a chatterbox and when I want to be a recluse, and for rolling with all kinds of punches, I thank my husband, Fred. I love you. Most of all, thank you to my family: Mom, Dad, Erica (not just my sister but the best reader I know), Matthew, Chris. I hope in my version of our story you hear how terribly much I love you. Belonging to our family is the proudest distinction of my life.

Endnotes

EPIGRAPHS THROUGHOUT
Ludwig Wittgenstein, *Philosophical Investigations*, eds. P. M. S. Hacker and Joachim Schulte, revised 4th ed. (Malden, MA: Wiley-Blackwell, 2009).

CHAPTER 1
p. 8.   the only full expression of pain: R. Selzer, "The Language of Pain," *The Wilson Quarterly* 18, no. 4 (Autumn 1994): 28–33.
p. 8.   turned to writing at fifty-eight: R. H. Epstein, "Richard Selzer, Who Fictionalized Medicine's Absurdity and Gore, Dies at 87," *New York Times*, June 15, 2016, http://www.nytimes.com/2016/06/16/books/richard-selzer-who-fictionalized-medicines-absurdity-and-gore-dies-at-87.html?_r=0.
p. 9.   But seronegative rheumatoid arthritis means: R. Gandhi, "Juvenile Rheumatoid Arthritis and Total Hip Arthroplasty," *Seminars in Arthroplasty* 19, no. 4 (December 2008): 261–66.
p. 13.   glucosamine supplements peddled: H. Matsuno, H. Nakamura, K. Katayama, et al., "Effects of an Oral Administration of Glucosamine-Chondroitin-quercetin Glucoside on the Synovial Fluid Properties in Patients with Osteoarthritis and Rheumatoid Arthritis," *Bioscience, Biotechnology, and Biochemistry* 73, no. 2 (February 2009): 288–92.

p. 13. Internet research will uncover: (1) J. A. Lee, M. J. Son, J. Choi, et al. "Bee Venom Acupuncture for Rheumatoid Arthritis: A Systematic Review of Randomised Clinical Trials," *BMJ Open* 4, no. 11 (November 7, 2014): 1–8. (2) J. M. Kahlenberg and D. A. Fox, "Advances in the Medical Treatment of Rheumatoid Arthritis," *Hand Clinics* 27, no. 1 (February 2011): 11–20.

p. 13. a leading treatment for RA was gold: T. Sokka and H. Mäkinen, "Drug Management of Early Rheumatoid Arthritis," *Best Practice and Research in Clinical Rheumatology* 23, no. 1 (2008): 93–102.

p. 15. Tantalizing mysteries abound: G. Tobón, P. Youinou, and A. Saraux, "The Environment, Geo-epidemiology, and Auto-immune Disease: Rheumatoid Arthritis," *Journal of Autoimmunity* 35, no. 1 (August 2010): 10–14.

p. 15. women's immune systems: R. G. Lahita and I. L. Yalof, *Women and Autoimmune Disease: The Mysterious Ways Your Body Betrays Itself* (New York: HarperCollins, 2005), p. xii.

p. 16. some four-thousand-year-old rheumatoid-looking bones: (1) R. Kolberg, "6 Skeletons Seem to Answer Riddle of Origins of Rheumatoid Arthritis," *Los Angeles Times*, November 6, 1988. (2) B. M. Rothschild, "Tennessee Origins of Rheumatoid Arthritis," McClung Museum of Natural History & Culture, April 1, 1991, http://mcclungmuseum.utk.edu/1991/04/01/tennessee-origins-of-rheumatoid-arthritis/. (3) Y. Alamanos and A. A. Drosos, "Epidemiology of Adult Rheumatoid Arthritis," *Autoimmunity Reviews* 4, no. 3 (2005): 130–36. (4) P. Entezami, D. A. Fox, P. J. Clapham, and K. C. Chung, "Historical Perspectives on the Etiology of Rheumatoid Arthritis," *Hand Clinics* 27, no. 1 (February 2011): 1–10.

p. 16. a female mummy named "Braids Lady": G. Fontecchio, L. Ventura, M. A. Fioroni, G. Fornaciara, and F. Papola, "HLA-DRB Genotyping of an Italian Mummy from the 16th Century with Signs of Rheumatoid Arthritis," *Annals of the Rheumatic Diseases* 65, no. 12 (December 2006): 1676–77.

p. 16. that featured the observations of Jan Dequeker: Ann Waldron, "Reflections in a Painter's Eye," *Washington Post*, May 29, 1990, https://www.washingtonpost.com/archive/lifestyle/wellness/1990/05/29/reflections-in-a-painters-eye/0e6138f9-024d-4112-a54b-3851792c2410/.

p. 16. Dequeker's diagnosis of Vespucci: James Elkins, *Pictures of the Body: Pain and Metamorphosis* (Stanford, CA: Stanford University Press, 1999), p. 155.

p. 17. 1.5 million adults: "Rheumatoid Arthritis," Centers for Disease Control and Prevention, 2006, http://www.cdc.gov/arthritis/basics/rheumatoid.htm; http://www.cdc.gov/arthritis/basics/faqs.htm.

p. 18.   revised RA classification criteria in 2010: "2010 Rheumatoid Arthritis
          Classification Criteria," *Arthritis & Rheumatism* 62, no. 9 (September
          2010): 2569–81.

p. 18.   use the old classification criteria, some the new: E. Minichiello,
          L. Semerano, and M. Boissier, "Time Trends in the Incidence,
          Prevalence, and Severity of Rheumatoid Arthritis: A Systematic
          Literature Review," *Joint Bone Spine* 83, no. 6 (2016): 625–30.

p. 18.   rates are, literally, all over the map: (1) Tobón, et al., "The
          Environment, Geo-epidemiology, and Autoimmune Disease:
          Rheumatoid Arthritis," 11. (2) L. Carmona, M. Cross, B. Williams, M.
          Lassere, and L. March, "Rheumatoid Arthritis," *Best Practice & Research
          Clinical Rheumatology* 24, no. 6 (December 2010): 733–45.

p. 18.   One theory to explain this correlation: M. Versini, P. Jeandel, T.
          Bashi, G. Bizzro, M. Blank, and Y. Shoenfeld, "Unraveling the
          Hygiene Hypothesis of Helminthes and Autoimmunity: Origins,
          Pathophysiology, and Clinical Applications," *BMC Medicine* 13, no. 1
          (April 13, 2015): 81.

p. 19.   rheumatoid arthritis in any prior decade—in the 1940s: H. M.
          Margolis, "Rheumatoid Arthritis." *American Journal of Nursing* 47, no.
          12 (December 1947): 787–93.

p. 19.   or in the 1950s: B. M. Cormier, and E. D. Wittkower, "Psychological
          Aspects of Rheumatoid Arthritis." *Canadian Medical Association Journal*
          77 no. 6 (September 15, 1957): 533–41.

p. 20.   anti-inflammatory corticosteroids were the standard treatment:
          Jim Morelli, "Corticosteroid Use in Rheumatoid Arthritis." The
          Arthritis Foundation, http://www.arthritis.org/living-with-arthritis/
          treatments/medication/drug-types/corticosteroids/ra-corticosteroid.
          php, accessed 1 December 2016.

p. 23.   The medical model of disability: S. Goering, "Rethinking Disability:
          The Social Model of Disability and Chronic Disease," *Current Reviews
          in Musculoskeletal Medicine* 8, no. 2 (June 2015): 134–38.

CHAPTER 2

p. 30.   Nannerl Mozart, Wolfgang's older sister: (1) Sylvia Milo, "The
          Lost Genius of Mozart's sister," *The Guardian*, September 8,
          2015, https://www.theguardian.com/music/2015/sep/08/lost-
          genius-the-other-mozart-sister-nannerl. (2) Elizabeth Rusch,
          "Maria Anna Mozart: The Family's First Prodigy," *Smithsonian*,
          March 27, 2011, http://www.smithsonianmag.com/arts-culture/
          maria-anna-mozart-the-familys-first-prodigy-1259016/.

p. 30.   "Our society is quick to judge": Julian Seifter, *After the Diagnosis:
          Transcending Chronic Illness* (New York: Simon & Schuster, 2010),
          p. 157.

p. 31.   numerous pianists with arthritis: (1) Holly Brubach, "The Pianist Leon Fleisher: A Life-altering Debility, Reconsidered," *New York Times*, June 12, 2007, http://www.nytimes.com/2007/06/12/arts/12iht-pianist.1.6104272.html. (2) Byron Janis, *Chopin and Beyond: My Extraordinary Life in Music and the Paranormal* (Hoboken, NJ: John Wiley and Sons, 2010), p. 161 (and throughout). (3) David Revill, *The Roaring Silence—John Cage: A Life*, 2nd ed. (New York: Arcade, 2014), p. 287 (and throughout). (4) R. A. Henson and H. Urich, "Schumann's Hand Injury," *British Medical Journal* 1, no. 6117 (1978): 900–03.

p. 31.   2008 study of an extended Finnish family: K. Pulli, K. Karma, P. Sistonen, H. H. H. Göring, and I. Järvelä, "Genome-wide Linkage Scan for Loci of Musical Aptitude in Finnish Families: Evidence for a Major Locus at 4q22," *Journal of Medical Genetics* 45, no. 7 (July 2008), 451–56.

p. 31.   "neither nature nor nurture can alone make a musician": Paul R. Farnsworth, *The Social Psychology of Music* (Ames: Iowa State University Press, 1969), p. 184.

p. 34.   Picker is featured: Joseph Straus, *Extraordinary Measures: Disability in Music* (New York: Oxford University Press, 2011), p. 43.

p. 35.   Victorian-era children were instructed: Thomas Tapper, *Franz Schubert: The Story of the Boy Who Wrote Beautiful Songs* (Philadelphia: Theodore Presser, 1916), p. 3.

p. 35.   Paul Wittgenstein was plenty famous: Alexander Waugh, *The House of Wittgenstein: A Family at War* (New York: Doubleday, 2009), p. 34.

CHAPTER 3

p. 48.   about children with identities they didn't get: Andrew Solomon, *Far from the Tree: Parents, Children, and the Search for Identity* (New York: Scribner, 2012), p. 2.

p. 51.   Signed into law by George H. W. Bush in 1990: "Americans with Disabilities Act of 1990, as Amended," sec. 12102 (2009), https://www.ada.gov/pubs/ada.htm.

CHAPTER 4

p. 63.   Byron Janis would quip: G. Spencer, "A New Harmony: Concert Pianist Byron Janis Shares His Insights on Coping with Arthritis," *Arthritis Today* 24, no. 6 (November 2010): 19.

p. 67.   Rainer Maria Rilke's writing about illness: Rainier Maria Rilke, *The Notebooks of Malte Laurids Brigge: A Novel*, translated by Robert Vilain (Oxford: Oxford University Press, 2016), p. 37.

p. 68.   "[i]llness is the night-side of life": Susan Sontag, *Illness as Metaphor and AIDS and Its Metaphors* (New York: Picador, 2001), p. 3.

p. 68.   "Sickness is a place": Flannery O'Connor, *The Habit of Being: Letters of Flannery O'Connor*, ed. Sally Fitzgerald (New York: Farrar, Strauss, and Giroux, 1988): p. 163.

CHAPTER 5

p. 71.   "It [is] a mark of refinement, of sensibility": Sontag, *Illness as Metaphor*, p. 31.

p. 72.   nineteen-year-old Schubert: Christopher H. Gibbs, *The Life of Schubert* (Cambridge: Cambridge University Press, 2000), p. 50.

p. 73.   "a man full of affection and goodness of heart": ibid, p. 21.

p. 74.   a great and prolific songwriter: ibid, p. 43.

p. 75.   extended the same privilege: ibid, p. 28.

p. 77.   Water has inspired and soothed: ibid, p. 57.

p. 78.   "Some look like a dab of warm": "Seborrheic Keratosis," American Academy of Dermatology, https://www.aad.org/public/diseases/ bumps-and-growths/seborrheic-keratoses, accessed October 13, 2016.

p. 80.   didn't get their own piano until Schubert was seventeen: Gibbs, *Life of Schubert*, p. 38.

p. 82.   When people write about this sonata: Chris Woodstra, Gerald Brennan, and Allen Schrott, *All Media Guide to Classical Music* (San Francisco: Backbeat, 2005), p. 205.

CHAPTER 6

p. 86.   "Chopin was tubercular at a time": Sontag, *Illness as Metaphor*, p. 28.

p. 87.   arsenic to pale their skin: Therese Oneill, *Unmentionable: The Victorian Lady's Guide to Sex, Marriage, and Manners* (New York: Little, Brown & Co, 2016), p. 111.

p. 88.   classic tactics used by women: Clifton D. Bryant, *Deviant Behavior: Readings in the Sociology of Norm Violations* (New York: Routledge, 1989), p. 435.

p. 91.   his lesson with the great Salieri: Gibbs, *The Life of Schubert*, p. 30.

p. 94.   Schubert's brother Ferdinand: ibid, p. 55.

p. 95.   tempered with practicality, backup plans: ibid, p. 51.

p. 96.   For two summers during his short life: ibid, p. 57.

p. 97.   unofficially exiled from Vienna: ibid, p. 56.

CHAPTER 7

p. 103.   researchers tried to create a unit of pain measurement: (1) J. D. Hardy and C. T. Javert, "Studies on Pain: Measurements of Pain Intensity in Childbirth" *Journal of Clinical Investigation* 28, no. 1 (January 1949): 153–62. (2) J. D. Hardy, H. G. Wolff, and H. Goodell, "Studies on Pain: A New Method for Measuring Pain Threshold: Observations on Spatial Summation of Pain," *Journal of Clinical Investigation* 19, no. 4 (July1940): 649–57. (3) J. D. Hardy, H. G. Wolff, and H. Goodell, "Studies on Pain: Discrimination of Differences in Intensity of a Pain Stimulus as a Basis of a Scale of Pain Intensity," *Journal of Clinical Investigation* 26, no. 6 (November 1947): 1152–58.

p. 103. Wong-Baker FACES pain-rating scale: Wong-Baker FACES Foundation website: http://wongbakerfaces.org/.

p. 104. Schubert was preoccupied with the idea, too: Gibbs, *The Life of Schubert*, p. 104.

p. 104. the problem of private language: Wittgenstein, *Philosophical Investigations*, p. 188.

CHAPTER 8

p. 123. Schubert's health began to fail in 1823: Gibbs, *The Life of Schubert*, p. 106.

p. 126. they named the parties after him: ibid, p. 11.

p. 129. Schubert's own elevated music teacher: ibid, p. 26.

p. 131. Robert Schumann's "finger tormentor": Henson and Urich, "Schumann's Hand Injury," p. 1156.

p. 131. his "cigar mechanism": Peter Ostwald and Lise Deschamps Ostwald, *Robert Schumann: The Inner Voices of a Musical Genius* (Boston: Northeastern University Press, 1985), p. 88.

p. 132. Hunchback!: Gibbs, *The Life of Schubert*, p. 24.

p. 133. After Paul Wittgenstein was shot: Waugh, *House of Wittgenstein*, p. 156.

p. 138. "Thank God I live at last": Gibbs, *The Life of Schubert*, p. 53.

p. 139. ultrasound has been used: D. Miller, et al., "Overview of Therapeutic Ultrasound Applications and Safety Considerations," *Journal of Ultrasound Medicine* 31, no. 4 (April 2012): 623–34.

p. 139. the Lung Flute: Lung Flute website: http://www.lungflute.com/.

p. 140. well-established benefits of music therapy: "Music Therapy with Specific Populations: Fact Sheets, Resources & Bibliographies," American Music Therapy Association, http://www.musictherapy.org/research/factsheets/, accessed 10 January 2017.

p. 140. many stutterers don't stutter when they're singing: R. Spain, S. Mandel, and R. T. Sataloff, "Care of the Professional Voice: The Neurology of Stuttering," *Journal of Singing: The Official Journal of the National Association of Teachers of Singing* 62, no. 4 (Mar 2006): 423–33.

CHAPTER 9

p. 142. "Butterfly and crab are both bizarre": Italo Calvino, *Six Memos for the Next Millennium* (New York: Vintage, 1992), p. 48.

p. 142. Even as Schubert's body failed him: Gibbs, *The Life of Schubert*, p. 106.

p. 142. "people with disabilities": Nancy Mairs, *Waist-High in the World: A Life Among the Nondisabled* (Boston: Beacon Press, 1997), p. 92.

p. 143. "Brother Body is poor": Rainer Maria Rilke, "Brother Body," reprinted in *First Things: A Monthly Journal of Religion and Public Life* 167 (November 2006): 20.

p. 145. the intersection of body modification and disability: Clinton Sanders and D. Angus Vail, *Customizing the Body: The Art and Culture of Tattooing* (Philadelphia: Temple University Press, 2007), Interview conducted May 12, 2012.

p. 146. Tattooing is still essentially fringe: Clinton Sanders and D. Angus Vail, *Customizing the Body: The Art and Culture of Tattooing* (Philadelphia: Temple University Press, 2007), p. 2.

p. 146. "keepsakes to mark my journey": John Irving, *Until I Find You: A Novel* (New York: Random House, 2006), p. 74.

p. 147. Sometimes these cadenzas were written out: S. P. Keefe, "A Complementary Pair: Stylistic Experimentation in Mozart's Final Piano Concertos, K. 537 in D and K. 595 in B-flat," *Journal of Musicology* 18, no. 4 (Fall 2001): 658–84.

p. 150. Leon Fleisher, who lost the use of his right hand: Brubach, "The Pianist Leon Fleisher."

p. 151. Schubert had been dead for a century: Alfred Brendel, *Music, Sense and Nonsense: Collected Essays and Lectures* (London: Robson, 2015), Kindle loc. 2499.

p. 151. But it is Beethoven's sonatas: Charles Rosen, *Sonata Forms, Revised Edition* (New York: W. W. Norton, 1988), p. 3.

p. 152. not just purposeful imitation of Beethoven: Gibbs, *The Life of Schubert*, pp. 158–159.

CAESURA/INTERRUPTION

p. 155. "whenever I attempted to sing of love": Gibbs, *The Life of Schubert*, p. 32.

p. 156. known as the "Unfinished" Symphony: (1) M. J. E. Brown and E. Sams, *The New Grove Schubert* (Oxford: Oxford University Press, 1983), p. 35. (2) Opal Wheeler and Sybil Deucher, *Franz Schubert and His Merry Friends* (Elyria, OH: Zeezok, 2008), p. 113.

p. 161. *Here will Jack always stumble:* Vladimir Nabokov, *Lolita* (New York: Putnam, 1955), p. 193.

p. 165. The winter after that final public concert: W. J. Dawson, "Review: Wolfgang Amadeus Mozart: Controversies Regarding his Illnesses and Death: A Bibliographic Review," *Medical Problems of Performing Artists* 25, no. 2 (June 2010): 49–53.

p. 166. Beth appears to recover: Louisa May Alcott, *Little Women* (New York: Black & White Classics, 1880), p. 239.

p. 168. Great pianists can come from healthy competition: Janis, *Chopin and Beyond*, p. 67.

p. 169. Labor replied that he'd already begun: Waugh, *House of Wittgenstein*, p. 87.

CHAPTER 11

p. 205.   sympathetically details Wittgenstein's notebooks: B. Howe, "Paul Wittgenstein and the Performance of Disability, *Journal of Musicology* 27, no. 2 (Spring 2010): 135–80.

p. 206.   Byron Janis kept his arthritis a secret: Janis, *Chopin and Beyond*, p. 164.

p. 211.   If music is in the spaces between the notes: Revill, *The Roaring Silence*, p. 156.

p. 212.   "pain sharpens the understanding": Gibbs, *The Life of Schubert*, p. 104.

CHAPTER 12

p. 213.   Methotrexate has long been: Kahlenberg and Fox, "Advances in the Medical Treatment of Rheumatoid Arthritis," p. 3.

p. 214.   go into remission when they are pregnant: (1) N. Neeman, M. D. Aronson, J. E. Schulze, and R. H. Shmerling, "Improving Pregnancy Counseling for Women with Rheumatoid Arthritis Taking Methotrexate," *American Journal of Medicine* 122, no. 11 (November 2009): 998–1000. (2) V. R. Tandon, et al. "Pregnancy and Rheumatoid Arthritis," *Indian Journal of Medical Sciences* 60, no. 8 (August 2006): 334–44.

p. 217.   Taylor Mali poem called "Undivided Attention": Taylor Mali, "Undivided Attention," *What Learning Leaves* (Newtown, CT: Hanover Press, 2002), p. 34.

p. 229.   Schubert leaves a great deal of musical opportunity: R. Levin, "Performance Prerogatives in Schubert," *Early Music* 25, no. 4 (November 1997): 723–27.

p. 229.   As for repeats in Schubert's sonatas: Brendel, *Music, Sense and Nonsense*, Kindle loc. 2205.

p. 230.   Schubert and his music specifically through the lens of illness: Straus, *Extraordinary Measures*, p. 64.

p. 231.   most beautiful songs is "An die Musik": S. E. Gontarski, *The Edinburgh Companion to Samuel Beckett and the Arts* (Edinburgh: Edinburgh University Press, 2014), p. 376.

p. 234.   It is writers who will save Schubert's sonatas: Rosen, *Sonata Forms*, p. viii.

p. 234.   Schubert's sonatas may always be penalized: Brendel, *Music, Sense and Nonsense*, Kindle loc. 3003.

p. 235.   "The mystery of illness stories": Arthur W. Frank, *The Wounded Storyteller: Body, Illness, and Ethics* (Chicago: University of Chicago Press, 1995), Kindle loc. 136.

DA CAPO AL FINE/START AGAIN:

p. 238.   he argues that true musical interpretation: Byron Janis, "In Praise of Infidelity," *Wall Street Journal*, January 6, 2010, http://www.wsj.com/articles/SB10001424052748703580904574638380890512334.